OSU'S UNFORGETTABLES

BY BRUCE HOOLEY

SP
SPORTS
PUBLISHING
L.L.C.

ISBN 1-58261-243-9

Director of Production: Susan M. Moyer
Interior design and senior project manager: Jennifer L. Polson
Book layout: Jennifer L. Polson and Jim Henehan
Developmental editor: Stephanie Fuqua
Dust jacket designer: Joseph Brumleve
Copy editor: Ashley Burum

To Sheri:
The woman of my dreams and the answer
to my prayer for a Godly wife.

And to my mom and dad:
the blessing of Christian parents and a loving home
enriched my life immeasurably.

ACKNOWLEDGMENTS

The author wishes to gratefully acknowledge the assistance of the following persons in the publication of this work:

Sue Ferguson, Jeff Rapp, Steve Helwagen, Mike Wachsman, Jon Spencer, Marc Katz, Bob Baptist, Bob Hunter, Terry Gilliam, Jim Knight, Eric Kaelin, D.C. Koehl, LeAnn Parker, Steve Snapp, Jim Sargent, Kelli Servizzi, Dave Hackenberg, Leslie Lane, Sam Nicola and John Porentas.

TABLE OF CONTENTS

OSU'S
UNFORGETTABLES

Gary
BRADDS

He Knew He Could Do It

One of the great untapped moneymaking opportunities of the 20th century went unrecognized in Columbus in the early 1960s.

Just imagine how much cash could have been raised by betting that the Ohio State center who succeeded Jerry Lucas would put up bigger scoring numbers than the greatest player in Buckeye basketball history.

That's what Gary Bradds did in 1963 and 1964, emerging from Lucas's shadow to win back-to-back Big Ten MVP honors and extend OSU's dominance of the league to a still-unmatched five straight championships.

The Buckeyes won shares of the conference title in both those seasons, but didn't participate in the NCAA Tournament either year due to the conference's tiebreaker rules.

Bradds was an All-American selection both seasons and the national player-of-the-year in 1964. Though not as physically-imposing as Lucas, Bradds never let his 180-pound frame preclude him from compiling scoring figures no player in the conference could match during his era.

Bradds's streak of six straight 40-point games as a senior in 1964 remains unprecedented in school history, as is the single-game mark of 49 points he recorded during that span against Illinois.

OSU nearly lost Bradds to Kentucky when he came out of tiny Greeneview High School in Jamestown, Ohio, but after enrolling and spending two days in Lexington, Bradds decided to return to his home state.

The move met with the consternation of legendary UK coach Adolph Rupp, who told Bradds he would never get on the floor with the Buckeyes as long as Lucas was around.

Bradds, though, never had any doubt he would succeed.

"He was one of the most confident people I've ever known with regard to basketball," former teammate Don Devoe said. "He told me matter-of-factly that he'd be an All-American at Ohio State, and he said it before we ever enrolled."

Bradds made good on that prediction by taking over in the middle after Lucas's graduation and averaging 28 points and 13 rebounds per game as a junior.

That production earned Bradds both league MVP honors and All-American selection, while helping the Buckeyes to a 20-4 overall record and a share of first place in the conference.

The next year, however, is when Bradds made an indelible mark on the school record book.

The Buckeyes started only 5-5 that season and saw their 50-game home winning streak end, but the team took its cue from Bradds once Big Ten play began and caught fire.

He made 20 of 30 field goal attempts in a home game against Purdue to score 47 points, after which he scored 48 against Michigan State.

No. 2 Michigan then invaded St. John Arena and Bradds' 40-point streak looked like it would end when he started just 1 of 10 from the field. Incredibly, he made 15 of his next 19 shots and 10 of 12 tries from the line to score 42 points and lead the Buckeyes to a 86-85 upset.

OSU next went to Indiana and used Bradds's 40 points for a 98-96 overtime victory.

Then came Illinois at home and the school-record 49-point effort and yet another win. Bradds shot 17-of-28 from the field, 15-of-16 from the line, and had 21 rebounds in that victory.

The streak lasted one more game, with Bradds getting 40 more points in a win over Wisconsin.

Afterward, Badgers coach John Erickson wondered, "Does he look at the basket or does he just have a string tied to the ball?"

Bradds's 30.6 scoring average led the league by more than 10 points per game, and he also championed the conference in rebounding (13.4) and field goal percentage (.523).

During his six-game streak of 40 or more points per game, he shot 58 percent from the field, helping him set a Big Ten scoring record for league games (474 points) and an OSU single-season scoring record (735 points) that stood until 1987.

"A lot of those 40-point games Gary had would have been a lot higher in today's game of basketball," said Bill Hosket, who succeeded Bradds in the pivot. "He had a phenomenal stroke from the outside. He scored so many of his points from the top of the key. But more than anything he did on the floor, I just remember him being a fine gentleman."

Bradds died of cancer in the early 1990s. Ohio State retired his number two years ago. He is one of only three basketball players so honored in school history—along with Jerry Lucas and Jim Jackson.

Bradds once scored 40 or more points in six straight games.

Jay BURSON

The Little Engine That Could

Jay Burson went from being a kid people weren't sure could play at Ohio State to one the Buckeyes literally couldn't win without, proving to everyone that he definitely belonged not only in the Big Ten, but among the finest players ever to wear the OSU uniform.

Coming out of New Concord John Glenn High School as Ohio's career basketball scoring leader, Burson still wasn't a lock to make an impact at Ohio State.

Sure, he had scored a record 2,598 points, but at just 6-foot, 150 pounds, Burson was believed by many to be too small to withstand the rigors of physical play in the Big Ten.

"I know a lot of others worried about that, but I never really did, because I never thought of myself as being small," Burson said. "I just thought of myself as being a basketball player. I was a big scorer in high school, but it didn't take me long to realize once I got to Ohio State that I was going to

have to do other things if I wanted to get on the floor."

Burson made the adjustment successfully enough to play in 32 of 33 games as a freshman. He started five times before settling into the role of the first backcourt substitute on a team that reeled off five straight victories to win the NIT after head coach Eldon Miller was fired late in the season.

Burson wasn't sure how the coaching change would affect him, but the arrival of Gary Williams from Boston College was "a really big boost to my career."

"Coach Williams liked to play more of an open-court style, which really suited my game and was more to my liking," Burson said. "We ran up and down and pressed a lot, which allowed us to compensate for some of my defensive deficiencies."

It also helped the Buckeyes surprisingly reach the NCAA Tournament that year, where they nearly knocked off No. 1 seeded Georgetown in the second round

before suffering an 82-79 defeat.

Burson averaged 12.5 points per game as a sophomore, setting the tone for a junior season in which he took over the top scorer's role from Dennis Hopson.

Burson's 18.9 average was invaluable to a team that lost to Connecticut in the NIT championship game.

The Buckeyes broke fast from the gate Burson's senior season, winning the ECAC Holiday Festival thanks to his MVP performance. He scored 37 points in a semifinal victory over Florida, with an OSU-record nine three-point field goals in 13 attempts, and then followed with a 23-point effort in the title game against St. John's.

Everything was running smoothly for the Buckeyes until an 83-75 loss at Iowa in mid-February, when Burson was fouled hard by the Hawkeyes' Ed Horton.

Though he stayed in the game, Burson suffered a broken neck on the play. The injury was discovered the following day, putting him in a halo brace and ending his season with OSU 17-7 overall.

That mark included the wins over St. John's and Florida in New York, plus a nationally televised win at Louisville, so the Buckeyes seemed destined to gain an NCAA Tournament bid despite Burson's injury.

His absence, however, deflated the team, which went on to lose its final seven regular season games and miss out on an NCAA berth. Burson went on to play with the Houston Rockets in the NBA.

"Jay was one of the scrappiest kids I ever saw," said Tony White, who played all four seasons with Burson. "He was always the smallest guy out there, but by the end of the game there was never any doubt who the toughest kid was. He just had a stubbornness that allowed him to think he couldn't lose out there.

"We really missed that when he got injured. It's one thing to lose your point guard. It's another to lose your leading scorer. It's a different universe to lose your leading scorer who is also your point guard. We had no chemistry and no cohesion without Jay.

"We couldn't get the ball where we needed to get it to run our offense. Consequently, our season just fell apart."

Burson still wonders what the Buckeyes might

Burson's slight stature was no impediment.

have accomplished that season had he not gotten hurt.

"We had everything set up perfectly," he said. "We had good seniors on that team who were hungry, and we were hard to play against. To see guys I'd been playing with for four years struggle without me, it was really tough."

Jim CLEAMONS

Leading the Kids to Victory

They were two men from different backgrounds and different eras, but they shared a common goal that united them and proved crucial to Ohio State's 1971 Big Ten championship basketball team.

As surely as Fred Taylor was the Buckeyes' head coach on the sideline, Jim Cleamons was OSU's head coach on the floor, and the results of their collaborative effort left no doubt that two heads were better than one.

Ohio State's expectations were relatively modest prior to Cleamons's senior year, what with three sophomores stepping into the lineup in an era when freshmen were ineligible and thus unable to gain varsity experience.

What forecasters didn't know was that Taylor and Cleamons had a bond that dated to the early days of their relationship, when a trust developed between them that would make the player an on-court extension of his coach and allow them to quench their mutual thirst for a championship.

"Coach and I had a heart-to-heart talk when I was a senior in high school on the day before I was going to make my decision where to go to college," Cleamons said. "We talked about my particular situation and his and what we both felt was important. At the end of that conversation, I knew I wanted to play for him because of how honest and frank he was, and how he allowed me to be the same way with him."

Cleamons pulled no punches in that talk, asking Taylor about rumors that black players weren't welcome at OSU and to explain why several had not succeeded academically over the previous few years.

"Fred didn't butter me up and tell me anything that wasn't factual," Cleamons said. "Some guys do that just to get you on campus, but then you get on campus and find out things are different. Fred was very honest and forthright."

Cleamons knew he had found a coach of his word when, as a freshman, he struggled academically and asked out of spring workouts to concentrate on his class work.

Taylor agreed and Cleamons's grade point average rose from 1.65 to 2.4 that quarter.

He averaged 16.6 points as a sophomore and 21.6 points as a junior, but both those years the Buckeyes fell short of winning the Big Ten, placing second and third, respectively.

That was frustrating to Cleamons, who had played on a state championship team at Columbus' Linden McKinley High School, and to Taylor, who had directed OSU to six conference titles in his first 11 seasons.

"The points were nice, but I didn't have a championship yet, and I wanted that more than anything," Cleamons said. "I hadn't won anything, and I desperately wanted to go out leaving some kind of a winning legacy."

The odds of that didn't appear promising, with Cleamons the lone returnee from the lineup of the previous season.

The Buckeyes' lost about 70 percent of their points and rebounds off that 1970 team, but replacing those aspects wasn't a huge concern with 7-0 Luke Witte and sharp-shooting guard Allan Hornyak becoming eligible as sophomores.

The mystery was how "The Cougar," as Cleamons was known, would adjust to playing point guard full-time after being in a scorer's role the previous two seasons.

The answer would come soon enough, after OSU's record sank to 4-4 after a loss to Indiana in the Far West Classic.

"I was scoring a lot at the start of that season, but we weren't winning," Cleamons said. "Our offense needed to get the ball inside to Luke, so if Allan and I were shooting all the time, that wasn't going to happen. That's why I made a conscious decision to stop shooting as much and concentrate on setting Luke and Allan up."

The switch worked for a 3-0 start in the Big Ten before an 82-70 loss to visiting Michigan State interrupted the Buckeyes' momentum.

Cleamons, though, kept the young team together, and it wouldn't lose again until the season's final game in the NCAA Tournament.

"The success we had that year was directly because of Jim Cleamons," said Hornyak, whose 22.5 scoring average led the team. "He sacrificed his own game for the good of the team. You talk about a leader, that man was a leader.

"Whatever we needed, he did it. He was a great defensive player and a great offensive player. He wasn't the best outside shooter, but he was a tremendous playmaker and rebounder."

Cleamons' influence was so important few thought OSU could survive when he broke a bone in his left wrist in a late-February win over Northwestern.

Cleamons was OSU's leader on its '71 conference winner.

The initial prognosis listed him as doubtful for the remainder of the season, but instead he returned after missing two games.

OSU needed him for a one-point win at Northwestern that preserved the Buckeyes' one-game lead in the standings and set up the season finale against visiting Indiana.

The Hoosiers owned an 85-77 win over Ohio State in non-conference play, but Cleamons wouldn't permit IU or the cast on his left wrist to ruin his dream.

"I wanted that championship," he said. "And I wasn't about to lose my last game in St. John Arena."

Robin
FREEMAN

I Did It My Way

Basketball players in the 1950s possessed an old-school mentality that left no room for questioning the orders of their coach.

Good thing Robin Freeman was different.

Had he followed instructions to the letter, Freeman would never have become the most prolific scorer of his era—not only at OSU, but in the Big Ten.

His 32.9 average in 1956 led the conference by more than five points per game and followed seasons in which the 5-11 Freeman averaged 21.2 points as a sophomore and 31.5 as a junior.

That left him with a per-game career average of 28.0, easily the best in OSU history, and made Freeman the Buckeyes' career scoring leader upon his graduation.

None of that would have happened if not for a reflex action his senior year at Cincinnati Hughes High School.

While averaging 17 points per game as a junior, Freeman tried

convincing his coach that the jump shot would enhance his game.

That suggestion drew a firm rebuke and orders to stick with the set shot.

"There was a fellow named Paul Arnzen, who played at Villanova," Freeman said. "I saw the success he was having with the jump shot, and I fooled around with it enough to know that I was as accurate with that, if not more so, than with most of my other shots.

"My coach just wouldn't let me shoot that way, but in the first game of my senior year, I went up and did it out of habit and it went in. Then I made another, and another, and after that, my coach didn't gripe any more."

Neither would OSU head coach Floyd Stahl, who incorporated Freeman's jumper into the Buckeyes' offense with forward Paul Ebert's skills in the lane.

They combined for 60 points in an early-season non-conference game against Miami on the first

Ohio State team to surpass the century mark.

Ebert scored 35 and Freeman 25, despite sitting out the fourth quarter, in that 106-81 victory.

"Basketball was in an evolving stage," Freeman said. "When I first started to play, everything that happened was a set play. That changed to a free-lancing style, where you had all kinds of options.

"You could throw it into the center, then get the pass back out and then either shoot it, make a move to the basket, run a give-and-go, all sorts of things. That worked to my strength with the jump shot, because I could drive my man to the basket and then stop quickly and shoot."

Freeman was not only a rarity shooting the jumper, he did so with the ball raised high over his head, released while fading away from his defender.

"I shot almost exclusively off the dribble," he said. "I didn't like my teammates to screen for me. . . . If they screened for you, that meant there would be two defenders in the area. I preferred to go one-on-one with my man.

"All I had to do was get him moving as fast as I was, then I'd stop and go up with the jump shot. I was pretty accurate with it out to 22 feet. That's where the majority of my shots came from."

Freeman shot 44 percent as a junior, when his season was cut short by a severe ankle sprain that sidelined him after just 13 games.

One of those was a 44-point performance at Oklahoma, which broke the OSU single-game scoring record Freeman set with 43 against Loyola of Chicago.

That explosiveness earned Freeman All-American honors, despite his abbreviated junior year, and positioned him to become a repeat selection as a senior.

That was a certainty given his continued scoring outbursts, which included games of 43 points against both Michigan State and Illinois and a new school-record 46 against the Spartans in the teams' other meeting.

Freeman totaled 723 points that season, which endured as the best in a single year at OSU until surpassed by Gary Bradds's 735 points in 1964 and Dennis Hopson's 958 in 1987.

The NBA's St. Louis Hawks tried to sign Freeman, but he turned down their $10,000 offer to enter law school and embark upon a career path that would eventually see him named a fellow in the American College of Trial Lawyers.

"Pro ball in those days wasn't paying anything like it does now," Freeman said. "Sure, it paid more than my dad made teaching school. But I wasn't sure the money would be there for very long. I knew I

Freeman set a OSU scoring record his senior year.

wanted to be an attorney, so I thought it would be a wiser decision to get started toward that.

"Basketball was extremely enjoyable for me when I played. The thing that gave me such a thrill was, here I was, a guy just 5-11, but I was on the All-American team with guys like Bill Russell, who was 6-9. I was a relative midget compared to him, but there was a place for both of us in the game of basketball."

Tracey
HALL

Willing to Do the Dirty Work

The number that meant the most to Tracey Hall Yarbrough during her Ohio State women's basketball career was never the one that wound up epitomizing her talents in the minds of most observers.

The Buckeyes' career scoring leader with 1,912 points when her career concluded following the 1988 season, Hall always took much greater pride in a figure buried in the center of the statistical summary.

"The thing I'm most proud of is that I was able to do the little things, like rebound," said Hall, a starter in each of OSU's 122 games during her four seasons, three of which resulted in first-team All-Big Ten selection and two of which ended with her being named conference MVP. "I figured everybody in college was talented enough to score and shoot the ball, so I took pride in doing the things that other people couldn't do. I wanted to be known as an overall player, and rebounding was a big part of that."

True to that focus, Hall's impact on the glass belied her 6 foot-0 size.

She wound up third in Big Ten history with 1,115 career rebounds, a figure attained with rock-solid consistency from her freshman debut in 1984-85 to her senior year in 1987-88.

Hall grabbed more than 250 rebounds each season, led by a high of 305 in 1987 when she led the league with an average of 10.7 boards in conference games.

"Tracey took great pride in her rebounding," said Nancy Darsch, who coached Hall as a sophomore, junior and senior. "She looked at that as something that no one could prevent her from doing by herself. She challenged herself and motivated herself that way. It was always a great source of pride for her to get her 8-to-10 rebounds a game."

Hall was the Big Ten's freshman of the year in the final season of coach Tara Van Derveer's tenure at OSU, when the Buckeyes went 18-0 in the Big Ten and lost in the

NCAA East Regional finals to Old Dominion.

No conference team went unbeaten again in league play until national champion Purdue turned the trick in 1999.

"My freshman year was probably my favorite season because of the people who were around," Hall said. "The seniors, the coaching staff, everybody just took the young players under their wing. We were very close as a team, and I learned a lot that year, things I was able to take with me throughout the rest of my career."

OSU also won the Big Ten in Hall's sophomore and junior seasons, thanks in no small part to her continued dominance of the league's field goal percentage numbers.

She led the league in that category her first three seasons with accuracy rates of .588, .586, and .636 in conference games only.

"I went to Ohio State not sure if I could play at that level," Hall said. "I didn't have a lot of confidence in my ability when I got there, so I tried to become a student of the game. I felt I had pretty good athletic ability, and I thought if I could put that together with hard work, I could make a spot for myself."

Hall did far more than that, dominating the league in the years that she played.

"Tracey Hall was ahead of her time," said former Iowa coach Vivian Stringer. "She was just a great athlete with great reach and great reactions. She is one of the greatest players I ever saw in this conference—just a tremendous, tremendous player who was really ahead of her time.

"A player like Tracey Hall would have been successful in any era of basketball, she was that athletic. You could take the game she had when she played and put her out there on the floor today and she would still be a dominant player."

Darsch concurs, but as Hall's coach, she was even more impressed with Hall's manner than her on-court performance.

"Tracey was one of the best players of her era, but she never flaunted it or gloated or celebrated in any way like some of today's athletes," Darsch said. "She was just an extremely hard worker with a lot of class. She was a great role model."

Hall was a scoring and rebounding force.

Hall's talents were rewarded with her induction into the Ohio State Athletic Hall of Fame in 1998.

"That is the biggest honor I've ever received in my career," Hall said. "I was just in shock when I received it. I was overwhelmed when I was honored as the Player of the Decade, but to get named to the Hall of Fame was even more amazing to me. That's an honor I will always cherish."

John HAVLICEK

More Co-Pilot than Back-Seat Driver

He played in the shadow of the greatest basketball player in Ohio State history, yet was not overshadowed himself. That says plenty about John Havlicek's abilities, but not as much as the testimony his own talents offered while performing for the Buckeyes' 1960 national champions and 1961 and 1962 NCAA runner-ups.

A compliment to three-time All-American Jerry Lucas during his OSU career, Havlicek would not flower completely as a basketball player until getting his chance with the Boston Celtics of the NBA, where he made his reputation first as the league's best sixth man and later as a solid starter on several of the eight championship teams he was a part of.

Havlicek finished his professional career having played more NBA games than everyone but Kareem Abdul-Jabbar and Elvin Hayes, playing 16 seasons in which he scored 26,395 points and averaged 20.8 per game.

Havlicek didn't show that high-scoring side of his abilities at OSU until his final season because the Buckeyes needed his other talents more. Being the consummate team player, he was only too happy to oblige.

Coach Fred Taylor made Havlicek the team's defensive stopper, a role he filled so admirably that Taylor once noted, "John had such a reputation as a defensive player that schools were printing in their media guides how many points their stars scored against him."

Not many schools were left with much to print, for Havlicek unnerved the best of his day.

Detroit's Dave DeBusschere scored 10 quick points against the Buckeyes in 1960 and seemed well on his way to meeting his averages of 25.6 points and 20 rebounds. Havlicek switched over, however, and DeBusschere finished with only 14 points and 10 rebounds.

The story was the same in the Final Four against St. Joseph's John Egan, a 22-point scorer who managed only eight against Havlicek.

"He was the best coordinated big athlete I ever encountered," said CBS television analyst Billy Packer, who as a Wake Forest guard watched Havlicek take apart All-American Len Chappel twice. "He was relentless. . .and a fierce competitor. We thought he was even better than Lucas."

Havlicek wasn't sure he was good enough to play basketball for the Buckeyes when he came out of Bridgeport High School, where he was All-State in football, basketball and baseball.

Scouts from Pittsburgh, Cleveland, Cincinnati, Baltimore, and the New York Yankees wanted him to play baseball, while OSU football coach Woody Hayes had other ideas.

"Woody told me once, 'He probably would have been the greatest quarterback in Ohio State history, I just couldn't get him to come out,'" Celtics coach and general manager Red Auerbach once said.

Havlicek remembers Hayes keeping true to his promise that, "if you come to Ohio State to play basketball, I'll never bother you."

"Woody really pursued me a great deal, but the sport I liked best was basketball," Havlicek said. "After having played in some high school all-star games with (future teammates Lucas, Mel Nowell, and Bob Knight), it became quite clear as to where I was going to go. I thought we had the nucleus of a great team.

"As it turned out, I couldn't have picked it or planned it any better."

Havlicek progressed from the team's fourth-leading scorer as a sophomore to its second-leading scorer as a senior, when his 17-point mark and continued defensive excellence made him a first-team All-American.

His hustle and determination defined those Buckeye teams that reached three straight NCAA championship games and endeared Havlicek to a legion of OSU faithful.

Said Taylor: "I used to get notes from mothers saying their sons were diving on couches at home, imitating John going after loose balls."

Havlicek wisely chose basketball over football.

Dennis HOPSON

Timing is Everything

Dennis Hopson possessed a multiplicity of skills with the basketball.

With a crystal ball, Hopson wasn't quite so talented.

What he foresaw as the worst break of his Ohio State basketball career wound up positioning Hopson to become the Buckeyes' career scoring leader, the Big Ten's most valuable player, and a consensus All-American as a senior.

The Toledo native now sees how favorably fate tilted toward him, but worry initially had him in a hammerlock when OSU went searching for a new head coach prior to Hopson's senior season.

"We'd just won the NIT with Coach (Eldon) Miller, and I'd played very well that year," said Hopson, who averaged 20.9 points per game for the Buckeyes that season. "You never know what's going to happen in that situation. I was nervous about what kind of coach was going to

come in and whether he was going to allow us to play or if he was going to hold us back."

Hopson's fears vanished with the hiring of Gary Williams from Boston College, a coach who came highly recommended to athletic director Rick Bay by former OSU All-American and Boston Celtics legend John Havlicek.

What transpired during Williams's and Hopson's one season together proved them the perfect fit for each other.

Williams brought a pressing defense and fast-paced offense to St. John Arena, and Hopson gave him a made-to-order catalyst for both strategies.

"You couldn't have picked a guy more perfect for what we wanted to do," Williams said. "Dennis had all the skills you could ever want offensively. He could beat anyone one-on-one, he was a great shooter, and yet he was an unselfish passer who wasn't afraid to give up the ball.

"Defensively, he had long arms and great quickness and anticipation, so he was the perfect guy to play at the point of the press. He caused teams a lot of headaches there, because you couldn't pass over him and you couldn't get by him."

It took all of four games for the college basketball world to witness the wide-ranging skills Williams knew Hopson possessed after just a few days of practice.

Ohio University was the foil on a night when Hopson recorded the first triple-double in OSU history, making 13-of-18 field goal attempts to score 27 points, while also grabbing 11 rebounds and passing out 10 assists.

Three games later, Hopson went off for 41 points and 14 rebounds against Dayton, then turned his assault on some out-of-state opponents at the Rainbow Classic.

Hopson did everything but the hula in that three-game tournament in Hawaii, scoring 36 in a loss to Arkansas, 28 in an upset of 13th-ranked Kansas, and 36 in a win over Florida that avenged a road loss to the Gators 10 days earlier.

"Dennis just played great out there, and that was really crucial to giving us the confidence that we could get into the NCAA Tournament," said Jay Burson, a freshman guard for the Buckeyes that year.

"Dennis obviously did a terrific job for us in those three games, but maybe more important than that was the way he handled himself off the court. He showed all of our younger guys how to remain focused in a tough situation where you're playing three straight days against tough competition away from home."

That poise would show itself again once the Big Ten season began and Hopson unleashed a string of five straight 30-plus scoring performances.

The highlight was his 36-point effort in an 80-76 upset of No. 1 ranked Iowa at Carver-Hawkeye Arena that was Ohio State's first victory ever over a top-ranked opponent on the road.

Midway through that season, Williams termed Hopson "the best player I've ever coached," and other Big Ten coaches chimed in with equally lofty praise.

"I put Hopson at the top of the league and then there's a big gap," Michigan State's Jud Heathcote said. "He does it all inside and out, shooting, rebounding and on defense."

Hopson not only wound up the Big Ten's leading scorer at 29 points per game, a figure that ranked second nationally, he also had 97 more rebounds than any of his teammates. He led OSU with an average of 8.2 rebounds per game, and finished second on the team with an average of 3.6 assists.

"The greatest testament to Dennis is that he averaged 29 points, eight rebounds and all those assists, and he did it without his teammates resenting him," Burson said. "He just made it look so easy. There wasn't any dissension on our team because everything that he did, he did it in the scheme of what we were trying to get done on offense. That's what made him a great player."

Hopson would have had it no other way.

"I had the green light, so I could shoot the ball whenever I wanted and Coach Williams wouldn't have said anything," Hopson said. "But it wasn't like I was a ball hog. That wasn't my style of play. I got my points in the flow of what we were doing as a team, and I took my rebounding and defense very seriously."

Hopson's scoring talents shone brightest, however, and reached a crescendo in the final home game of his career.

A 36-point effort against Florida International enabled Hopson to pass both Jerry Lucas and Herb Williams on the OSU career scoring list. A 32-point effort in the Buckeyes' NCAA first-round win over Kentucky pushed Hopson past Purdue's Rick Mount as the Big Ten's single-season scoring leader.

"Those scoring records weren't something I set out to do or even thought I could do at the start of my senior year," said Hopson, whose 958-point season gave him 2,096 points for his career. "No one expects to average 29 points a game. That's crazy. Things just worked out right for me in Coach Williams's system."

Hopson played professionally for both the New Jersey Nets and Chicago Bulls before retiring from the NBA.

Hopson averaged 29 points his senior year.

Allan
HORNYAK

The Bellaire Bomber

The descriptive phrase commonly called upon to summarize the skills of the deadeye shooter was more than mere hyperbole in the case of Allan Hornyak.

The uncanny accuracy Hornyak displayed from the perimeter during a three-year career at Ohio State moved many to describe the "Bellaire Bomber" as someone who could shoot the lights out in St. John Arena.

What those admirers didn't know, however, was that Hornyak honed the left-handed jumper that would give him 1,572 points and a 22.8-point scoring average in 69 career games by, quite literally, shooting with the lights already out.

"We used to play all the time when I was a kid down in the Valley," Hornyak said of his formative years growing up across the Ohio River from Wheeling, W. Va., in Bellaire, Ohio. "We'd play all day until it got dark, and then we'd keep on playing, because we had a fluorescent net. That's all I could see sometimes."

Small wonder, then, that Hornyak grew into a scorer of unparalleled achievement at St. John High School in his home town, and later transferred those talents to OSU as part of the Buckeyes' 1971 Big Ten championship team.

His 41.9 scoring average as a high school senior led the nation and, incredibly, represented a reduction from the numbers Hornyak put up through the first 10 games of that season.

Thanks to consecutive games of 86—yes, 86—and 61 points and his 60 percent shooting from the field and 80 percent accuracy from the line, Hornyak began that year with an average of 48.6 points.

That stellar conclusion to his prep career left Hornyak with 2,385 points in 78 games—just 75 points less than the total accumulated by Jerry Lucas before he became a three-time All-American at Ohio State.

The hubbub over Hornyak becoming a Buckeye had plenty of time to build once he rejected

offers from every other major basketball power in America and chose to play for Fred Taylor at OSU.

Freshmen weren't eligible to play in 1970, so Hornyak spent the season getting to know his new teammates, including 7-footer Luke Witte.

"I didn't pay much attention to who the other guys were that I would be playing with when I was recruited," Hornyak said. "I didn't even know Fred had signed a 7-footer until after I decided to go to Ohio State. I looked at quite a few other places, including Kentucky and North Carolina, but it came down to just wanting to play close to home. Plus, I knew with what Ohio State had leaving, I was going to get the chance to play as a sophomore."

Indeed, the loss of four senior starters off OSU's roster took 71 percent of the scoring away, but scoring wouldn't be a problem with Hornyak joining the lineup.

He offered 23 points in the opener to serve immediate notice that the glow-in-the-dark shooting talents he displayed in high school would indeed transfer to the collegiate level.

After a 4-4 start, the players settled into their roles and began a sustained run to the conference championship.

Senior Jim Cleamons provided expert leadership at the point. Witte gave the Buckeyes a solid low-post presence, and Hornyak proved adept at coming off teammates' screens and stretching defenses with his long-range jumpers.

"I suppose the majority of my shots would have been three-point field goals today," Hornyak said. "It was tough, unless you had a layup, for a guard to get an inside shot in the Big Ten. The guys were so big and could really jump.

Hornyak had 32 points in OSU's final non-conference game and then scored 30 in the Big Ten opener at Iowa, where the Buckeyes won for the first time since 1964.

A home loss to Michigan State four games later interrupted the team's momentum, but Hornyak's 25 points in the rematch a week later helped OSU gain revenge and embark on a 10-game winning streak that would eventually claim the league title.

Hornyak's stellar road scoring spree continued throughout that surge, giving him an average of 26.5 points in the league games OSU played away from home that season.

He was never better than in the game that gave Ohio State first place in the standings, a 91-85 victory at eighth-ranked Michigan.

With Cleamons nursing a hairline fracture in his wrist, and therefore unable to take on many offensive responsibilities, the Buckeyes turned to Hornyak, and he delivered with 17 points in the first 5:20 and 37 overall on 16-of-28 shooting.

A 91-75 win over visiting Indiana in the regular-season finale secured the Big Ten title and sent OSU into an NCAA first-round game against second-ranked Marquette, which boasted a 27-0 record and 39-game winning streak over two seasons.

OSU fell into a 24-11 hole and still trailed by five, 57-52, with less than three minutes to play.

The Buckeyes then rallied, however, and took a one-point lead with just over one minute left.

That margin still prevailed when Hornyak went to the line with six seconds remaining and hit the two free throws that rendered meaningless a Marquette basket at the buzzer.

Hornyak's textbook jumpshot.

The Buckeyes' future seemed limitless at that point, with sophomore stars Witte and Hornyak in the fold for two more seasons and the team seemingly on the verge of a fifth Final Four berth in 12 years.

OSU, however, had reached its high point right then, for an overtime loss to Western Kentucky followed in the Mideast Regional final and the Buckeyes never reached the NCAA Tournament thereafter.

Hornyak certainly couldn't be blamed for that, averaging 21.6 points as a junior and 24.0 as a senior to earn All-American honors. He eventually played professional basketball with the Cleveland Cavaliers.

Witte, however, was never the same after being mugged in a midseason brawl at Minnesota in 1972, an attack that Taylor often said removed his enthusiasm for coaching.

"I wasn't the victim up there at Minnesota the way Luke was," Hornyak said.

Bill HOSKET

A Remarkable Season

Yogi Berra gets the credit for that time-worn sports cliché, "It ain't over 'til it's over," but Bill Hosket and his teammates proved that sometimes when it's over, it still ain't over.

Back in March of 1968, Hosket and the Buckeyes handed in their uniforms after a successful 17-7 season in which they made a mockery of predictions that placed them as low as ninth in the preseason forecasts of the Big Ten basketball race.

Head coach Fred Taylor was so certain his team would finish second in the league to Iowa that he held the postseason banquet on March 5, even though the Hawkeyes still had one game to play.

Last-place Michigan appeared no real threat to upset Iowa in Iowa City and thus close the half-game gap in the standings separating Ohio State from a share of first place.

But four days after the Buckeyes turned in their uniforms,

Michigan indeed sprang the upset that positioned Hosket and his teammates for one of the greatest rags-to-riches stories in OSU lore.

"When you think back on it, that was really a pretty amazing season," said Hosket, the Buckeyes' captain that year and the team's leading scorer and rebounder. "We all thought we were done playing. Iowa had the championship all sewn up. But then we got that one more chance, and we really made the best of it."

Hosket led the way in Ohio State's 85-81 win over Iowa in the Big Ten championship playoff game at Purdue, scoring 24 points and collecting 11 rebounds to give Taylor his sixth conference title of the decade.

That league title alone would have made the 1968 season memorable, but the Buckeyes had much more in store for their fans as recipients of the Big Ten's lone berth in the NCAA Tournament.

Hosket had 18 points and 20 rebounds to help dispatch Ohio

Valley Conference champion East Tennessee State in the first-round of the Mideast Regional at Kentucky's Memorial Coliseum.

That 79-72 victory set up a showdown with third-ranked Kentucky, unbeaten on its home floor that season, for the regional championship and a berth in the Final Four.

"Kentucky had a much better season than us," Hosket said. "They were very talented and had some great players, like Dan Issel and Mike Pratt. We were just a bunch of ordinary players that Fred made into a pretty good team.

"He redesigned his entire offense that season. He had to, because four of us played center in high school. After we got done playing, we used to kid Coach Taylor and tell him, 'We were the team that got you into the Hall of Fame.'

"It's one thing to win championships with guys like (Jerry) Lucas and (John) Havlicek. But when we showed up at the Final

Four in '68, people started to realize, "This guy must be a great coach.'"

Hosket's deadpan assessment of his talents belies the abilities of the '68 Buckeyes.

He and 6-foot-7 Dave Sorenson were a lethal tandem in Taylor's double-stack attack, and Steve Howell was an accurate perimeter shooter who kept teams from collapsing inside. Denny Meadors, Mike Swain, Craig Barclay and Jody Finney completed the rotation and provided the intangibles that tied the package together.

Still, OSU trailed Kentucky, 81-80, with five seconds left in their regional title game as Hosket set up beneath the basket for an inbounds pass.

"We set up a play we'd run all year," Hosket said. "Either Kentucky defended it differently or we broke down, but Steve Howell was supposed to take the shot and Sorenson and I were supposed to get in position for the rebound.

"I looked for Steve, because he was always open, but this time he wasn't. I didn't have any place to throw the ball until Issel dropped his arm to complain to the referee about a five-second count. I threw the ball right where his arm was."

Sorenson grabbed the pass and banked in a tough shot from the side to give the Buckeyes a stunning 82-81 victory.

North Carolina ended OSU's hopes for a national title with an 80-66 win in the Final Four semifinals, but Hosket and his teammates bounced back to edge the University of Houston and All-American Elvin Hayes in the consolation game, 89-85.

Hosket scored 19 in that win to cap a season in which he was the unanimous All-Big Ten and All-Mideast Regional, averaging 20.1 points and 11.4 rebounds.

That marked the third straight season in which he led the Buckeyes in both categories, ending his career as the second-leading rebounder in school history (910) behind Lucas and the fourth-leading scorer with 1,441 points in 74 games.

The 6-foot-8 Dayton native was so impressive his final year that U.S. Olympic coach Henry Iba selected for the team that won a gold medal in Mexico City.

Hosket finished his career in style.

After that, the New York Knicks made Hosket their first-round draft choice in advance of winning the NBA championship the following season.

"I think back on my career and a great deal of what I was able to do after Ohio State was a result of what happened after we thought our season was over my senior year," Hosket said. "I had a decent year, but the fact that Michigan upset Iowa and gave us a chance to get into that playoff game for the conference championship gave me added exposure.

"We got the chance to play in the NCAA Tournament, then beat Kentucky and got to the Final Four, where we beat Houston. That took me to the Olympics in very good condition. Playing on the gold-medal team, getting drafted by the Knicks—all of that happened or was helped by the fact that Michigan beat Iowa and gave us that extra chance.

"I would have missed out on a lot of great experiences and a lot of great memories if that hadn't happened."

Jimmy HULL

Stylish With a Comb and Basketball

Most everyone has been taught that the Great Depression struck in the 1930s.

Within the Ohio State basketball program, however, it struck even sooner.

After winning their first Big Ten championship in 1925, the Buckeyes went into a tailspin the likes of which could have prompted their most ardent supporters to leap off the ledge of a building.

OSU finished above fifth in the conference only once in the 12 years after claiming its initial league title. Given a crash like that, the Buckeyes didn't need a New Deal as much as they needed a new attitude.

That's what senior captain Jimmy Hull gave them prior to the 1938-39 season, taking a leadership role on a squad that suffered from dissension throughout his previous two seasons as a starter.

Hull led the effort to bolster the Buckeyes' harmony, taking his cause so far as to insist team members all cut their hair the same way.

That camaraderie knit together what had previously been a fragmented roster and helped OSU recognize the potential it began flashing during Hull's junior season in 1937-38.

Hull set a new school scoring record against Big Ten competition with 134 points in 12 conference games that season, including a 23-point effort against Chicago that was the highest single-game total by a Buckeye against a league member.

A quick shooter who freed himself by faking drives, then backing away from his defenders, Hull broke the OSU mark set by Johnny Miner in 1925.

Still, no one suspected that a year later Hull would join Miner as the Buckeyes' second All-American and almost lead OSU to the first NCAA Tournament championship.

After all, Ohio State's modest 12-8 record in 1938 gave no hint of such success, nor did its 7-5 mark in the Big Ten.

That earned the Buckeyes a third-place finish, their second-highest since winning the conference championship 13 years earlier.

Hull must have seen something, however, because he issued a stunning prediction when OSU returned from a West Coast road trip early in the 1939 season.

The Buckeyes won only twice in six games and were met upon arrival at the train depot by reporters seeking an explanation for the team's slow start.

Hull shocked them by predicting a Big Ten championship for OSU, and was so strong in his belief that he made head coach Harold Olsen promise the players a diamond-studded watch fob if they followed through on their captain's forecast.

An upset victory in the conference opener at Indiana lent some credence to Hull's claim, but a loss in game three at Illinois moved the Buckeyes back into a tie for first place with the Hoosiers.

They stayed there by the narrowest of margins until Indiana came to the Fairgrounds Coliseum seeking—and getting—revenge with a 46-34 victory.

The Hoosiers looked unstoppable, having lost only that one game so far to OSU, with only two games left in league play.

OSU went to Wisconsin facing a must win and got it when Hull exploded for a school-record 27 points. Indiana suffered an upset that same night at Purdue, giving the Buckeyes a share of first place.

The Hoosiers then lost again in their regular season finale at Michigan, and OSU took the title all by itself with a 16-point home win over Purdue. That seemed a storybook way for Hull to go out until word came that the NCAA wanted the Buckeyes as one of eight teams in its inaugural post season tournament.

It didn't hurt that Olsen was the chairman of the NCAA committee for the event, which was drawn up to rival the success of the already established National Invitation Tournament in New York.

These days, the NCAA Tournament is every collegiate player's goal. But things were much different in Hull's era, as he told author Bob Hunter in the 1981 book, *Buckeye Basketball.*

"As soon as the season was over, we were invited to participate in the NCAA, and it was like, 'What's that?'" Hull said. "We didn't even know what it was all about. Two or three of our players didn't even want to go. The state high school basketball tournament was going on, and we wanted to see that. We were tired. We had reached our goals."

Of course, OSU couldn't beg out of a tournament Olsen helped formulate, so it headed off to The Palestra in Philadelphia.

The Buckeyes posted back-to-back wins over Wake Forest and Villanova, with Hull getting 28 points in 28 minutes of the victory that put Ohio State into the first NCAA championship game.

Hull's outburst against Villanova carried a heavy cost, for he sprained his ankle in the victory and

Hull took OSU to its first Final Four.

couldn't practice the week leading up to OSU's game against Oregon for the title. Although he played in the game, Hull wasn't himself and neither were the Buckeyes, who fell short in a 46-33 final at Patten Gymnasium on the campus of Northwestern University.

Hull's exploits that season earned him the unique honor of having a tree planted in his honor by the athletic department in Buckeye grove, a distinction given before and since solely to Ohio State's football All-Americans.

Hull is the only non-football Buckeye to be honored in that fashion, but the tree planting wasn't the last Ohio State heard of Jimmy Hull.

On April 23, 1940, he appeared before the school's athletic board and proposed the establishment of a Varsity "O" club. The board approved the plan Hull proposed and voted to present gold watch keys to award winners, later changing to sweaters and finally to jackets, which in 1958 became the symbol for participation in a varsity sport at OSU.

Jim JACKSON

Special Didn't Begin to Say It

It's an image burned into the minds of those who witnessed it and those who didn't—the kind of moment that years afterward multiplies tenfold the 13,190 who were packed into St. John Arena, because everyone who wasn't there that day wishes they were.

Though he would play in 93 games over three seasons, get Ohio State a pair of Big Ten championships during his career, and carry the Buckeyes to three NCAA Tournament berths, the defining moment of Jim Jackson's era occurred on Feb. 17, 1991.

Seven seconds remained in a crucial conference showdown with Indiana that Sunday afternoon when Jackson received an inbounds pass in the backcourt and dribbled toward the basket with OSU trailing, 78-76.

He had already done yeoman's work keeping the Buckeyes in contention, moving to point guard early in the game when teammate Mark Baker went down

with an ankle sprain, yet also doing enough work on the boards to earn 11 rebounds.

This time, though, Jackson wasn't passing and he wasn't going to leave a rebound for anyone else.

He powered past Chris Reynolds, drove into the lane, rose over Matt Nover and Eric Anderson, and gently laid the basketball in at the buzzer.

St. John throbbed and a CBS television audience swooned as Jackson, fist pumping and eyes flashing, screamed, "C'mon, baby. YEAH!"

In that instant, it was no longer mid-afternoon, it was one of those special instances that for the duration of Jackson's career were known affectionately to OSU loyalists as, "J.J. Time."

What fans saw Jackson do as a freshman, tipping in missed free throws to author upsets of Top Ten members Illinois and Michigan, they would see him do again that day against IU, completing the script in a 97-95 double-

overtime triumph against the Hoosiers with his characteristic flourish.

Jackson's assist to Treg Lee off a drive to the hoop with four seconds left in the second overtime made the difference, just as so much of his artistry stood at the root of OSU's 70-23 mark over his career.

The Buckeyes hadn't experienced that much success in a three-year span since 1961-63, and the two Big Ten titles Jackson led OSU to in 1991 and 1992 were the school's first titles in 20 years.

All that caused Randy Ayers, Jackson's coach, to say this when Jackson finally decided to leave OSU with one season of eligibility remaining to enter the NBA draft:

"Jimmy was just a special player," Ayers said. "I feel very fortunate to have had a player of his talents during my first three years."

You didn't have to be a coach

to appreciate Jackson's talents. Even the competition—the most ardent competition Jackson faced—Hosketspoke highly of his ability and his manner.

"He's one of the three or four best players I've ever seen in our league," Indiana coach Bob Knight said of Jackson after competing against him for the last time. "He's one of those rare kids who can really play.

"Obviously, he knows he can play, and he has a lot of confidence in his play, but he doesn't act like it. I think the kid is a hell of an example of what a great college player should be. He's as good an example for kids to emulate as I've seen in the Big Ten."

Jackson was always his own harshest critic, finding holes in his game that no one else could locate.

After he progressed from Big Ten Freshman of the Year in 1990 to the league's Player of the Year in 1991, he turned his back on being a first-round NBA draft selection to come back to the Buckeyes as a junior.

"My all around game has to get better," Jackson said at the time. "I need to improve my ball handling, get stronger, and hit the outside shot with more consistency. I want to get quicker with my lateral movement and become more a complete player."

Privately, many wondered if Jackson had left himself much room for improvement with his All-American sophomore year, but he showed just how far he could come by growing his game tremendously before playing as a junior.

OSU fans held their collective breath that summer when Jackson had to sit out the medal round of the Pan-American Games when some slight discomfort in his left foot proved to be a weak bone on the verge of breaking.

Jackson wore a protective boot for six weeks and came back stronger than ever, despite missing the team's overseas trip that summer.

He increased his scoring average from 18.9 points as a sophomore to 22.4 as a junior, a figure that led

Jim Jackson was a two-time Big Ten MVP.

the Big Ten and made him a runaway winner of the league's Player of the Year award once again.

Jackson was named conference Player of the Week three times that season, increasing his total to a record seven times for his career, and led the Buckeyes to the NCAA Southeast Regional finals before falling to Michigan in overtime.

Shortly after that, Jackson declared himself eligible for the NBA draft and was taken as a lottery pick by the Dallas Mavericks.

"Jimmy was our focal point," Ayers said of the role Jackson played throughout his career. "He was the guy a lot of what we did revolved around. He was so important to us after we got that good strong (1992 recruiting) class. After that, we needed that one great player who could pull everything together, and Jimmy was that player."

Ken JOHNSON

No One Would Have Believed It

In every out-of-the-blue tale of triumph, where success sprang from humble beginnings, it seems there's always someone who foresaw the greatness that no one else anticipated.

Many times it's a mother or father, quite often a coach, and occasionally the only believer is the very person who musters the magic to climb from ordinary to extraordinary.

In the case of Ken Johnson—who came to Ohio State a timid teenager and departed four years later as the most feared shot-blocker in Big Ten basketball history—all the people who anticipated that transformation could have reclined comfortably in a Volkswagen Beetle.

Inside the glove compartment.

"Oh, my goodness, not in my wildest dreams did I expect to achieve all the things I was able to do individually and with the team," the 6 foot-11 Johnson said. "It was all just a tremendous blessing."

Johnson's ascent to a better-than-1,000-point career scorer, the seventh-leading rebounder in school history, and a shot-blocking artist the likes of which the Big Ten had never seen before nearly ended before it began.

He was so distraught in his first year at OSU that he nearly packed up and headed back home to Detroit.

That's where Johnson played his high school basketball, chiefly because as a 6 foot-7 freshman he was pressured into it by his peers.

"I was always talked about for being tall and skinny," Johnson said. "When I started playing basketball, I was awkward. I had no hands. I was really clumsy. I didn't know anything about it. (Basketball) was kind of like an enemy to me. It got to the point where I'd hear people laughing at me and I'd be like, 'Man, what am I doing here?'"

Johnson again found himself asking that question his true freshman year at Ohio State, when he couldn't play or practice with the Buckeyes after failing to meet the NCAA's immediate eligibility requirements.

"Walking around campus, I felt like I had a label on me," Johnson said. "I felt like people were looking at me, thinking, 'There goes that Prop (48).'"

Johnson's ego took even more of a blow as a sophomore, when he finally took the court and found a new head coach in place of the man who recruited him.

Jim O'Brien saw a mountain of talent in his new center, but virtually no basketball knowledge and even less desire.

"Kenny was just raw," O'Brien said. "I really couldn't tell if he even wanted to be on our team or not. He didn't seem tough enough and he didn't seem to want it bad enough."

Having already dumped a handful of holdover players for poor grades or bad attitudes, O'Brien took a risk with Johnson that wound up paying off like a penny stock that becomes a blue chip.

"I was on him and on him and on him," O'Brien said. "Every day, it was, 'Ken, how bad do you want this? Are you going to quit on us?' I figured, 'What have we got to lose?' We weren't very good anyway, and we weren't going to ever get good if the guys in the program didn't really want to be here.

"I wasn't trying to run him off. It was all about finding out if he was willing to make the commitment to doing the things he needed to do to get better."

Slowly, and in very infrequent bursts, Johnson began responding and flashed glimpses of the potential deep within him.

More importantly, with every sliver of success he experienced, Johnson's confidence began to grow.

Call it fate or call it luck, but the big man ended his first year with his best game of the season-a 15-point, 10-rebound, 4-block effort against Indiana in a loss at the Big Ten Tournament.

Still, no one saw Johnson being anything but a bit player on the Buckeyes in 1999, when all the preseason optimism centered on the addition of Boston College transfer Scoonie Penn.

While Penn proved as good as advertised, Johnson was the Buckeyes' unadvertised special.

His confidence and aggressiveness grew with every blocked shot, and it wasn't long before opponents learned the futility of challenging him around the basket.

St. John's, perhaps imbued by the bravado of its New York City base, chose to attack Johnson in the South Regional finals that March and watched helplessly as he took over the game.

Johnson not only blocked seven shots, but scored in double figures for only the fourth time all season, getting 12 points on six-of-nine shooting to help get the Buckeyes to the Final Four.

Johnson's 100 blocks ranked fifth in the country that season and set the stage for a senior year in which he led the nation with 161 blocks to set a Big Ten single-season record and easily win the league's defensive player-of-the-year award.

That seemed a storybook way for his career to end, until the story got even better.

OSU appealed to the NCAA and it granted Johnson an additional year of eligibility to recapture the one he lost as a freshman.

He responded with career-best averages of 12.5

Johnson (No. 32) records one of his 444 blocked shots.

points, 7.3 rebounds, and 125 more blocks to put the league's career record in that category—which he already possessed—virtually out of reach.

Those numbers earned Johnson a second straight defensive Player of the Year award and consensus first-team all-conference honors.

"When you think about all the great players who've played in Big Ten history, to think that Kenny blocked more shots than any of them, that just blows my mind," O'Brien said of Johnson's 444 career rejections. "Could anyone in 100 years ever have imagined Ken Johnson doing what he did, based on the type of player he was when he first got here?

"You'd have to be crazy to say to yourself, 'We'll get to the Final Four, win a Big Ten championship, and he's going to end up the leading shot-blocker in the history of this league.' Are you serious? No one would have said that.

Clark
KELLOGG

Special K in Every Way

It's a proven technique in the movie industry to whet the appetites of ticket-buyers with a preview that feeds their desire to see a particular show.

Clark Kellogg wasn't a theater major at Ohio State, but he nevertheless gave Buckeye fans an unforgettable coming attraction and followed with a career that didn't disappoint.

Before he ever donned a scarlet and gray uniform, Kellogg carved his own legendary niche in St. John Arena history with a 51-point performance in the state championship game of his senior season at Cleveland's St. Joseph's High School.

Already the most desired recruit in the state, if not the nation, Kellogg only inflamed the appetite of OSU loyalists with that effort against Columbus East in March of 1979.

Later that spring, he sent expectations soaring with the announcement he would, indeed, play for the Buckeyes.

"It's one thing to hear about a player, but it's another thing entirely to see him exhibit his skills," Kellogg said. "That state championship game my senior year was as grand a stage as you could ever want as a high school player. The only bad thing is, we didn't win the game."

Just as Kellogg's state single-game scoring record wasn't enough to gain his team the Class AAA title, the addition of his multi-faceted skills to a talent-laden OSU lineup didn't work the way most expected.

Instead, the payoff for his presence was more back-loaded than anticipated.

Logic suggested Kellogg would make his greatest contribution as a freshman, when his addition figured to give the Buckeyes the one element they lacked to make a run at the national championship.

After all, with center Herb Williams, forward Jim Smith, and guards Carter Scott and Kelvin Ransey, OSU seemed to have everything except a skilled small forward.

The 6-foot-8 Kellogg filled that void perfectly, helping the Buckeyes reach their first NCAA Tournament in nine years and take the race for the Big Ten title down to the final day at Indiana.

The 13th-ranked Hoosiers, however, came away with a 76-73 victory over the 10th-ranked Buckeyes to deny OSU's title dream. Later, UCLA's second-round upset en route to reaching the NCAA final ended Ohio State's hopes of winning the national championship.

"That season didn't pan out the way we wanted it to," Kellogg said. "It was still very exciting, and I had a productive freshman year, but we came up a little short of what we thought we could achieve."

If OSU's 21-8 finish in 1980 was a disappointment, what happened to the Buckeyes the following season was downright crushing.

A team expected to win the conference instead struggled to a 14-13 mark without the steady hand of Ransey at the point.

Kellogg increased his scoring from 11.6 as a freshman to 17.3 and upped his rebound average from 8.0 his first year to a Big Ten-best 11 per game as a sophomore, but neither of those achievements tempered his frustration over the Buckeyes' struggles on the floor.

"There were some dynamics within that team that just didn't work," Kellogg said. "There are certain things about team chemistry that can't be explained, but sometimes having talent just isn't enough. By the time I was a junior, I was more capable of being a leader on a team that lacked experience, but had all the intangibles you need to be successful."

Besides his leadership, Kellogg gave the Buckeyes plenty of tangible production in the 1981-82 season.

His 16.1 scoring average led the team and ranked third in the Big Ten, while his 10.5 rebounds led the league for a second straight season.

"He was our leader out there," OSU coach Eldon Miller said. "Our players looked to him in crucial situations. He was just a complete player. No one in the Big Ten did more for his team than Clark."

Even though he was the Buckeyes' only returning starter, Kellogg made sure Ohio State's conference title dreams didn't depart with the graduation losses of Williams, Smith, Scott and Todd Penn.

"Without a doubt, Clark was our star," said Ron Stokes, a freshman guard that season. "When you have a great player, it takes a lot of pressure off everyone else. We knew if we got the ball to Clark at crunch time, he would make the plays on his own. He absolutely took over a lot of games down the stretch."

Kellogg had shown the capacity to dominate before, of course, having gone for 42 points the previous season against Northwestern.

But as a junior, he was the target of every opposing team's defense and yet still delivered the victories OSU needed to stay in the Big Ten title chase until the final day.

The Buckeyes were just 4-4 in the league nearing the midpoint of the conference schedule, and had lost four of five games.

Kellogg scored 17 points to go with his 15 rebounds in a 50-49 overtime win against visiting Michigan State, putting the Buckeyes ahead for good with a three-point play in the extra period.

OSU took off from there, winning eight of nine to pull into a tie with Minnesota atop the standings.

Fate, however, dealt the Buckeyes a road game at Minneapolis on the final day—just as had been the case Kellogg's freshman season when OSU had to play at Indiana to finish the year.

A loss to the eighth-ranked Gophers and a first-round upset loss against James Madison in the NCAA Tournament wrote a disappointing conclusion to the season, but no one had expected the 21-10 record Kellogg carried the Buckeyes to in what was supposed to be a rebuilding year.

"It was good to go out with a surprise on the upside after the disappointment of my sophomore year," said Kellogg, who made himself eligible for the NBA draft after his junior season and was a first-round pick of the Indiana Pacers. "Being able to leave as the Big Ten MVP, being able to compete for a Big Ten title two out of three years, that helped make my years at Ohio State really special."

Kellogg ruled the glass.

Nikki LOWRY

Determined To Succeed

Nikita Lowry came to Ohio State in 1985 already equipped with a feature manufacturers in her native Detroit wouldn't bring to their automobile plants for a few more years.

Even before she reported to campus, it became apparent that Lowry, a 6 foot-0 forward for the Lady Buckeyes, had shift-on-the-fly engineering.

How else to explain her rapid adjustment to adverse circumstances that would throw most high school recruits for a loop—a quality that would serve her well later in her OSU career.

The coach who recruited Lowry, Tara Van Derveer, accepted the same job at Stanford before Lowry could report and play a single game.

"I knew I wasn't going to go to California," Lowry said with a laugh. "That was way too far. So, I decided to make the best of it at Ohio State, work hard and hope things worked out."

A pair of Big Ten scoring titles

and All-America selection her senior year suggests Lowry indeed made the most of her time as a Buckeye, during which her teams won one outright conference championship and shared two others.

That Lowry was able to complete her career in such accomplished fashion was a testament to her determination to endure.

Between her junior and senior seasons, while playing for Team USA in the World University Games, she landed awkwardly on her left leg when fouled on a fast-break layup.

"My knee buckled and I went down," Lowry said. "I thought I hurt my ankle, because that's where I felt the pain. But when the doctors got a look at it, they came to find out it was my knee. I'd torn my anterior cruciate ligament and messed myself up pretty good."

Arthroscopic surgery wasn't as advanced in those days, so Lowry's option was to have full surgery to

repair the injury, redshirt a year while rehabilitating, and hopefully then regain her previous form in a fifth season of eligibility.

Or, she could work to strengthen the muscles around the damaged area, wear a brace, and hope the joint held up throughout her senior year.

"I wanted to finish with the players I came into Ohio State with," Lowry said. "That's why I decided to strengthen the knee and see what I could do."

Measuring up to her junior season wouldn't have been easy, even on a healthy knee.

Lowry had averaged a conference-best 22.2 points, becoming the first OSU women's player to average more than 20 points in a season since Frani Washington in 1979, while also leading the league in field goal percentage (.616) and steals (3.1) and tying for the conference lead in rebounding (8.4).

Trouble was, as a senior, Lowry was to have even more pressure to produce, because All-American

Tracey Hall, whom she played beside in the frontcourt for three seasons, had just graduated.

"I made up my mind to play, but I wasn't going to play if I couldn't play like I had the year before," Lowry said.

"I remember there were times I'd take off trying to do something and the coaches would yell at me to take it easy.

"I told them several times, 'I either go or I don't go. I can't play half-speed.' They finally accepted that and let me go and things worked out. I got used to the brace I was wearing and was able to hold up."

Lowry did more than survive; she thrived, leading the league in scoring again with a 19.1 average and helping the Buckeyes to a share of first-place in the conference and 24-6 overall record.

"Nikki showed a lot of courage the way she played her senior year," head coach Nancy Darsch said. "She was always a very smooth player, one who never looked like she was working hard, even when she was.

"She was just so effortless at what she did. She had good strength inside and was very smart in there. She was instinctive. She could create shots for herself and for her teammates. She also could shoot the three, so she was really the first player in the Big Ten to exhibit that inside-outside combination."

Lowry later became an assistant coach at OSU before taking over as the head coach at Detroit and then New Mexico.

Lowry played through pain her senior year.

"I really enjoyed all my years at Ohio State, but my senior year was the most special," Lowry said. "It meant a lot to me to play through a situation I had never been forced to face before. Basketball was very precious to me, and when I got injured I felt like it was being taken away from me. I took it as a personal challenge to fight, not fold."

Jerry LUCAS

An Open and Shut Case

Statistics can often be arranged to prove anything, whether the statement is factual or fictional. Sometimes, though, no matter how the numbers are shuffled, the result cannot be denied.

Such is the case with acknowledging Jerry Lucas as the greatest Ohio State basketball player of all time.

There have been and perhaps will be other OSU players who shot more, scored more, dunked more, and demonstrated more flash with their game than Lucas.

Put plainly, however, there has never been a better player in a Buckeye uniform than Lucas, and it's unfathomable to believe there ever will be.

The truest measure of his greatness lies not in the impressive scoring, rebounding, and shooting totals Lucas compiled, but in the manner in which he accumulated those numbers.

If ever there was a player whose contributions came within the context of the team game, it was the graceful 6-foot-8 Lucas, whose three years of varsity action for the Buckeyes from 1959-60 to 1961-62 not so coincidentally coincided with the most successful era in school history.

Ohio State won 78 of 84 games during Lucas's career, winning the NCAA championship his sophomore season and losing in the NCAA championship game both his junior and senior years.

He was the Final Four MVP in 1960 and 1961, winning the award for the second time despite OSU's failure to win the event, something that has happened only four times since.

The Buckeyes breezed to the Big Ten title all three of Lucas's seasons, going 40-2 in conference games and winning a record 27 in a row over the three-year span.

Lucas led the nation in field goal percentage all three years and led the nation in rebounding his final two seasons.

Statistics were not kept to record assists in those days, or Lucas would likely have led the nation in that category, too.

That's no exaggeration, for while Lucas averaged 24.3 points per game for his career, he averaged only 16 field goal attempts per game as a sophomore, 15 as a junior and 14 as a senior.

Head coach Fred Taylor was once asked by a West Coast reporter if he wished Lucas would shoot more.

"Is Los Angeles big?" Taylor deadpanned.

It was no accident that Lucas's scoring average declined each season, from 26.3 as a sophomore to 24.8 as a junior, to 21.8 as a senior.

"The more I played, the less I cared about points," Lucas said. "Anybody can score if his teammates set him up."

Predictably, Lucas's rebound totals increased each season. He collected 442 boards his first year, 470 his second season, and 499 as a senior.

Those totals not only make Lucas the Big Ten's career rebounding leader to this day, they give him the three highest single-season rebounding totals in conference history.

Early in his senior year, Lucas read an account of his performance in a 21-point victory at third-ranked Wake Forest that said he collected "everything but the paint off the backboards."

After that game, OSU headed to a four-day tournament in Los Angeles that featured five of the best teams in America.

"Maybe I'll get the paint there," Lucas told writers.

Sure enough, in the second round against UCLA, Lucas grabbed a tournament-record 30 rebounds to better the previous mark of 25.

His 30 boards were more than the entire UCLA team, and Lucas also scored 30 points on 11-of-13 field goal shooting and eight-of-eight shooting at the free throw line.

Only four of Lucas's baskets in that victory came off teammate passes. Instead, he regularly returned their passes to foster their own scoring chances and contented himself with converting via the offensive glass.

Afterward, legendary UCLA coach John Wooden came to the Ohio State locker room to congratulate Lucas.

"I want to tell you that you are the most unselfish athlete I have ever seen," Wooden said. "Our team played its very finest, but (you) were magnificent. It was a pleasure to lose to such a man. I have never said such a thing before. I never expect to again."

After Lucas scored 38 points in the tournament championship game the next night against USC, vanquished coach Forest Twogood said of Lucas, "That was the greatest performance I ever saw. Most

Lucas was a two-time Final Four MVP.

star players always want the ball, but Lucas is like a man who gets drunk without drinking. He scores 30 points without getting ball."

Lucas' play regularly inspired such praise from opponents.

"I've never seen a pro who was any better," legendary St. John's coach Joe Lapchick said after a loss to OSU.

"He was the best player I ever coached," California's Pete Newell said after Lucas helped lead Team USA to the 1960 Olympic gold medal in Rome.

When Lucas left Ohio State, he had lost only eight basketball games in 13 years, dating to when he took up the sport as a fourth-grader in Middletown.

Lucas was the most coveted recruit in the nation, and was so talented that the Cincinnati Royals of the NBA drafted him every year after he graduated from high school until he finally joined the team following his graduation from Ohio State.

Offers of cars, money and a lucrative job for his father never swayed Lucas, whose focus was always on life after basketball and not the sport itself.

"I stopped even reading the letters from the schools," he said. "I came from an ordinary family. I could picture myself with a new car, my dad with a lot of money, and right away I could see myself getting into a lot of trouble.

"I felt I had a good future. A wrong decision could have ruined everything. You have to look at the future in life. . . . I knew I wanted to go to school in Ohio, and Ohio State was the only school out of all of them that talked about academics first. The rest talked about athletics."

Johnny MINER

Good Thing He Didn't Hold a Grudge

Michael Jordan gained some measure of fame for—among other things (OK, many other things)—being cut from his high school basketball team.

His Airness, of course, went on to sink the winning shot in the waning seconds of an NCAA championship game, win six NBA titles, and redefine the game as perhaps its greatest individual player in history.

But in one respect, at least, MJ had nothing on Johnny Miner.

OSU's first basketball All-American, Miner went one better than Jordan by being cut—not from his high school team—but from the Buckeyes' roster the first time he tried out.

In the fall of 1921, Miner was fresh out of Columbus East High School, a 5-foot-8, 130-pound wisp whose shooting skills most likely could have helped an OSU team that would finish 8-10 overall.

The head coach back then, however, was George "Red" Trautman, who had been a fine all-around athlete on the Buckeyes' baseball, football, and basketball teams from 1911-14.

Judging basketball talent, or at least potential, apparently wasn't Trautman's strength.

He cut Miner the first night he tried out, giving Miner the thought that perhaps his future in the sport would be better spent playing the semi-professional circuit in Ohio.

Some friends talked him out of that, encouraging Miner to preserve his amateur eligibility because Trautman was soon to be replaced by new coach Harold Olsen.

Olsen's arrival signaled a renewed commitment to basketball by the university, since he had been an all-conference guard on one of the seven Wisconsin teams that won the Big Ten championship over a 10-year period.

Olsen spotted Miner playing in an intramural game one day and was so impressed that he went to the team's locker room at halftime and asked him to join the Buckeyes.

"I was just trying out for the team," Miner told Bob Hunter, author of the 1981 book, Buckeye Basketball. "I was small, they used to call me, 'Little Johnny Miner.' I didn't particularly know whether I would make it or not. Those players who were there, they looked awfully big to me. I didn't expect to make it."

Miner more than made the team this time. He joined with Olsen finds Mel Shaw and Harold "Cookie" Cunningham to make OSU an immediate Big Ten championship contender.

The Buckeyes finished 12-5 overall and 7-5 in the league in 1924, tying with three other teams for fourth place behind tri-champions Wisconsin, Illinois, and the University of Chicago.

OSU lost three of its first four conference games that season, but made a run at the title with six straight victories.

Consecutive road losses at

Minnesota and Wisconsin to end the year wound up costing the Buckeyes a share of first place.

OSU lost four of its five conference games by a combined nine points—any one of which would have provided a piece of the title had the result wound up differently.

So, when the Buckeyes came together for practice the next season, expectations for the school's first Big Ten title were running high.

Overflow crowds wedged into the frigid Fairgrounds Coliseum to watch the Buckeyes win their first three games that season.

OSU split its next four to stand 5-2 overall and 2-1 in the Big Ten, then ran the table with victories in its last nine games to wind up 14-2 and 11-1.

That left the Buckeyes alone atop the conference,

Miner was OSU's first basketball star.

three games in front of second-place finishers Indiana and Illinois.

Miner led the Big Ten in scoring with 133 points in 12 games for an 11.08 average, numbers that made him the Buckeyes' first basketball All-American.

Scoonie PENN

Here I Come to Save the Day

As long as they'd been together, they should have been on the same wavelength—so perfectly in tune that the point guard was, by now, a seamless extension of his head coach.

That's what everyone thought would be the case when James "Scoonie" Penn put a transfer year behind him and became eligible to take the floor for the Ohio State basketball team.

Penn had followed head coach Jim O'Brien from Boston College to OSU and was expected to figure prominently in the revitalization of a program that had hit bottom just six years after winning back-to-back Big Ten championships in 1991 and 1992.

At first, however, Penn sounded more like his coach's evil twin than his alter ego.

While O'Brien was preaching patience and stressing the goal of following an 8-22 season in 1998 with an above-.500 finish in 1999, Penn was talking bigger things.

Much bigger things.

"I've been to the NCAA Tournament my first two years and I don't plan on missing it this year," Penn said when practice began that October. "That's our goal, to get into the NCAA Tournament."

No one knew then that it was Penn, not O'Brien, who was being conservative.

The Buckeyes didn't just make the NCAA Tournament that season, they made it all the way to the school's first Final Four in 31 years.

And every inch of the way, Penn was the 5-foot-10-inch fireball of a jockey whipping the Buckeyes along.

His ballhandling and passing skills turned Jason Singleton and Ken Johnson into scoring threats inside, and Penn's 16.9 scoring average gave OSU a backcourt threat to go with reigning Big Ten scoring leader Michael Redd.

The biggest change, though, was Penn's ability to drive his teammates through the sheer force of his will.

"Scoonie brought a lot of leadership and made a difference in how guys approached the game," Redd said. "He brought a winning passion to our program."

Penn was frequently the smallest player on the floor, but he was a seven-footer in terms of confidence.

"I knew our team needed me the most in the biggest games," Penn said. "I never knew how many points I was going to score. It might be a lot of points, it might not. But I knew that some how, some way, I was going to play a role in those games. That was my job as the point guard and a leader on that team, and that was fine with me."

Whatever OSU needed, whenever the Buckeyes needed it, he provided the spark.

Just 4-3 in the league in late January, facing four of its next five games on the road, Penn awoke the Buckeyes from their doldrums by leading them to successive victories at Illinois, Purdue, Iowa, and Indiana.

No Ohio State team had ever won at those four schools in the same season, and the 1999 Buckeyes surely wouldn't have without Penn averaging over 19 points in those victories.

He had 20 at the half in OSU's final regular season game at Penn State, but took a hard fall early in the second half and suffered a deep bruise on his backside.

The injury not only hampered him in that eventual loss, but in the Big Ten Tournament, where OSU suffered a second-round upset to Illinois.

Suddenly, a season full of so much promise hinged on how well Penn could recover from a damaged derriere.

He still wasn't himself in Indianapolis, where the Buckeyes breezed past Murray State and Detroit, setting up a South Regional match up with top-seeded Auburn.

The Tigers had lost only three times in 32 games, and appeared home free against OSU when Johnson, Singleton and Penn all gained their fourth personal fouls by 12:26 of the second half.

The Tigers quickly moved to a 52-46 lead before O'Brien made a daring move and reinserted Penn at 10:14.

"You don't want to lose the game with your best player on the bench," O'Brien said.

You sure don't.

And OSU didn't.

Penn offered an immediate three-pointer, then scored in transition, and the Buckeyes were alive.

He wound up making six of his last eight shots and scoring 26 points in a 72-64 victory that put OSU into the finals against St. John's the following day.

Penn was no less spectacular against the Red Storm, getting 22 points, eight rebounds and eight assists to win regional MVP honors.

He also knocked the ball away from St. John's Erick Barkley in the final seconds as Barkley drove toward the basket with his team down by two points and less than 10 seconds left.

OSU's storybook season ended with a loss to eventual NCAA champion Connecticut at the Final Four, but that defeat did nothing to spoil the fairy tale that saw the Buckeyes go from 8-22 in 1998 to 27-9 in 1999.

Nor did the loss at the Final Four do anything to lessen the expectations for the following season once

Penn turned his back on leaving school early for the NBA and came back for his senior year. (He was eventually drafted by the Atlanta Hawks after his senior season.)

Once again, he was outstanding, averaging 15.6 points, making first-team All-Big Ten and leading the Buckeyes to a co-championship of the conference with eventual national champion Michigan State.

Although he played only two seasons, Penn cracked the 1,000-point mark in career scoring at OSU and wound up the Buckeyes' career leader with 153 three-point field goals.

Only 11 other players before Penn scored more points in their final two seasons with the Buckeyes than his 1,076, with Kelvin Ransey the only point guard among that group.

"When you think about his impact, you'd be hard-pressed to come up with any other guy who impacted any program the way Scoonie impacted our program," O'Brien said.

Penn was the consummate leader.

Kelvin RANSEY

Establishing a New Standard

None of the typical standards prove suitable for measuring the completion of Kelvin Ransey's primary goal upon enrolling at Ohio State.

There were no Big Ten championships, no NCAA titles, and no Final Four berths to show for the era Ransey directed the Buckeyes from the point guard position.

But to conclude that the Toledo native's career was anything but a resounding success would be as farcical as it would be unfair.

A three-time first-team all-conference selection and a consensus All-American as a senior, Ransey's talents earned something more lasting than considerable individual recognition for himself.

His wide-ranging abilities and invaluable leadership directed the Buckeyes back to the national spotlight and positioned the program for ongoing success throughout the remainder of the 20th Century.

"The thing that I am the most proud of in my career was playing a role in changing the focus toward Ohio State basketball," Ransey said. "Looking back to my first year, we barely got 6,000 people to come to our games. But by my senior year, we were the hottest ticket in town.

"The interest in basketball was really high at that time, which made me feel good, knowing I had accomplished what I set out to do."

Ransey's 1,934 points ranked second in OSU history upon his graduation behind only Jerry Lucas's 1,990, and Ransey's 516 assists remain the school's career record.

He led the Buckeyes in scoring each of his last three seasons, including a 21.4 mark as a junior and a 16.2 mark as a senior when Ransey sacrificed his offense to balance the team's attack and involve other players.

"Kelvin was such a terrific scoring point guard," said Clark Kellogg, a freshman on that 1980 Ohio State team. "He took so much pressure off our other guards and everyone else on the team, because he could go get his own shot whenever we needed a basket."

No one at OSU knew what a gem first-year coach Eldon Miller acquired when he lured Ransey to campus out of Macomber High School for the 1977 season.

Miller was hired in April, well after most top high school players had committed elsewhere.

But few, if any coaches in the Big Ten, came up with a recruit as talented as the 6-foot-1 Ransey, who became the cornerstone for a renaissance in the Buckeyes' fortunes.

Miller added center Herb Williams, forward Jim Smith, and guards Carter Scott and Todd Penn the following season, then plucked Kellogg the year after that to give OSU what many believed was the most talented starting five in the nation for that 1980 season.

By then, Ransey's reputation as the team's leader was already cemented, growing off his repeated big game performances his first three years.

As a junior, he scored 26 points in New York's Madison Square Garden to bring the Buckeyes back from a 17-point second half deficit and provide an upset of then No. 1 Duke.

"I'll never forget that," Ransey said. "That was one of the best games we ever played. It had always been my dream to play in Madison Square Garden, because my favorite players were Walt Frazier and Earl Monroe with the New York Knicks. I always felt if I played in the Garden, I was going to have a good game."

Ransey fulfilled that promise, although his achievements that night and the following night, when he scored 38 points in a triple-overtime loss to Rutgers, were obscured by the firing of legendary OSU football coach Woody Hayes that same weekend.

The Buckeyes rolled to an 8-0 start in the Big Ten that year, but lost three of four games to imperil their hold on first place. They wound up losing the 1979 championship by one game during a three-game skid at the end of the regular season.

"We didn't expect to start as fast as we did in the conference, and I really don't think we handled it very well," Ransey said. "We didn't realize how much teams were going to come after us that second half of the season, and we just wilted a little toward the end."

Adding Kellogg, the most coveted Ohio recruit in years, supplied the final piece believed necessary to win the Big Ten title in 1980.

OSU started 5-0 in the league, but then lost four of six to bring the conference title down to a winner-take-all, regular season finale at Indiana.

The Buckeyes had a 58-51 lead in the second half, but IU forced overtime and then got the break it needed for a 76-73 victory when Williams fouled out down the stretch.

"I don't like to say anything bad about officiating, but I still say that was a phantom call," Ransey said. "Herb never touched their guy. I think we would have been home free if that hadn't happened, but losing Herb really hurt us in that game."

Williams and Ransey came back to score 25 points apiece in OSU's NCAA Tournament debut, an 89-75 victory over Arizona State on the Sun Devils' home floor.

That brought on a second-round game against UCLA, a team that was lightly regarded, but wound up reaching the national championship game with a lineup that featured four eventual NBA players.

Ransey did all he could to prevent the Buckeyes' elimination, scoring 29 points before fouling out with 29 seconds left in a 72-68 loss.

Miller bade farewell to his four-year stalwart at point guard by terming him "the most complete player I've ever been around," an assessment the Portland Trail Blazers didn't quarrel with upon making Ransey the fourth pick overall in the 1980 NBA draft.

He played six seasons before retiring to enter the ministry, working with his brother in Toledo for over a decade before starting the Spirit of Excellence Church in Oxford, Miss.

"If there is one regret I have it is that I didn't have the same love for the game as many of the great players," Ransey said. "If I had loved the game a little more, I would have worked harder at it, but my heart was always set on the ministry.

"Those Ohio State years were great years. I definitely enjoyed college basketball a lot more than the pros, because of the atmosphere, the excitement and the enthusiasm. Every night that you played in college, it was just wonderful."

Ransey led a OSU hoops resurgence.

Larry SIEGFRIED

Sacrifice Worth The Struggle

The years have framed a story of Ohio State's 1960 NCAA championship team as a unit that sprang to instant competitiveness because of the addition of sophomores Jerry Lucas, John Havlicek, and Mel Nowell.

What's often ignored is that those three joined a formidable talent already on the roster who, if not for his willingness to sacrifice personal goals, likely could have undermined the considerable success the Buckeyes enjoyed the final two seasons of his career.

While Lucas, Havlicek, and Nowell were indeed as good as advertised, Larry Siegfried was no returning slouch when he reported for his junior year.

As a sophomore, Siegfried had averaged 19.6 points per game and earned All-American status in almost single handedly driving Ohio State to a respectable 11-11 record in head coach Fred Taylor's rookie season.

Siegfried had been a scoring machine in his high school days in

Shelby, once getting 58 and 60 points in consecutive games during a senior year in which his 36-point average ranked second in the state only to Lucas.

It's no wonder, then, that OSU went 24-3 and breezed to the NCAA title in 1960 with talent like that at its disposal.

But what's overlooked is that the Buckeyes' success then—and in 1961 when they won a second straight Big Ten championship and lost to Cincinnati going for back-to-back NCAA titles—came about only after Siegfried sublimated his high-scoring desires.

"I struggled with that," Siegfried said. "I hated (Taylor), because he was infringing on my selfish ways, but he was the coach. He threatened to bench me because I was struggling with (the team concept). We were blowing people out, but I was getting only eight or 10 shots a game."

The choice Siegfried eventually made for the good of the whole wasn't lost upon his teammates.

"Larry had to sacrifice a great deal," Havlicek said. "He showed that he wasn't just interested in personal stats."

Siegfried's average fell from 19.6 points per game as a sophomore to 13.2 as a junior.

The following year, he captained the Buckeyes and scored 15.2 per game to finish his career with 1,228 points.

"I never reached my full potential, but we had a team," Siegfried said. "From a selfish, egotistical standpoint, maybe I should have gone to another school where I could have had amazing stats. But my reward was fitting in when I joined the Boston Celtics. That was the epitome of everything I had learned at Ohio State."

Siegfried was the third pick in the 1961 NBA draft by the Cincinnati Royals, but his bitterness over losing to Cincinnati in the NCAA championship game that March prompted him to sign with the Cleveland Pipers of the upstart American Basketball League.

That endeavor folded after one season and Siegfried didn't make it to the NBA until Havlicek sold Red Auerbach on picking up his former Ohio State teammate in 1963.

Siegfried became a mainstay on five Celtics' championship teams, filling a myriad of roles for the team, depending upon whether his scoring, ball handling or defensive skills were most needed.

"The more pressure you put on Larry, inside, he loved it and responded to it," Havlicek said. "He might complain, but you knew he was going to give it everything he had."

That same statement still typifies Siegfried's memories of his Ohio State career.

Although he sometimes sounds torn by the individual accolades he sacrificed, he knows the choice was ultimately worth the price.

"I couldn't do everything I wanted to," Siegfried said. ". . . It forced me to adjust my game, and because of my desire to compete and succeed, I moved myself into that role. Was I frustrated? You bet I was. But never reaching my individual potential is not the issue. It's the team (that matters).

"I'd do it over again, but I'd do it better, because I'd enjoy it. By the time I arrived in Boston, I was a team player. There were no (inner) struggles. I could enjoy the ride. But when I was at Ohio State, I was still struggling."

Siegfried was a mainstay on the 1960 NCAA championship team,

Katie
SMITH

Small-Town Girl, Big-Time Talent

It had a script that seemed too corny for Hollywood, but not for Columbus. Otherwise, the story of Katie Smith's Ohio State basketball career would have been fantasy and not reality.

Coming out of the small town of Logan, Ohio, Smith wasn't swayed by the attention she received as the most sought-after recruit in the nation in 1992 and chose to play for the Buckeyes.

OSU fans, keenly aware Smith could have played anywhere, never forgot that loyalty and lavished their affection upon her through-out an achievement-laden career that began with a Cinderella trip to the NCAA championship game her freshman season.

"Ohio State was a very special place for me," said Smith, whose career total of 2,578 points stands as the Big Ten women's record. "The fans made it so that I cherished every moment."

Smith more than reciprocated, playing with a fearless style that made her impossible to guard one-on-one and risky to double-team because of her unselfishness.

"Katie could hurt you a lot of ways," said Nancy Darsch, Smith's coach at OSU. "She could shoot the three-pointer. She could post up. She could score in transition and she could really hurt you at the free throw line. All of those things were part of her game, and all of them accounted for why she was so hard to stop."

Smith started in the first game of her freshman season in 1992 and was a consistent force throughout her career.

She failed to reach double figures in only five of 124 career games, and she scored 30 or more points 11 times, leading the Buckeyes in scoring every year of her career.

Her 21.3 average led the Big Ten as a junior, and she finished second in the league with a 21.9 average as a senior, when her 745 points broke Frani Washington's record of 711 set in 1978-79.

Smith's four single-season averages ranked among the top seven single-season scoring efforts in OSU women's history when she graduated, including the third-best (639 points in 1994-95) total ever by a Buckeye.

Smith, though, was far more than just a scorer.

She had over 100 assists in a season three times and led the Buckeyes in that category as a junior and a senior, years when she also led the team in steals.

"I tried to do a lot of different things," Smith said. "The thing I was most proud of was my ability to be a distributor and a creator, someone who set things up for my teammates. Sometimes that was by a pass. Sometimes, it was by being a decoy.

"I always tried to be a player who just took advantage of what was there for me, whether it was a shot or something for somebody else."

That's how former Iowa coach C. Vivian Stringer remembers

Smith from the season in which the then-Buckeye freshman led the Buckeyes to a Final Four semifinal victory over the Hawkeyes.

"Katie was just such a strong player, even for a freshman," Stringer said. "She came in and made Ohio State a complete team, not just because she could score, but because she lifted the games of the players around her."

"Katie was always a very unselfish player," Darsch said. "There were a lot of facets to her game that people didn't see or appreciate, because they focused on her scoring, but her coaches noticed it and her teammates noticed it."

Smith broke Machelle Joseph's Big Ten scoring record of 2,405 points late in her senior season.

"When I think about the players who played before me in the league, that's when having that record really makes an impression on me," Smith said.

She played on the U.S. Olympic team in 2000 and is one of the top young players in the WNBA, leading scoring during the 2001 season while playing for the Minnesota Lynx.

"I'll never forget my years at Ohio State," Smith said. "They gave me some great memories."

Smith shows her perimeter skills.

David BOSTON

He Learned His Lesson

He did not play for Woody Hayes, but David Boston's Ohio State football career personified perhaps better than any other Buckeye in history what the legendary coach most loved about the sport.

Beyond the strategizing, beyond the hitting, beyond the winning, football for Hayes was always a metaphor of life and how it should be lived.

"When you get knocked down," Hayes used to say, "you have to keep getting back up."

Boston did that to such a degree that he ascended off the mat to heights previously unreached by any wide receiver to wear the scarlet-and-gray.

He left OSU following his junior season in 1998 in possession of 12 receiving records in school history, but none of them were as precious as the legacy Boston secured as a player who learned from his mistake and worked hard enough to erase its memory.

"I think David grew the most of any player I saw in my time at Ohio State," said Ahmed Plummer, an all-conference cornerback with the Buckeyes who was Boston's teammate from 1996-98. "When he came in as a freshman, he was really young and very inexperienced.

"He was always a great athlete with great talent, but he didn't have the savvy to go with it that he did when he left. He wasn't impatient any more. He had learned from his mistakes. He had the mental maturity to go with his physical maturity, and that's what made him the toughest receiver I ever had to face."

Boston completed his career the way all players hope to go out, by saving his best games for the conclusion of his final season.

At Iowa in the next-to-last game of 1998, he recorded a career-best 231 all-purpose yards and scored a pair of receiving touchdowns.

His bon voyage came in the Sugar Bowl on Jan. 1, when Boston caught 11 passes for 105 yards on a gimpy ankle sprained the previous week to emerge as the game's MVP in OSU's 24-14 victory over Texas A&M.

In between those performances came the defining moment of Boston's career—his 10-catch, 217-yard, two-touchdown effort in a 31-16 victory over Michigan.

No receiver had ever caught passes for more yardage against the Wolverines, even though no receiver had ever carried as much baggage into a game with the maize-and-blue.

Only the season before, Boston had been the fall guy for OSU's 20-14 loss at Ann Arbor, having engaged in some pregame banter about eventual Heisman Trophy winner Charles Woodson that Woodson said motivated him to play well.

That flare-up cost Boston some of the respect he had coming for a sophomore season in which he broke Cris Carter's single-season school record of 69 catches with 73 grabs.

Suddenly, Boston entered his junior year with a cloud over his considerable achievements.

He had, after all, scored a touchdown the very first time he touched the ball in a game as a freshman, then came back the following week to score three times in OSU's second game. By the time his freshman year was over, Boston was the toast of Columbus, having caught two touchdown passes in the Buckeyes' first Rose Bowl victory in 24 years, including the game-winner against Arizona State on a five-yard pass with 19 seconds left.

"David was just a powerful receiver," said Chuck Stobart, who coached OSU's wide receivers during Boston's career. "He could outmuscle cornerbacks and make the play. That strength and the speed he had to make plays after the catch was very evident to us as soon as he got to campus, but David didn't rely on just that.

"He made himself a better player every year he was here. He just worked and worked and worked on his technique and his route-running. He never let success go to his head. Those last three games he played for us—Iowa, Michigan, and Texas A&M—were David Boston at his finest."

Boston, who was a first-round draft pick for the Phoenix Cardinals, never hid from the criticism he received after the Michigan game in 1997, instead choosing to face his detractors head on and silence them with the onslaught he unleashed on the Buckeyes' receiving records.

He reset the single-season reception and receiving yards marks he had taken possession of the previous year and boosted himself atop the career lists in both those categories, as well as touchdowns (34) and 100-yard games (13).

"When I broke a record, to me it was a team

Boston's best game came against Michigan.

accomplishment," Boston said. "I always believed that if I just went out and played hard, those things would happen. I didn't think when I came to Ohio State that I would end up with Cris Carter's receiving records.

"You look at those numbers when you're a freshman and they're so big, you don't even think about them. When I finally got there, it was hard to believe. I mean, Cris was such a great athlete, it was just an honor to be associated with him."

Keith BYARS

You Can Take It to the Bank

There is a delicate balance in sports between the confident expression and words weighted with too much bluster.

Every so often, however, a statement artfully balances upon that tightrope and inspires warm memories of the moment it recalls.

Such was Babe Ruth's famous called shot in the 1934 World Series and Joe Namath's victory guarantee prior to the 1969 Super Bowl. Ohio State's storied football tradition is not without its own such incident, one marked by these famous words from 1984 Heisman Trophy runner-up Keith Byars:

"We're coming back, Dayton, Ohio. We're coming back."

Byars's profession of faith could have been dismissed as bravado, coming as it did with the Buckeyes in a 24-7 hole late in the first half of an Oct. 13, 1984 game against Illinois at Ohio Stadium.

Byars, however, wasn't one of those guys who spoke just to hear his own voice.

What he said, he meant, primarily because he committed himself to making it happen.

Before the sun would set on the Horseshoe for that Homecoming game, Byars would author what then was the single greatest performance by an OSU running back.

He rushed for a school-record five touchdowns and a school-record 274 yards to deliver a 45-38 victory that proved crucial to the Buckeyes' winning the Big Ten championship and Rose Bowl berth that season.

So, what was Byars thinking when he came to the sideline that October afternoon, having just scored to signal that vestiges of a pulse did indeed exist on the Ohio State sideline, despite its slow start against Illinois?

"I said what I said because I really believed it," Byars said. "I felt we were going to come back

and win that game. Up until we scored our first touchdown, we were getting embarrassed in our own backyard. That just wasn't supposed to happen at Ohio State.

"Once I scored, the floodgates just opened. You could sense the whole mood in the Stadium change. They put the camera on me, expecting me to say, 'Hi, mom.' Well, my mom was in the stands. She already knew I loved her. So I made a statement to all my friends and people watching all over the country. 'Hey, trust me. We're coming back.' And we did."

Byars's awe-inspiring performance against Illinois included one of the most memorable touchdown runs in school history, his 67-yard scamper to a fourth TD that featured him running out of his shoe and going the distance in his sock.

"He was just magnificent that day," OSU coach Earle Bruce said. "We got behind, but I don't think any of our kids thought we were out of it because we knew we had Keith. He just made great run after great run that day and wouldn't let us lose."

Byars led the nation in rushing that season with a then-school-record 1,764 yards. He also led the nation in scoring (144 points) and all-purpose yardage (2,441), but finished second to Boston College's Doug Flutie for the Heisman.

Flutie had the good fortune to author his signature performance after Byars, throwing a last-play, Hail Mary touchdown pass to defeat Miami on Thanksgiving Day.

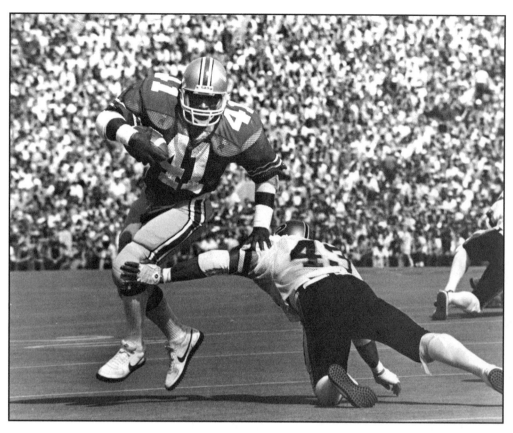

Byars led the Buckeyes to the Rose Bowl.

"It was all about timing," Byars said. "Unfortunately, my (regular) season was over by then, and all the voters were sitting at home eating their turkey watching that Boston College game. That was the last thing they remembered before the final vote, so it swayed things in Flutie's direction.

"I know in my heart I should have won that Heisman. Even today, I run into a lot of people who say, 'You should have won that Heisman,' and it means a lot to me. I may not have it in my living room, but I have that Heisman in my heart."

Byars came to OSU from Dayton's Roth High School and played fullback his first season just to get on the field. He played so well, however, that coaches were hesitant to move him to tailback until Byars got a chance there in the spring due to a teammate's injury.

By that fall, Bruce was certain he had a budding All-American, so certain that he entered a nationally-televised non-conference battle at Oklahoma with a secret he couldn't wait to spring on the college football world.

"All we heard about leading up to that game was (Oklahoma tailback) Marcus Dupree," Bruce said.

"Everybody kept talking about their guy, but we had Keith and I knew he was better than Marcus Dupree. I told my friends, 'You watch. We have a tailback better than Marcus Dupree. Keith Byars will make Marcus Dupree look sick. He'll run for more yards than Marcus Dupree.' That's how sure I was that Keith Byars was a great football player."

Byars did indeed outgain Dupree, setting the stage for a three-year career in which he would rush for 3,200 yards, then third-best in OSU history.

Byars's totals would have been much higher had he not broken a bone on the outside of his right foot in fall camp as a senior, which limited him to just three starts and 213 rushing yards.

Once again his dreams of winning the Heisman Trophy were shattered.

"I thought we had a shot to win everything with him as a senior," said Bruce, whose Buckeyes went 9-3 and finished No. 11 in the nation that year. "He was so good. A healthy Keith Byars playing like he was as a junior, we could have gone undefeated."

Byars eventually had a long pro career with the Philadelphia Eagles and Miami Dolphins. He is retired and lives in Florida.

Cris CARTER

No One Can Pick Just One

The one thing everyone who played with or coached Cris Carter can agree on is that he consistently amazed them throughout his Ohio State football career with his athleticism and uncanny ability to make the impossible occur.

The thing none of Carter's teammates or coaches can agree on, however, is a singular defining instance of his greatness.

Ask quarterback Jim Karsatos, and he'll vote for a one-hand grab Carter made in the 1985 Citrus Bowl against BYU.

Ask guard Jim Lachey, and he'll cite one of the nine grabs Carter made for a record 172 receiving yards in the 1985 Rose Bowl.

Ask Earle Bruce, who coached Carter during his three-year career at OSU from 1984-86, and he'll choose either a circus grab at Indiana in 1986 or any one of a number of unfathomable receptions Carter made behind the locked doors of daily practice.

"Cris is the only guy I've ever seen who would get an ovation for something he did in practice," Bruce said. "His teammates would literally stand there and clap after some of the things he did."

Bruce felt like applauding at halftime of the IU game in Bloomington in 1986, when the Buckeyes were locked in a tight struggle with an opponent they routinely rolled over.

"Cris stood up and said, 'We're not losing to these guys as long as I'm here,'" Bruce said. "Then he went out there in the third quarter and made an unbelievable catch, one of those where he hung in the air and brought it one-handed, that put us on the five-yard line. We scored and won that game. That's the kind of leader he was."

Carter's impact on the Buckeyes' passing game was immediate, setting him on a path that would lead to 164 career receptions for 2,725 yards and 27 touchdowns in his three seasons.

All were OSU career records, as were Carter's single-season catch and touchdown totals as

both a sophomore and junior before his career was cut short by the disclosure that he had signed with an agent. He eventually was taken in an NFL supplemental draft by the Philadelphia Eagles, and also played for the Vikings until he recently retired.

Despite that, his legacy at Ohio State is secure, not only because of the 58-catch, 950-yard season Carter enjoyed in 1985, or the 69-catch, 1,127-yard season he had in 1986, but because of the flair with which he accomplished everything he did.

"The catch I'm talking about in the Citrus Bowl, I was actually trying to throw the ball away," Karsatos said. "When I saw it on film, I couldn't believe it. He went up and caught the ball with one hand, tucked it in, then it looked like he just levitated back inbounds. I thought I threw that thing so hard and so high that no one would have a chance at it.

"That was Cris, though. He was just so much smarter than everybody else. He knew how to manipulate the defensive back. He knew if he took a step one way, they would have to respect his speed, and with the jumping ability that he had, it was impossible to cover him once he got the guy to turn his hips. He'd get himself between the man and the ball, and there was just no way to stop him, he was so strong, and yet so incredibly graceful."

Carter's ability at wide receiver proved the perfect compliment during his era to the wide-ranging talents of tailback Keith Byars, who as a Dayton native was only too happy to see his friend from Middletown show up to play for the Buckeyes.

"When Cris first came in, he was one of the most polished receivers people ever saw," Byars said. "There have been a lot of great receivers at Ohio State, but in my opinion, none of them had the total package as freshmen that Cris did.

Carter's catches were often unbelievable.

"I remember when he was being recruited, people were telling him, 'You shouldn't go to Ohio State. That's a running school.' His attitude was, 'It's a running school because they don't have me. Once they see what I can do, they'll start throwing it.' He was right, too. He gave us a reason to start throwing the ball."

Howard CASSADY

The Man of the Hour

He is an indispensable part of any successful enterprise, linking the origin and conclusion of an endeavor via a role typified by the name assigned his placement in the production.

He is "the middle man," that tie binding the start to the finish so that the two relate in a way they otherwise wouldn't.

Such is the function Howard "Hopalong" Cassady serves in the timeline of Ohio State football during the 20th century.

The success of the Buckeyes that began with Chic Harley just prior to 1920 would one day grow into the dominance OSU enjoyed throughout the late 1960s and into the mid-1970s.

Cassady was the bridge between those eras.

Like Harley and Archie Griffin, the most decorated Ohio State player of the century, Cassady came out of a Columbus high school to star in the backfield for the Buckeyes.

Without Cassady, though, there might not have been a Griffin, for without Cassady, there wouldn't have been a national championship in 1954 and therefore almost certainly wouldn't have been the leeway for Woody Hayes to retain his job and build the program into the machine it became.

Hayes was on the ropes when Cassady arrived out of Central High School in 1952, having gone 4-3-2 in a rookie season that ended with a 7-0 loss to Michigan.

Ohio State had gone through three coaches in the seven years prior to that, the last three of which ended with much more successful seasons than the one Hayes produced during his debut.

The grumbling wouldn't stop the instant Cassady arrived on campus, but from the minute he took the field as a freshman, a seed began to flourish that would bloom by the time he graduated.

In his first collegiate game, the season-opener in 1952, Cassady came off the bench to score three touchdowns in a 33-12 victory over Indiana.

He became a starter from that day forward, and later in the year was crucial to OSU's 23-14 upset of No. 1 Wisconsin and 27-7 victory over Michigan, the Buckeyes' first win in the series in eight years.

That sensational freshman season, in which Cassady tied for the team lead with six touchdowns, only foreshadowed the success that was to follow. Two years later in 1954, he led OSU to an unbeaten season and the national championship.

Calls for Hayes's firing were again at fever pitch entering that year because of a 20-0 loss in Ann Arbor to end the 1953 season. Cassady silenced them with a brilliant season in which he rushed for 764 yards and led the team in receiving with 148 yards.

His biggest play, however, was an 88-yard interception return for a touchdown against second-ranked Wisconsin in the season's fifth game, a play Hayes later termed "the most spectacular play in 20 years of football in our stadium."

OSU trailed, 7-3, prior to Cassady's momentum-shifter, but went on to a 33-14 victory aided not only by Cassady's interception, but also by his 39-yard touchdown run.

"That was a great win for us," Cassady said. "Wisconsin was really a great team. They were ranked very high and had Alan Ameche, who would win the Heisman Trophy that season. Beating them really gave us a springboard for the rest of our schedule."

The Buckeyes closed the 1954 season with a 21-7 comeback victory over Michigan that turned on Cassady's 52 yard touchdown run, and a 20-7 win in the Rose Bowl over USC, a game in which Cassady slogged for 92 rushing yards on a field muddied by day-long rains.

It was no surprise, therefore, that Cassady finished a strong third in the Heisman Trophy voting that year, just 28 points behind runner-up Kurt Burris of Oklahoma and 258 points back of Ameche.

That made "Hoppie" the overwhelming favorite for the coveted honor in 1955 and he didn't disappoint, offering his best season yet.

"The Heisman wasn't talked about in those days the way it is now," Cassady said. "There wasn't the attention given to who would win it in the pre-season. I sure wanted to win it, though. If you were a competitor, you wanted to win everything you could."

The Buckeyes lost a pair of non-conference games that year to Stanford and Duke, but nevertheless defended their Big Ten championship thanks to Cassady's 958 rushing yards.

He broke Harley's Ohio State scoring record in his final game at the Horseshoe, getting the mark on a 45-yard touchdown run, one of Cassady's three touchdowns that day against Iowa.

"I scored three touchdowns my first game in Ohio Stadium and three touchdowns in my last one," Cassady said with a laugh. "I guess I didn't get any better."

The Buckeyes couldn't go to the Rose Bowl that year because of the league's no-repeat rule, so their season finale at Michigan was for the pride of de-

Cassady won the 1955 Heisman.

fending their league title and making sure the Wolverines couldn't go to Pasadena, either.

"That was the win I enjoyed the most in my career," said Cassady, who rushed for 146 yards on 28 carries and one touchdown in the 17-0 victory, running his career-scoring total to 222 points. "They never crossed the 50 on us. If they had beaten us, they would have gone to the Rose Bowl. But because they lost, Michigan State got to go."

Cassady headed off for New York and the Downtown Athletic Club, where his 2,219 points—a 742 margin over second-place finisher Jim Swink of TCU—made him the first Heisman winner to get more than 2,000 points and gave him the largest victory margin ever.

"Being a Heisman winner is great," said Cassady, who was eventually a first-round draft pick for Detroit in 1956. "You get invited back to the banquet every year and that really makes it special. You get to vote, so you stay involved with the award. You have a lot of camaraderie with all the other winners and it becomes like a second family."

Neal COLZIE

Gone, But Not Forgotten

I t's an ironic tragedy that the skills which typified Neal Colzie's football career at Ohio State also served as an epitaph for a life cut short.

When he was intercepting passes and returning punts for the Buckeyes in the early 1970s, Colzie's speed and quickness frustrated opponents powerless to cope with his array of here-one-minute, gone-the-next skills.

In a much deeper fashion, Colzie's death of a heart attack at the age of 48 left his teammates grasping to cope with their sorrow over losing a friend who flashed through their lives and vanished all too soon.

"Coach (Woody) Hayes used to say that the finest people you were ever going to meet in your life were in the locker room with you as teammates," said John Hicks, OSU's Outland and Lombardi Trophy winner in 1973. "Neal Colzie was proof of that."

Colzie set a host of Ohio State records during his three seasons of eligibility, coming along in 1971 at a time when freshmen were ineligible to compete on the varsity.

The following season, that rule changed and the Buckeyes got a huge boost from eventual two-time Heisman Trophy-winner Archie Griffin's addition to the lineup. On the defensive side, Colzie was making his mark as a first-year contributor, as well, batting down a pass on the final play at Wisconsin to preserve a 28-20 victory.

"Neal was probably one of the most natural DBs we ever had at Ohio State," Griffin said. "He was completely at ease out there at his position. He just had a very fluid style, very relaxed, as a coverage guy. But once he got his hands on the ball, look out."

Colzie made plenty of good things happen for the Buckeyes, not just with his 15 career interceptions, but with his shifty moves and darting speed on punt returns.

As a junior in 1973, he set an Ohio State record that still stands with eight punt returns for 170 return yards in a 35-0 victory over Michigan State.

Among those runbacks was a 43-yard effort for a touchdown, one of two Colzie took back for a score in his career.

The other was a 78-yard effort in the 1973 season-opener against Minnesota.

Colzie also scored twice on interception returns that year, going 55 yards against Indiana and 19 yards for another TD against Northwestern.

"Neal was an extremely quick guy, very fast, with good anticipation and intelligence," said Randy Gradishar, OSU's All-American middle linebacker in 1972-73. "He was just great on the corner covering guys one-on-one. It got to where teams didn't throw to his side very much, because he earned the reputation as someone it was good to avoid."

Michigan tempted fate in that regard on its first possession of the second half in the 1973 game that wound up in a 10-10 tie.

Wolverines' quarterback Dennis Franklin tried Colzie on a snap from the OSU 22-yard line and suffered an interception that turned back a scoring drive, helping the Buckeyes survive and eventually win the Big Ten athletic directors' vote to play in the Rose Bowl.

Colzie made them look good by returning a punt 56 yards to set up Ohio State's go-ahead touchdown in its 42-17 win over USC in Pasadena.

Franklin tried Colzie again the following year in Ohio Stadium shortly after the Buckeyes claimed a 12-10 lead that would prevail at the finish. This time, Michigan went deep after reaching the OSU 39-yard line, thinking it might victimize Colzie because he had spent most of the previous week in the hospital battling the flu.

Instead, Colzie intercepted and the drive was turned away to help return the Buckeyes to the Rose Bowl. That's where Colzie made the final interception of his career, one that could have made the difference between an 18-17 defeat and victory if not for a questionable officials' flag.

OSU was in front, 17-10, when Colzie picked off a pass from Pat Hayden and returned it to the Trojans' 10-yard line.

In his exuberance over making what appeared to be a game-breaking play, Colzie spiked the ball to the turf as he was shoved out of bounds and drew a 15-yard penalty that pushed the Buckeyes back to the 25-yard line.

"Have you ever seen that called before? I haven't," Hayes lamented afterward. "I didn't even know it was in the rule book."

OSU got no points out of the turnover when it threw an interception of its own, something the conservative Hayes likely wouldn't have tried had his team maintained possession at the Trojans' 10-yard line.

That wrote a frustrating finish to Colzie's career, which saw him make All-Big Ten his final two years and All-American as a senior in 1974.

The Oakland Raiders chose Colzie in the first round of the NFL draft the following spring.

He played on the Raiders' Super Bowl XI championship team and also played for the Miami Dolphins and Tampa Bay Buccaneers in a nine-year professional career.

"Neal was a fun-loving guy and a great teammate," Griffin said. "It's a shame we lost him so early."

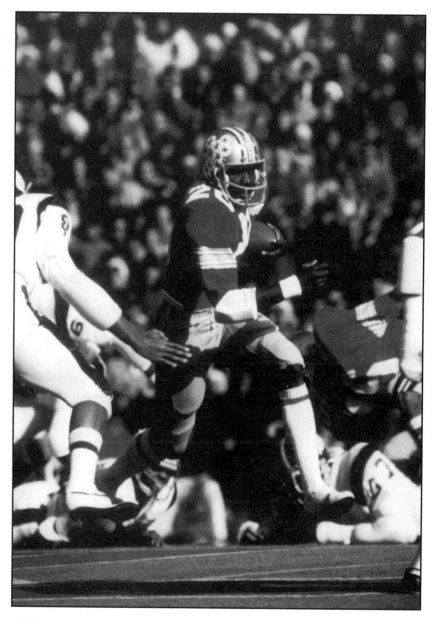

Colzie breaks away on a return.

Tom COUSINEAU

A Bright Spot in Hard Times

There's been no shortage of football success at Ohio State over the years to require a search of middling seasons to locate individual heroes.

Think of an OSU championship team at the Big Ten or national level and a host of names immediately come forward because of their role in those achievements.

The Buckeyes' tradition is so rich, so storied, and so encompassing that to distinguish oneself amid a year fans would just as soon forget speaks loudly to how special a player must have been.

Such is the case with linebacker Tom Cousineau, who set a standard for linebackers at Ohio State that lent fuel to that position's already-vibrant legacy.

Cousineau came along on the heels of great OSU linebackers Ike Kelly and Randy Gradishar, starting on the 1976 and 1977 Big Ten championship teams that, respectively, won the Orange Bowl and lost in the Sugar Bowl.

Cousineau was the choice as defensive MVP in that 27-10 victory over Colorado in the Orange Bowl after a season in which he led the Buckeyes with 184 tackles (102 solos, 82 assists).

He likely would have gained that distinction as a junior, too, had he not missed all of one game and part of another with a shoulder injury.

Despite that, Cousineau finished second on the team with 129 stops, including 20 in the Sugar Bowl against Alabama to cap a season in which he repeated as a first-team All-Big Ten selection and gained first-team All-American honors.

The best, however, was yet to come.

Although Ohio State's 1978 finish was forgettable, resulting in a 7-4-1 record and the firing of head coach Woody Hayes after a loss in the Gator Bowl, the excellence Cousineau brought to the field each game provides a shining light by which to remember that year.

The free-spirited native of Fairview Park in suburban Cleveland reported for practice that fall sporting a tattoo and an earring that raised his legendary coach's eyebrow, but there was never any doubt in Hayes about what kind of linebacker wore the No. 36 jersey.

"He is the best conditioned athlete we have ever had at Ohio State," Hayes said early that season. "He is a complete football player, because besides his many physical talents, he also has intelligence and great desire."

Cousineau foreshadowed the tremendous performance he would offer in 1978 by making a school-record 29 tackles in the opener, a 19-0 loss to visiting Penn State.

"It would have meant a lot more to me if we had won the game," Cousineau said. "I had been looking forward to that game all summer, so it really hurt to lose."

Cousineau's disappointment over the Buckeyes' season-opening defeat would be revisited all too often that year, for the Buckeyes struggled to a 2-2-1 mark out of the gate to fall far off the pace the program had grown accustomed to throughout the late 1960s and early 1970s.

Even so, Cousineau didn't let the team's failure prevent him from playing at an inspired level each week.

In a 35-35 tie with Southern Methodist, he recorded a school-record 16 solo tackles (28 overall) en route to boosting his season tackle total to 122 after just five games.

"Tom was pretty special," said George Hill, OSU's defensive coordinator that season. "He reminded me a lot of Randy Gradishar. Tom was just a great linebacker. He was a great hitter. He could defend equally well against the pass or the run.

"He could stop a big fullback up the middle, and yet he had enough mobility to get to the outside when he had to. Wherever the ball was, that's where Tom would usually be."

By the time the 1978 season ended, Cousineau had recorded four of the top six and six of the top 10 single-game tackle totals in OSU history.

"Personally, I would rather have had a few less tackles and a few more wins," Cousineau said.

His 211 stops overall (101 solo, 110 assists) as a senior established a new single-season record at OSU and also left Cousineau the Buckeyes' career leader with 569 career tackles.

Such achievements made a sage of Cousineau's father, Tom Sr., who played college football at Indiana and then became a high school football and wrestling coach.

"My father used to take me to high school wrestling practice with him when I was in the third, fourth and fifth grade," Cousineau said. "I'd wrestle the guys on the varsity and I'd get my butt kicked. I'd end up with a bloody nose and crying. A lot of people thought my father pushed me too hard, but I was never forced to do anything."

Cousineau's love for contact made him a consensus All-American again in 1978 and enticed the Buffalo Bills into making him Ohio State's first ever No. 1 NFL draft selection overall.

"Being taken No. 1 was something I'd been looking forward to in football since I started playing in third grade," Cousineau said.

Buffalo couldn't meet his contract asking price, however, and Cousineau opted to play his first three professional seasons in the Canadian Football League.

He returned in 1982 to play for his hometown Cleveland Browns, getting a $3.5-million, five-year contract that made him the highest-paid player in the NFL.

After his retirement, Cousineau returned to OSU and spent one season as an assistant coach.

That was in 1988, exactly 10 years after his play established a standard Hayes once ranked with the finest to ever grace Ohio Stadium.

"He made a great contribution to our team for four years," Hayes said upon Cousineau's graduation. "We never had a man who played with greater intensity, nor one who got himself into better shape, both mentally and physically, to play the game."

Cousineau continued OSU's linebacker tradition.

Bob
FERGUSON

The Made-to-Order Fullback

The stars must have been lined up perfectly on the night of Bob Ferguson's birth, because for a player of his size, speed and ability, there could have been no better place for him to be born than within a short drive of Columbus, Ohio.

If ever someone were placed on earth with the purpose of playing fullback for Ohio State, it was Ferguson, a 225-pound bulldozer who piled up outrageous numbers at Troy High School near Dayton and continued to produce them for the Buckeyes.

"Bob Ferguson was the prototypical Ohio State fullback," said Paul Warfield, an NFL Hall of Famer who played with Ferguson in the backfield on OSU's 1961 undefeated national championship team.

"He fit perfectly into Ohio State's image, which was to have a powerful running game. Bob created the necessary yards and took time off the clock and scored

touchdowns, which just wore the opponent out over the course of a game."

Ferguson began his varsity career in 1959, which ended with a 3-5-1 record that was OSU's first losing finish in 11 seasons.

The Buckeyes bounced back in a big way the following year, however, and it was Ferguson who led the charge.

Running behind massive tackle Jim Tyrer, Ferguson gave OSU fans a taste of the exploits he would offer regularly over the next two years by rushing for three touchdowns and 157 yards on 20 carries in a 20-0 win over Southern California the season's second week.

"Bobby wasn't satisfied with his own performance," head coach Woody Hayes said afterward. "He told me he can play a better ballgame, and I believe he can."

Ferguson would, indeed, play better games before his career concluded.

He finished his junior season with 853 rushing yards and scored

at least one touchdown in every game, but that wasn't his most eye-opening statistic.

On 160 carries that season, Ferguson was thrown for a loss exactly once, and for all of one yard.

That consistency earned him All-American recognition and made Ferguson a contender for the Heisman Trophy in 1961, an honor he made serious inroads toward achieving.

He carried an OSU record 35 times in the season opener against TCU, gaining 137 yards.

Fourteen of his carries and 42 of Ferguson's rushing yards came on the Buckeyes' only scoring drive in a 7-7 tie.

Hayes's reliance on Ferguson set the tone for a season in which he would carry 202 times for 938 yards and 11 touchdowns, giving him 26 for his career.

"Woody's favorite play was called, 26," Warfield said. "It was basically a fullback off-tackle play. The way it was designed, Bob was to run toward the tackle and read his block. He could then break the play back over guard or tackle.

"Bob was just a master at running that 26 play. He had heavy thighs and a low center of gravity. He could really run up in there and create movement. He made the pile move, as they say."

Ferguson scored four TDs in a single game twice his senior year, including his finale against Michigan in a 50-20 Buckeyes romp in Ann Arbor.

"Only one team did a good job of stopping him that year," Warfield said. "Oddly enough, it was Indiana, which was one of the worst teams in the league. We played them the week before we played Michigan in Ann Arbor.

"There used to be a hamburger joint or diner in Bloomington called Fergie's. Well, the night before the game, one of Indiana's team captains talked at their pep rally about how their entire defensive unit was going to make Fergie burgers out of Bob Ferguson.

"They stacked their entire defense to stop them, and Woody was just stubborn enough he wouldn't give up on running that 26 play. Bo Schembechler, who was our offensive coordinator, finally convinced him to fake the Ferguson and throw a pass.

"Well, we did that and there was no one within a

Ferguson seldom went backward with the ball.

mile of our end, Chuck Bryant. So when we came into the locker room afterward, Woody told us we could have thrown the ball all day on them. A lot of us sat there wondering, 'Well, then, why didn't we?' The answer was simple, of course. Woody believed that if you threw the ball, only three things could happen and two of them were bad, and he also believed he had the best weapon on the field in Bob Ferguson."

Wes FESLER

He Had It All and Could Do It All

Wes Fesler's career as an Ohio State football player and later as head coach was the stuff that inspires full-length feature films.

A three-time All-American end for the Buckeyes, Fesler had unparalleled athleticism that made him a star throughout his playing career.

Then, as OSU's head coach from 1947-50, he directed the team to a Big Ten championship and Rose Bowl title, while also presiding over perhaps the most legendary defeat in school history.

How screenwriters in the golden age of movie making overlooked Fesler's life story is a mystery, for his is unquestionably one of the most storied tales in Ohio State athletic lore.

The handsome, wavy-haired Fesler played his first season for the Buckeyes in 1928 and immediately treated fans to the type of performances that had been scarce in Columbus since the early part of that decade.

Only once since 1921 had OSU finished above sixth in the Big Ten, and in five of those six years had combined for only six conference victories.

Fesler's arrival made the Buckeyes instantly competitive, which was glaringly apparent when he caught a touchdown pass to spark the team's 19-7 victory over Michigan in Ohio Stadium.

That win was OSU's first over the Wolverines in six seasons, but wouldn't be its last against its archrival during the Fesler era.

The very next season, Fesler's 19-yard touchdown reception from Allen Holman was the only score in the Buckeyes' 7-0 victory at Michigan.

It was the only score because Fesler also saved the day defensively, racing across the field to tackle Michigan's speedy Willie Heston Jr. after he broke loose and headed toward the end zone on a 40-yard run.

What open-mouthed awe that didn't inspire, Fesler took care of several weeks later when North-western was on the one-foot line on fourth down, seeking to pad its 6-0 lead over the Buckeyes.

The Wildcats' snap hit halfback Don Calderwood on the chest and bounced into mid-air. Fesler swooped in and grabbed the football before it hit the ground and raced 99 yards the other way to give the Buckeyes their only touchdown in an eventual 19-7 defeat.

Plays like that are what caused Fesler's teammate, Dick Larkins, who went on to become Ohio State's athletic director, to later comment, "He was the greatest athlete I've ever seen. I've never seen a human animal as well coordinated.

"In those days, you didn't bring the ball in 15 yards from the sideline when a play ended close to the sideline. You played it from where it was. I was a less than average end. When the ball was near the sideline and I was playing end, Fesler would always switch to the tough side."

Fesler's athleticism was evident beyond the football field.

He also lettered three years at OSU in both baseball and basketball and was an all-conference selection in the latter in 1931.

Head coach Sam Willaman decided to capitalize on Fesler's all-around ability in 1930 by using his senior at fullback, in addition to his regular spot at end.

In a 27-0 victory over Navy, Fesler played fullback and end on offense, end on defense, punted, rushed the football and also passed to Larkins for a touchdown.

The next week, Fesler threw for one score and set up another with his passing in a victory over Pittsburgh.

The Youngstown native also had a flair for the dramatic, saving perhaps his finest effort for the final game of his career at Illinois.

The Buckeyes hadn't scored on the powerful Illini for three seasons, but Fesler scored 12 points himself in the first quarter and OSU made that stand up for a five-point victory.

After his graduation, Fesler played professional baseball in the St. Louis Cardinals organization for one year before beginning a coaching career that saw him serve one season as a football assistant at OSU, eight years as the head basketball and assistant football coach at Harvard, two seasons as head football coach at Connecticut Wesleyan, one year as head basketball coach at Princeton, and one year as head football coach at Pittsburgh.

He returned as the Buckeyes' head coach in 1947 and in his third season directed the team to a conference championship and 1950 Rose Bowl victory over California.

Fesler's teams went 21-13-3 during his tenure, a record dragged down by professional teams in Cleveland and Philadelphia raiding his roster of players with remaining eligibility.

Fesler's final season as head coach resulted in junior halfback Vic Janowicz winning the 1950 Heisman Trophy, but also in Fesler's surprising resignation on Dec. 9.

He had taken considerable criticism for ordering a punt on third down in the Snow Bowl, a kick Michigan blocked for its only touchdown in the 9-3 victory.

Fesler accepted a job with the John Galbreath Realty Company in Columbus, saying it had been "a wonderful honor to have been the director of the football program at my alma mater."

Columbus was in an uproar for weeks over the 42-year-old Fesler's resignation.

He received a 45-second ovation at the team's awards banquet and was awarded the first lifetime membership in the Columbus Quarterback Club.

"I know," OSU president Howard Bevis told the crowd, "that many of you will join in accord when I say that Wesley Fesler was a good coach."

Fesler played and coached at OSU.

Tim FOX

A Happy Ending All Around

Some greats in the history of Ohio State football owed their arrival on campus to superior high school careers or perhaps even a deep allegiance to the Buckeyes formed as a youth.

Tim Fox had elements of those things, but the factor which played heaviest in Fox attending OSU was a girlfriend's engaging manner with a random restaurant customer.

If not for her, Fox might have wound up at Kent State or Indiana or Bowling Green or Navy and never treated Buckeye fans to his swashbuckling secondary play on OSU's four consecutive Big Ten championship teams from 1972-75.

A four-year starter and 1975 All-American safety, Fox wasn't even on the minds of Ohio State head coach Woody Hayes or his recruiters after being injured midway through his senior season at Glenwood High School.

"Ohio State was talking to me a little bit that fall, but then I got hurt and never heard from them again," Fox said. "As it turned out, my girlfriend was a year older than me and so she was a freshman at Ohio State when I was a senior in high school. She was working as a waitress in Canton when she ran into this guy, Harry Myers, who claimed to be a friend of Woody.

"He said he would tell Woody about me. Well, I thought this was just some guy kidding around with a cute waitress, but I met him, and then he came to see me play basketball. The next thing I know, I got a call from George Hill."

Hill was Hayes's defensive coordinator, and after a look at Fox playing basketball and a scan of some game tape, he extended the next-to-last scholarship the Buckeyes awarded that year.

OSU's expectations for Fox weren't too high that fall. His biography didn't appear in the school's football media guide, nor did his name appear on the roster.

He did, however, end up starting by mid-season and so impressed Hayes that Fox was assigned shadow duties on Minnesota tailback Rick Upchurch in a crucial mid-season game against the Gophers.

"Woody was scared to death of Rick Upchurch's speed," Fox said. "He played wide receiver in the pros, but he was their tailback then. They ran the option, so basically, wherever he went, I ran with him. I supposedly had pass coverage, too, but if they would have thrown it at me that day I would have been in trouble. I was completely focused on Upchurch."

OSU won that day, 27-19, and went on to win the first of four straight Big Ten championships that season.

Fox, Archie Griffin, linebacker Ken Kuhn, and punter/ placekicker Tom Skladany were freshman starters for the Buckeyes in that first season of the restoration of freshman eligibility and would become the leaders in a class that powered OSU's dominance in the first half of that decade.

Eight of the 13 recruits in that class started as sophomores, 10 eventually made All-Big Ten and five made All-American.

That was also the era of allowable touchdown celebrations, a fad popularized first by quarterback Cornelius Greene's end-zone two-step.

Griffin got in on the act with his own scoring shuffle, but Fox, a ballcarrier in high school, had a style that surpassed both his teammates.

"I never would have done it if not for Corny doing his thing," Fox said. "We called him Flam (short for flamboyant). He was one of the first guys to do an end-zone dance, so I decided if I ever scored, I was going to do my own thing."

That thing became known as "The Fox Flip," a forward somersault from a standing position to a two-foot landing.

"Tim had great speed and tremendous athletic ability," Griffin said. "He could jump like crazy. I think about that Fox Flip he did when he'd get in the end zone. That blew my mind."

Fox executed the move perfectly on consecutive weeks late in the 1975 season after scoring on an interception against Illinois and a punt return against Minnesota.

"There were very few guys who could do a flip to the front," Fox said. "I've had people come up to me and say, 'Hey, I remember your back flips. Well, it wasn't a back flip, it was a front flip. I was a diver and did some gymnastics when I was growing up, so it just seemed like the thing to do. Woody loved it because it was an athletic move."

OSU went 40-5-1 during Fox's career, an .880 winning percentage that is the best of any class to play four seasons in school history.

The only void in the Buckeyes' achievements during that era was their lack of a national championship, something that eluded the team via a 10-10 tie against Michigan in 1973 and Rose Bowl losses after both the 1974 and 1975 season.

"The biggest disappointment in my athletic career, even after playing 12 years in the NFL, was not winning that national championship our senior year," Fox said of the upset UCLA inflicted in Pasadena. "We had already beaten them by 21 points in their home stadium earlier that year."

That setback, however, can't dull the pleasant memories Fox has of his Ohio State career or the lessons he learned playing under Hayes.

"It was just a tremendous, tremendous advantage to play for him," Fox said. "The fact of the matter is, life is a game. You compete with people every day to try to earn your living in some manner or fashion. Woody prepared you for that.

"He got you just at the age where you were forming your work ethic and habits. I've talked to other guys, and even though we've been removed from him for a long time, those ethics remain."

That's not all Fox took away from his OSU career, either.

Remember that waitress?

Fox married her and they live happily today in New England, where he played the bulk of his career in the NFL and works for a financial printing and management company.

OSU fans flipped for Fox.

John FRANK

The Toughest Nut in the Forest

The day may yet come when Ohio State fields a tight end with better statistics than John Frank, but the passion with which he played for the Buckeyes left an indelible impression that will endure forever.

Frank's numbers remained the best for a player at his position more than two decades after his 1983 graduation from OSU, but the passes he caught and the touchdowns he scored were never the most memorable thing about the 6-2, 225-pounder from Mt. Lebanon, Pa.

"I wish I could have given his intensity to every athlete I coached," Earle Bruce said of Frank, a three-year starter at tight end from 1981-83.

A first-team All-Big Ten pick as both a junior and senior, Frank left OSU with the third-best single-season reception total in school history (45 in both 1981 and 1983) and the second-highest total of career catches (121).

His nine career touchdown receptions remain the record for a tight end, and Frank would undoubtedly have the mark for tacklers left strewn in his wake if official statistics were available in that category.

"He was really something after he caught the ball," Bruce said. "He just didn't know how to give up."

Frank once explained his determination and drive by saying, "I have a little Woody Hayes in me."

Few who watched Frank catch the ball, then turn and virtually dare defensive players to confront him, doubted that.

"I guess I would describe myself as a Type A personality," Frank said. "I did everything with a lot of intensity. That was particularly true in football. I gave it all I had every play, because I never wanted to let the team down. I liked to think of myself as a complete player."

Although undersized for a tight end, Frank worked extensively to become a devastating blocker, and was an inspiration to his teammates with the attitude he displayed.

"John was an outstanding student and he brought that same work ethic to the way he studied film," said All-American tackle Jim Lachey. "He always knew the game plan like the back of his hand, and once the whistle blew, he was ready for action. That was his mentality. He was a warrior. He was always front and center. He had a lot of athletic ability, but he also got a lot of things done with intensity and sheer will power."

Frank started on three victorious bowl teams, contributing to wins over Navy in the Liberty Bowl, Brigham Young in the Holiday Bowl, and Pittsburgh in the Fiesta Bowl.

He broke through as a starter his sophomore season in 1981 in quarterback Art Schlichter's final year, catching 45 passes for 449 yards and three touchdowns.

The following season, OSU struggled to replace Schlichter,

and Frank's catches sank to 26, although his per-catch average increased from 9.9 yards as a sophomore to 12.5 yards that year.

As a senior, with Mike Tomczak firmly entrenched at quarterback, Frank led the Buckeyes with 45 catches for 641 yards and was at his best in the team's biggest games.

He caught seven passes for 108 yards and two touchdowns in a win at Oklahoma, caught five passes for 115 yards and one score in a win over Michigan State and caught 10 passes for 123 yards in a 24-21 loss at Michigan.

Frank's teammates voted him the Buckeyes' MVP and his coaches voted him the team's most inspirational player.

"I always had my goals in mind," Frank said. "When I left Ohio State, I wanted to be able to say I studied hard, I didn't miss a block, and I did everything that was expected of me."

Frank's expectations extended to the classroom, where he was a 3.9 student in pre-med and a first-team Academic All-American as a junior and senior after being a second team pick as sophomore.

One of his research papers was published in a medical journal between his junior and senior years.

"Coming out of high school, I not only wanted to play major college football, but become a doctor," Frank said. "I made up my mind in my junior year of high school. I knew all along that I would be involved in some form of science.

"Going the medical route was a big decision. I realized it would involve disciplined studying in college, but I always knew that if I went to college blindly, without a goal, I would be making a big mistake."

Frank was so dedicated to his goal of becoming a doctor that he didn't hide it from NFL scouts, even though it might have benefited him to do so.

His hometown Pittsburgh Steelers were considering him until Frank met with then-Steelers coach Chuck Noll, who asked about his future plans.

Frank remembers Noll's reaction when he detailed his plans for a medical career:

"It was like a switch turned off," Frank said.

The San Francisco 49ers weren't scared off and took Frank in the second round of the 1984 NFL draft.

He played five seasons before giving up football after winning a second Super Bowl ring in 1989, leaving the game as he was approaching the peak years of his career for fear that an injury would end his hopes for becoming a surgeon.

"I didn't want to be an ex-athlete my whole life," Frank said. ". . .It came to the point where I needed to be a full-time med student. I was afraid of being too immersed in the NFL."

He completed medical school at Ohio State and spent six years in residency at Loyola University of Chicago, then spent time in Israel and Switzerland before beginning his own cosmetic surgery practice in San Francisco.

"I really didn't know that much about Ohio State until I visited," Frank said. "But once I drove over and realized I was only three hours from home, once I saw the campus, once I went to a game and saw what Ohio State football was about, I just said to myself, 'This place has my name on it.'"

Frank never shied from contact.

Joey GALLOWAY

Nothing Slowed Him Down

Of all the sizzling runs and breath-taking plays Joey Galloway made during his Ohio State career, perhaps none was more startling than the one he offered in street clothes in January 1994.

With the bright lights of the NFL beckoning him to join other OSU players of that era who bypassed their remaining years of Buckeye eligibility to turn professional, Galloway faked as if he would take the million-dollar handoff and instead ran in the other direction.

His decision to stay in school disappointed NFL franchises in need of a game-breaking wide receiver, but forever endeared Galloway to OSU loyalists who had begun to believe love for the alma mater to be extinct among elite athletes.

"At the last minute, I sat down with myself and thought about it and decided I should finish my education before I left," Galloway said. "That way, I'd always have it."

Besides his degree, Galloway left OSU with two of the best seasons a wide receiver had enjoyed in school history.

As a junior in 1993, he was the game-breaker on a team that went 10-1-1 overall, captured a share of the Big Ten championship and won the school's first bowl game in seven seasons.

Galloway caught 47 passes for 946 yards and 11 touchdowns that year, while also scoring twice on rushing plays.

His team-high 78 points made him the first wide receiver since Robert Grimes in 1952 to lead OSU in scoring.

That success also made Galloway a safe bet to bypass his senior season and enter the NFL, particularly since he had already flirted with the one factor that typically chases players out of school.

Two games into his sophomore season, Galloway tore the anterior cruciate ligament in his knee on a kickoff return against Bowling Green.

That ended a year in which the Buckeyes figured to make him the focal point of their pass offense based on the eight catches for 88 yards he had in the Hall of Fame Bowl at the end of his freshman season.

"At first I couldn't believe it," Galloway said of the injury. "I thought, I've come this far and worked this hard and now I have to take a whole year off. But after that, I just looked at it as an opportunity to see what good could come from it. Basically, it gave me a year to sit back and learn."

Galloway rehabilitated from the injury in six months, an unheard of time period for an athlete of that era.

Typically, skill players needed nine months to a year to recover, and many lost a step or two of their speed in the process.

Not Galloway.

Doctors had to fight to keep him off the field in spring ball, and when fall camp opened in

1993, he was running as fast, or faster, than ever.

OSU quarterback Bob Hoying expected Galloway to keep on running, right into the NFL, after his third-team All-American junior season, only to be pleasantly surprised upon learning that he would have his favorite target back for another year.

"A lot of guys on the team thought he was going pro," Hoying said. "When they wave all that money at you, it can be a tough decision."

Defenses concentrated their schemes to stop Galloway his senior year, but he still came up with 44 catches for 669 yards and ran his career touchdown catch total to 19, then second in OSU history.

Galloway also spent considerable time that season speaking to youth groups in and around Columbus, trying to get the youngsters to devote themselves to their studies and avoid legal entanglements that could compromise their future.

Those off-field efforts and his solid performance in the classroom contributed to Galloway being awarded one of the 15 postgraduate fellowships from National Football Foundation and College Hall of Fame.

He also won a National Association of Collegiate Athletic Directors Foundation scholarship.

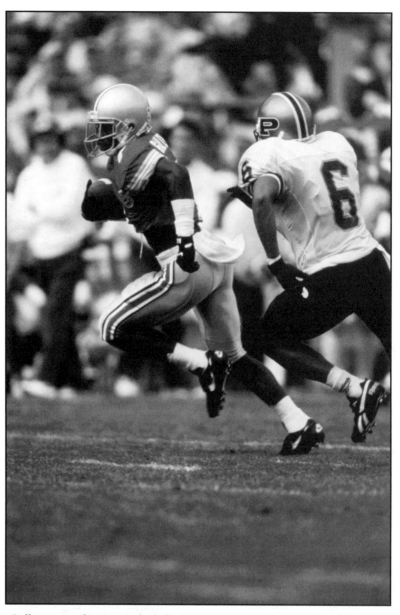

Galloway speeds away to daylight.

"Joey Galloway was more than a first-rate football player," OSU coach John Cooper said. "He was a first-class person. We probably never got the maximum out of Joey as a football player, because we weren't as sophisticated throwing the ball when he was here.

"He was probably one of the most talented players we ever had here. I don't think any of us realized how good he was until it was too late."

Galloway was eventually drafted in the first round by the Seattle Seahawks and was later traded to the Dallas Cowboys.

Eddie GEORGE

Another Link in the Heisman Legacy

The path to the Heisman Trophy was well-worn throughout the 1990s, or at least it was until Eddie George came along.

In an age when slick publicity campaigns often decided the winner of college football's most coveted award, George was a throwback, not only in the way he played, but in the way he rose to the pinnacle of his sport during the 1995 season.

The native of Philadelphia came into his senior year without the spotlight of national attention illuminating his talents.

George's name wasn't just absent from the lips of Heisman voters that September, he wasn't even a preseason all-Big Ten pick.

And even though he got off to an impressive start, more than halfway into the 1995 season George still wasn't the clear-cut Heisman choice on his own team.

None of that mattered by the end of October, however, for by then George had made the

transition from "Eddie who?" to the first name on most voters' lips.

A 207-yard rushing performance against Notre Dame in week three came on the heels of George's 219-yard game against Washington.

That established George as someone worthy of note in a Heisman field that until then looked like a two-man battle between Florida quarterback Danny Wuerffel and Nebraska quarterback Tommie Frazier.

Trouble was, right about the time George started doing the things worthy of making himself a top candidate, so did teammates Terry Glenn and Bob Hoying.

"We really didn't know which one of them was going to be the guy to promote for the Heisman," then-OSU coach John Cooper said. "Eddie got off to a great start, but so did Terry, and Bobby was just steady the whole way."

Glenn's emergence from anonymity as a sophomore to assaulting the OSU single-season

record book as a junior came in such spectacular fashion it looked like he might take over as the Buckeyes' Heisman contender.

But slowly, steadily, and with numbing efficiency, George began to assume that role with a 100-yard performance week after week after week.

"Our team was able to do whatever it wanted offensively," George said. "We had a great line, so we could move people off the ball if we wanted to, and we had a great quarterback in Bob Hoying and great receivers in Terry Glenn and Buster Tillman. Teams couldn't stack their defense to stop any one thing. That really contributed to my success."

While that was true, it was also true that George's success wasn't solely a factor of the talent around him.

"Eddie George had the best work ethic of any player I ever coached," Cooper said. "When he came to Ohio State, most people thought he would end up being a linebacker or a fullback. He had great size, but his speed wasn't quite what you want a tailback to have.

"Eddie didn't hit many home runs as a junior, but he worked to make himself faster. He was probably no faster than 4.6 or 4.55 when he first came in. It's a real tribute to him that he added that speed element to his game, because his last year, he hit a lot of home runs for us."

George's propensity for producing the big play was crucial to his Heisman campaign, with no single play more responsible than the 64-yarder he broke on the first play of the third quarter against Illinois.

The Illini's defense featured two of the top three picks in the NFL draft that season in defensive end Simeon Rice and linebacker Kevin Hardy, but George followed the dominant blocking of tackle Orlando Pace and the rest of the OSU line to a single-game school record 314 yards on 36 carries.

That performance coincided with the mailing of Heisman ballots to voters across the country and led to George compiling a huge early lead that gave him the trophy by 264 points over Frazier.

George's effort against Illinois was also important for personal reasons, since it symbolized better than any other game against any other opponent could how far he had come in his career.

Four years earlier, as a true freshman, George had fumbled twice against the Illini on the one-yard line in an 18-16 Buckeyes loss.

Those mistakes took George out of his role as OSU's designated short-yardage back and essentially kept him buried on the bench until he reemerged as a junior and began laying the groundwork for the superlative senior season that would follow.

"The way Eddie played against Illinois that year really put the cap on what a great career he had," Cooper said. "He was a guy who could have quit after all the adversity he went through as a freshman,

but he worked and worked and worked and make himself the Heisman Trophy winner."

That put George in elite company at OSU, joining Les Horvath, Vic Janowicz, Hopalong Cassady, and two-time winner Archie Griffin among the Buckeyes' Heisman fraternity.

As such, Ohio State honored George during the 2001 season by retiring his jersey, No. 27, in halftime ceremonies at Ohio Stadium. By then, George had become a top running back in the NFL and lead the Tennessee Titans to the Super Bowl the year before.

The capacity crowd rose and repeated its familiar "Ed-die . . . Ed-die . . . Ed-die," chant that rang out repeatedly at the Horseshoe his senior season.

George took it all in and wiped a tear from his cheek as a videotape of his career highlights played to robust applause.

George made himself a breakaway threat.

Joe
GERMAINE

Cool as the Other Side of the Pillow

The images still flicker across the movie screen of the mind, cut and spliced in staccato fashion to recall the artistry Joe Germaine brought to his career as an Ohio State quarterback.

The 56 touchdown passes, thrown with the authority and accuracy that made him the Big Ten's passing efficiency leader all three seasons he played, are part of the montage.

So is the calm, confident way Germaine stood in the pocket, unfazed by the intent of on-rushing defenders whose arrival he consistently frustrated with his rapid-fire release.

But amid the myriad of precision throws and skillful reads, one indelible image of Germaine lingers as a testament not just to the skills he exhibited, but to the source of his success.

Flash back to Pasadena, New Year's Day, 1997, and envision the mayhem breaking out as David Boston high-stepped into the end zone with the 5-yard touchdown

pass from Germaine that hands OSU a 20-17 victory over Arizona State.

Teammates are tossing their helmets in the air, hugging each other in unchecked exuberance.

Scarlet-and-gray loyalists are exulting in the aisles over the Buckeyes' first Rose Bowl victory in 23 seasons.

And there is Germaine, helmet on, chin-strap buckled, calmly clapping his hands as he jogs to the sideline—like a guy whose team just bumped a three-touchdown lead to four in a meaningless non-conference game.

That flat-line nature, the unwavering grip Germaine held upon his emotions, delivered him from adversity that would have crippled the confidence of lesser players or embittered them so deeply they never could have recognized their potential.

Instead, Germaine used being initially overlooked for a starting job and later being forced to split time with teammate Stanley Jackson to stoke the fire within.

"In the beginning, I had coaches tell me that other people were better than me, but I'm not the kind of guy to let that get me down," Germaine said. "I used that as motivation. It prompted me to work harder and things worked out for me. Those tough times definitely made me a tougher person and, I think, a better player.

"Of course, I wanted to start and play more, what player doesn't. But the most important thing to me was winning, and we were winning. It was difficult coming off the bench, because you really couldn't get into the flow. But that was my job and I had to make it work."

Germaine did that so well he made OSU head coach John Cooper appear a savant.

"I never saw Joe play before we signed him," Cooper said. "I just didn't like to waste scholarships. If we had one to give, I wanted to give it to somebody."

OSU has had shiftier quarterbacks, like Rod Gerald and

Cornelius Greene. It has also had more charismatic quarterbacks, like Rex Kern and Tom Matte. But never have the Buckeyes had a better quarterback than Germaine, whose Howdy Doody features belied the cold-steel mentality of Dirty Harry.

If records are the barometer of greatness, Germaine had them, setting 11 school marks, including eight his senior year in 1998.

If awards are the measuring stick, Germaine had those, winning Rose Bowl MVP as a sophomore and Big Ten MVP as a senior.

If victories are the standard, Germaine had those, directing the Buckeyes to 11-1 and 10-3 records while splitting time at his position as a sophomore and junior, and an 11-1 record, 10 weeks at No. 1 and an eventual No. 2 national finish as a senior.

And for a closing argument, consider that Germaine is the only quarterback in Ohio State history to lead his team to two Jan. 1 bowl wins—the 1997 Rose and the 1999 Sugar.

The first of those came against the favorite team of his childhood, Arizona State.

Germaine wanted to play for the Sun Devils, but they didn't recruit him because their quarterback spot was already filled by Jake "The Snake" Plummer.

Plummer guided ASU to one of his trademark late touchdown drives in that '97 Rose Bowl, but he left Germaine 1:40 on the clock to erase the resultant 17-14 deficit.

That was enough for Germaine to drive OSU 65 yards for the winning score.

"It's weird and it's funny how things worked out," said Germaine, who passed for 139 yards and two touchdowns in OSU's 20-17 win. "Being from Arizona and going halfway across the country to play football at Ohio State, then I go play against my hometown team in the Rose Bowl. That was a day I'll never forget."

Germaine's heroics in Pasadena still didn't win him the starting job over Jackson in 1997, when the Buckeyes finished 10-3 and lost to Florida State in the Sugar Bowl.

By his senior season, however, Jackson was gone and Germaine could fully display his talents.

"He played as good or better than any quarterback I ever coached," Cooper said. "Joe could pick any defense apart. He'd just stand in there, go through his progression, and *boom*."

Germaine set Ohio State records with 3,030 passing yards, 384 attempts, 230 completions, and seven 300-yard passing games, including four in succession.

He ended the regular season by passing for 330 yards, three touchdown and no interceptions in a 31-16 win over Michigan that matched the Buckeyes' biggest home margin against their archrival since 1968.

Then in the Sugar Bowl, Germaine passed for 222 yards and another score, again without an interception, in a 24-14 victory over Texas A&M. He eventually played pro ball with the St. Louis Rams' Super Bowl championship team, and now plays for the Kansas City Chiefs.

"The wins and the awards were great," Germaine said. "It was nice to be recognized by people and to be recognized by your teammates. But that wasn't really the most special part of it. I'm just happy I was able to be a part of the tradition at Ohio State. That's what I'll take with me forever."

Germaine showed uncanny poise in the pocket.

Terry GLENN

An Ace in the Hole

Every coach covets a secret weapon to spring on an unknowing opponent.

There are, however, some secrets that are too good to keep.

Terry Glenn was that kind of secret.

Prior to the 1995 Ohio State football season, head coach John Cooper and wide receivers coach Chuck Stobart could have played opossum with their gut feeling that Glenn would more than adequately fill the spot vacated by Joey Galloway.

Neither Cooper nor his assistant could keep the good news to themselves, however, broadcasting to anyone who would listen that Glenn had the talent to be just as good as Galloway.

Both of them were wrong, of course.

Glenn performed—statistically, at least—better than any receiver in a single season ever had at OSU.

"I told some people when we lost Galloway, 'Look out, we have a guy coming up who had a chance to be just as good,'" Cooper said. "Of course, I had no idea Terry was going to be that good. No one could have predicted that. He had as good a year as any wide receiver I've ever seen."

Glenn's ascent from walk-on to winner of the Fred Biletnikoff Award, given to the nation's outstanding receiver, was more than a tale of triumph on the football field.

His mother was murdered when Glenn was 13, leaving he and his sister to grow up without a parent.

Glenn's high school coach at Columbus Brookhaven, Greg Miller, and the family of teammate Charles "June" Henley, took him in and shepherded him through his formative years.

Glenn still was an unknown commodity at OSU entering his junior season, having caught only 15 passes for 266 yards and no touchdowns his freshman and sophomore seasons combined.

"Terry might not have been mature enough at that time to really contribute, but when he got his chance, he really stepped forward," Stobart said. "He could catch the ball in any position, was very quick off the line and was fast enough to run by guys, even if they played well off of him."

Glenn wasted no time after becoming a starter to show that the confidence his coaches placed in him was merited.

He had 105 receiving yards in the opening victory over Boston College and caught seven passes for 91 yards and his first career touchdown the following week against Washington.

Glenn's emergence reached full flower in week three at Pittsburgh, where his 253 receiving yards set an OSU single-game record and nearly matched the output of his first two seasons as a Buckeye.

Four of his nine catches went for touchdowns that day, establishing another OSU record.

It seemed impossible for Glenn, or anyone, to top that performance, but the following week he electrified a then-record Ohio Stadium crowd with an 82-

George made himself a breakaway threat.

yard catch-and-run for one of his two touchdowns in a 45-26 victory over Notre Dame.

The Buckeyes opened the Big Ten season the following week at Penn State and Glenn's theatrics were sensational. He caught nine passes, astounding the Beaver Stadium crowd and even himself with his leaping grabs that worked for 175 yards and two touchdowns in a pulsating 28-25 win.

"I'm still in shock over some of those catches," Glenn later said of his performance against the Nittany Lions. "I look at those films and wonder, 'Is that me? Did I do that?'"

Glenn certainly did, and only a separated shoulder later that season could slow him up.

He missed all of one game, three quarters of another, and half of two others with that injury, yet still wound up setting Ohio State single-season

records with 1,411 receiving yards and 17 touchdowns.

The 17 TDs obliterated the former mark of 11 scores shared by Cris Carter and Joey Galloway, the player both Cooper and Stobart hinted Glenn would capably replace.

"To see someone come from the background that Terry did and make a success of himself is really what coaching is all about," Cooper said. "He had tremendous speed and tremendous athletic ability and he didn't waste it. He made the most out of his ability and his opportunity."

Glenn was selected as the Biletnikoff winner over USC's Keyshawn Johnson, who would become the No. 1 pick in the NFL draft that season. Glenn went with the seventh overall choice to the New England Patriots, the first of three Buckeyes among the first 14 picks that season.

Archie GRIFFIN

A Winner in Every Way

It is a measure of Archie Griffin's most abundant and endearing quality that he still reflects genuine amazement at his popularity, not only in Columbus, but also with college football fans everywhere.

The tangible elements that made Griffin the only two-time Heisman Trophy winner in history—his artful balance, darting quickness, and uncanny sense for daylight—have faded with the passage of time.

There is, however, one trait that contributed significantly to Griffin's success at Ohio State and still defines him:

His humility.

For all the rushing yards he gained, touchdowns he scored, and honors he received during a four-year career at OSU from 1972-75, Griffin's lasting legacy should be a quotation from his coach, Woody Hayes.

"He's a better person than he is a football player," Hayes once said. "And he's the best football player I've ever seen."

The only player in history to start in four consecutive Rose Bowls, the first player ever to have his number retired at Ohio State, Griffin characteristically deflects the credit for his considerable achievements as a Buckeye.

"I was just extremely fortunate to come along and be at the right place at the right time," said Griffin, who returned to Ohio State as an athletic administrator following a nine-year career with the Cincinnati Bengals. "As a team, we were able to make those things happen."

The only thing OSU didn't accomplish during Griffin's era was winning a national championship.

As could be predicted, he would, to this day, gladly trade one or both of his Heismans for a single finish as the nation's No. 1 team.

The Buckeyes were edged for that honor Griffin's sophomore season because of a 10-10 tie with Michigan, his junior season by an 18-17 Rose Bowl loss to USC,

and his senior season by a 23-10 loss in Pasadena to UCLA.

"We played for it every year," said Griffin, whose teams went 40-5-1 during his career. "That's the one regret I have about my career, that we didn't win the national championship. We had great teams, teams that people have kind of forgot about because we didn't finish with that No. 1 label. Getting that would have proven how good we were."

The memories Griffin created need no massaging, from the then single-game record 239 yards he gained in his second game as a freshman to the NCAA-record 31 consecutive 100-yard performances he offered during his career.

"At times, I've thought about how it almost seemed destined to happen, the way that first game came about and all," Griffin said. "I mean, I was born at The Ohio State University Hospitals. I played football there and got a quality education there. I came back there to work. There's been that bond there between myself and the university all my life."

Griffin ended his OSU career with a then-NCAA record 5,177 yards, having never gained less than 100 yards from the ninth game of his freshman year to the final regular season game of his senior year.

He was listed as the Buckeyes' fifth-team tailback on Sept. 30, 1972, and hadn't even spent the previous night with the team in its Columbus hotel, when Hayes inserted him in the first quarter at the insistence of running backs coach Rudy Hubbard.

Archie Griffin rushed for 5,177 career yards.

"I didn't even think I would get in that day, because I played one play in the opener and I fumbled," Griffin said. "Rudy really pounded the table to get me in there. Coach Hayes always said, 'If you believe in something, you have to pound the table,' so Rudy pounded the table."

Hubbard never had to make the same hard sell again, for it took only that one afternoon for Hayes to brighten considerably on the new NCAA freshman eligibility rule.

"I have never known whether I was for or against the freshman rule until now," Hayes said after Griffin's breakout performance against North Carolina. "Archie has convinced me it's OK."

Griffin might have won three Heismans if not for the abundance of individual talent on the Buckeyes in 1973. He finished fifth in the voting as a sophomore, with teammates John Hicks second and Randy Gradishar sixth.

Had any of the three Buckeyes pooled all the votes the trio received, they would have won the award over Penn State's John Cappelletti.

Griffin swept to his first Heisman the following year by a 1,920-819 margin over USC's Anthony Davis, winning the voting in every section of the country.

The following season, despite OSU losing three linemen to graduation, Griffin followed his 1,695-yard performance as a junior with a 1,450-yard output reduced by the limited playing time he saw in the second half of numerous lopsided Buckeye victories.

Voters weren't fooled and again made Griffin an overwhelming winner of the Heisman, giving him 1,800 votes to runner-up Chuck Muncie of California's 730.

"It's a very special thing being a Heisman Trophy winner, just like it was a very special thing to be a member of the teams I was on at Ohio State," Griffin said. "One couldn't have happened without the other. We had great talent on those teams, but more than that, we had great people and a great coach in charge of the program. I was just fortunate to be a part of that."

Randy GRADISHAR

The Man in the Middle

He began his turn working in the family grocery store at age 11, sweeping floors, stocking shelves and—he was certain—getting a first glimpse at the rest of his adult life.

It didn't take long before Randy Gradishar realized something:

"I didn't want to spend the rest of my life in the grocery business."

He wouldn't, of course, going on to become a two-time All-American linebacker at Ohio State and a seven-time All-Pro with the NFL's Denver Broncos.

Still, throughout it all, there was one lingering aspect of the grocery business Gradishar couldn't escape.

Just about every time he'd blitz, blunt a ballcarrier's advance into the line, or bounce a tight end to the turf, you could almost hear the call come from the sideline:

"CLEAN UP ON AISLE ONE!"

Gradishar's excellence in the middle laid another stone in the foundation of Ohio State's linebacker tradition—one that's traced from Ike Kelly to Jim Houston, Gradishar, Tom Cousineau, Chris Spielman, and Andy Katzenmoyer.

Many would argue that Gradishar was the best of that group.

None could argue that he was the most unheralded when he walked on campus.

"I remember coming to Ohio State from Champion, Ohio, where our football program was only three or four years old at the time," Gradishar said. "All the guys in my class came in as all-state, all-this, all-that. They were all-everything and I was all-nothing. I started wondering, 'What am I doing here?'"

At 6-foot-3 and just 190 pounds as a freshman, Gradishar didn't inspire much awe with his physical presence.

But once he got on the field as a sophomore, it became apparent that coach Woody Hayes had invested a scholarship wisely.

"When I first saw Randy, what impressed me was his running," said two-time Heisman Trophy-winner Archie Griffin, Gradishar's teammate in 1972 and 1973. "We had a running test we had to take, where the backs were supposed to run a mile in 5:45. I had never run a mile before, so I really practiced that summer and thought I might be able to make it by the time I got to camp.

"Well, the first time I tried it, Randy finished in about 5:20. I thought, 'My goodness, I've never seen a big guy run that fast.' It was unbelievable."

Gradishar's speed and instincts helped him lead the Buckeyes in tackles from 1971-73 on a defense that dominated opponents both his junior and senior seasons.

OSU won the Big Ten and advanced to the Rose Bowl both years, with the Michigan games predictably the highlight of both seasons.

OSU's 14-11 victory over the Wolverines in 1972 will forever be known as the "goal-line stand game."

A capacity crowd in the Horseshoe that afternoon witnessed an unprecedented defensive performance in which the Buckeyes faced 12 Michigan snaps inside the six-yard line and eight inside the three-yard line, yet yielded only one touchdown.

The Wolverines trailed, 7-3, early in the second quarter and had the football first-and-goal at the OSU one-yard line, yet didn't score on four running plays.

In the third quarter, Michigan had a first down at the Buckeyes' five-yard line and needed four plays to reach the end zone. The Wolverines then added a two-point conversion to get within 14-11.

That lead survived until the fourth quarter, when an interception gave Michigan possession at the Buckeyes' 29-yard line.

The Wolverines moved toward a winning touchdown, gaining another first-and-goal at the five-yard line with nine minutes left.

A field goal seemed a certainty, since all Michigan needed was a tie to claim the Rose Bowl berth, given OSU's earlier Big Ten loss at Michigan State.

Michigan coach Bo Schembechler, however, chose to challenge Gradishar and the Buckeyes' defense, and that choice proved fatal.

"At that point, it's stop them or probably lose the game," Gradishar said.

Michigan gained one yard on first down, two on second, and all but the last few inches it needed on third down.

"On fourth down, I saw their quarterback, Dennis Franklin, take a false step," Gradishar said. "I was only about a yard and a half off the line of scrimmage, and when the ball was snapped, the hole just opened. He faked like he was going to hand off, and then he tried to come through. I met him, along with everybody else, and we'd stopped them again."

There was, however, no stopping USC in the Rose Bowl, with the Trojans bolting from a 7-7 halftime tie to claim a 42-17 victory and unanimous selection as the national champions.

Gradishar and the Buckeyes would get another shot at the Men of Troy the next season, however, and the defensive domination OSU showed all season would rewrite the script.

Ohio State registered four shutouts and allowed only three points in two other games that season, outscoring opponents 371-43 heading into Pasadena.

That dominance moved Big Ten athletic directors to give the Buckeyes the Rose Bowl berth after a 10-10 tie at Michigan, a decision swayed by the broken collarbone Franklin suffered late in the game.

"I had some friends in the Michigan area, so Woody gave me permission to stay there after the game," Gradishar said. "We were numb. We didn't know what to feel. You know how to react to a loss or a win, but a tie? What did that mean?"

The next day, he found out.

"I was driving back to campus and it came on the radio that we had been selected to play in the Rose Bowl," Gradishar said. "At that point, I just went nuts."

The storybook finish continued from there with a sixth-place finish in the Heisman Trophy race and atonement in the Rose Bowl via a 42-10 win over USC.

"As far as a way to end my career, you couldn't have asked for anything better than that," Gradishar said. "To beat Michigan at Michigan and then come back and beat USC after the way they beat us the year before, that was just a fantastic way to go out."

Gradishar was a two-time All-American.

Chic HARLEY

He Made It All Possible

There was a time before passions stirred in Columbus at the mere mention of the word Michigan.

That was before the Buckeyes and Wolverines ranked among the greatest rivalries in college football, when the series was nothing more than a colossal mismatch.

Then Chic Harley came along.

A 5-foot-9, 156-pound halfback from Columbus, Harley's impact on the OSU football program was as immeasurable as his importance in energizing the spirit of what makes Ohio State-Michigan special.

Before Harley, the Buckeyes played before crowds so sparse at tiny Ohio Field that local high school games drew more interest.

Before Harley, OSU hadn't won or even contended for a Big Ten championship.

And before Harley, Ohio State was a depressing 0-13-2 against Michigan, the team its fans most wanted to defeat.

The Wolverines weren't so much a rival in those days as they were destroyers.

After all, Michigan had beaten the Buckeyes by the embarrassing margin of 369-21, with 11 shutouts, in the schools' 15 meetings over 22 years.

That changed when Harley arrived on campus from Columbus East High School.

He led Ohio State to a 7-0 record and first-ever conference title as a sophomore in 1916 and followed that up by playing brilliantly on a 1917 squad that finished 8-0-1 and again won the league championship.

Harley's daring runs from the single-wing, his exploits as an accomplished punter and devotee of the drop-kick, and his smothering performance as a defensive back brought Ohio State football into the national spotlight for the first time.

He was the Buckeyes' first three-time All-American and set a school scoring record of 201 career points that stood until

Heisman Trophy winner Howard "Hopalong" Cassady broke the mark in 1955.

Harley's points came via 23 career touchdowns, 39 extra-points and eight field goals.

Ohio State not only hadn't beaten Michigan, it hadn't beaten either Illinois or Wisconsin until Harley came along in 1916.

He took care of the Illini in the third game that season by thrilling the Ohio Field partisans with a 12-yard scramble for a touchdown on a mud-soaked field that tied the score in the final minute.

Harley then calmly went to the bench, changed into dry shoes, and drop-kicked the winning point in the 7-6 victory.

That win so excited OSU fans that 12,500 packed into Ohio Field for Homecoming the following week, hoping to see an upset of powerful Wisconsin.

The Badgers were 4-0 and had outscored their opponents by a collective 91-10 margin.

Harley, though, scored on a 27-yard run to tie the score, 7-7, after Wisconsin went in front. He then made the game-winning play early in the fourth quarter.

Backed up to his own 20-yard line on a punt, Harley sped past his pursuers for an 80-yard touchdown and kicked the point-after to provide the decisive margin in an eventual 14-13 victory.

That win still didn't assure the Buckeyes their first Big Ten title, which came down to the final game of the regular season against visiting Northwestern.

Both teams were 6-0, and early in the fourth quarter nothing was decided, given the prevailing 3-3 tie.

That's when Harley went to work, scoring on a 63-yard run around right end and a 15-yard sweep. He also set up another touchdown with a 28-yard pass completion. The resultant 23-3 final completed an unbeaten season, but the Harley legend was far from complete.

As a junior in 1917, he led the Buckeyes to a 9-0-1 overall mark—spoiled only by a 0-0 tie with Auburn—and was voted an All-American for the second time.

There was, however, still one thing Harley hadn't accomplished.

He hadn't beaten Michigan.

Of course, he hadn't played the Wolverines, either.

Finally, after a year spent in the military, Harley returned and captained coach John W. Wilce's 1919 Buckeyes that ventured onto the road for the first time that season for an Oct. 25 game at Ann Arbor.

Both teams were unbeaten and unscored upon, but the Buckeyes had a 7-3 lead in the fourth quarter when Harley took care of the suspense. He followed teammate Pete Stinchcomb's 24-yard run to the Michigan 42 by going around the end and scoring on the next play.

Now in a deep hole, the Wolverines tried to pass, but Harley would have none of that. He wound up with four interceptions that day and also punted 11 times for a 42-yard average.

Finally, the Michigan monster had been felled.

After that, the only mystery was whether the great Harley could complete his OSU career without a defeat.

He nearly did, but Illinois edged the Buckeyes, 9-7, in the final game of the 1919 season before a record crowd of 17,000 at Ohio Field.

OSU athletic director Lynn W. St. John told reporters he could have sold 50,000 seats to that game, which provided the impetus for building Ohio Stadium three years later at the then-astronomical capacity of 60,000.

The Buckeyes have never had problems filling it, thanks to the inflamed passions of their fans that trace to the era when Chic Harley was the first of many OSU unforgettables.

Harley started OSU's football success.

John HICKS

It Didn't Matter if They Knew

It is the football equivalent of the chicken-and-the-egg dilemma, deciding whether a great blocker makes a great ball carrier or vice versa.

Whether one can exist without the other is debatable, because how would a lineman's excellence in the trenches be revealed except for a rusher darting through the holes up front?

And how would a back gain any yardage and the recognition that comes with it if not for the space to exhibit his talents?

One player clearly needs the other to succeed, and no one knows that better than two-time Heisman Trophy winner Archie Griffin.

While Griffin has gained most of the lasting fame from his era and the achievements the Buckeyes gathered during his career, he will tell anyone who asks that his ascent to immediate stardom at OSU couldn't have happened without tackle John Hicks and Co. clearing the way.

"John and the other guys who

blocked for me were really the key to us having such great offenses in those days," Griffin said. "John was the key to our offensive line. He was the leader of everything up front for us. He was an emotional person. He was a confident person. He was the guy who fired us up."

Hicks was so certain of his ability to dominate that he did something that drove his tailback crazy.

"I'd come up to the line, look at my guy and say, 'Hey, we're coming at you with this one,'" Hicks said. "That used to drive Archie nuts. He'd say, 'John, don't tell them what we're doing.' The way I looked at it, I didn't care if they knew or not, because even if they knew, they weren't going to stop us."

Hicks's confidence was well placed in his own talents, for as a senior in 1973 he offered arguably the greatest season of any lineman in college football history.

Not only did he win both the Outland and Lombardi trophies as

the best interior lineman in the country, he also finished second in the Heisman Trophy balloting to John Cappelletti of Penn State by a 1,057-524 margin.

Had Hicks gathered the 326 votes Griffin received for finishing fifth and the 282 teammate Randy Gradishar received for finishing sixth, the OSU tackle would have pulled off an unprecedented parlay of college football's three major awards.

"Those honors I received that year caught me totally off guard," Hicks said. "In coach Hayes's system, you didn't have individual goals. All I wanted to be was an All-American, and once I made that, I forgot about everything else."

"I remember being in a cab in New York for the Bob Hope All-American show when someone came on the radio and said Cappelletti from Penn State had won the Heisman. Someone in the cab said, 'Who finished second?' When someone said I did, I couldn't believe it."

Hicks's only concern entering his senior season was avenging OSU's 42-17 loss in the Rose Bowl from the previous season.

He had come to Ohio State in 1969 when freshmen were ineligible, and suffered ligament damage to his knee after starting the first six games of 1970, which caused him to miss the rest of that season and all of 1971.

The loss in the Rose Bowl following the 1972 season left Hicks only one more chance to gain a victory in Pasadena before the conclusion of his OSU career, and the way he blocked that fall showed a singlemindness to accomplish that goal.

The Buckeyes rushed for a then-school-record 3,908 yards and went undefeated, finishing No. 2 in the nation with a 10-0-1 record marred only by a 10-10 tie with Michigan.

"Whenever we needed a tough yard that year, we ran behind John," Griffin said. "We usually were in Robust in those situations, with the halfbacks blocking for the fullback, but there wasn't any doubt where the play was going. We were going to run behind John.

"When we tied Michigan, the athletic directors in the Big Ten voted for us to go to the Rose Bowl, so we went out there with something to prove. I know all the guys who played in that game against USC the year before wanted to do something about evening the score."

OSU put the cap on its unbeaten season by avenging its previous Rose Bowl loss with an equally lopsided victory over USC, 42-21.

"That was the worst whipping any of us every took during our careers and we promised Woody we would do something about it," Hicks said. "We dedicated that year to him."

OSU fell behind the Trojans, 21-14, but stormed back to score two touchdowns in both the third and fourth quarters to claim an easy victory.

Hicks and the line blocked well enough for Griffin to gain 149 rushing yards and freshman Pete Johnson to gain 94 yards and score three touchdowns.

OSU rushed for 320 yards and gained 459 overall in the victory.

"I'll always wonder how many yards we could have gained if Big John hadn't told them where we were going to run," Griffin said.

Hicks played professionally with the New York Giants and was elected to the college football hall of fame in 2001.

Hicks was the best offensive lineman of his era.

Les HORVATH

The Start Of Two Great Traditions

There have been six Heisman Trophies and at least a share of as many national championships in the history of Ohio State football, but Les Horvath has the distinction of standing alone as the player who initiated both legacies.

Horvath, a native of Parma, helped lead the Buckeyes to a 9-1 record in head coach Paul Brown's second season in Columbus and the 1942 national championship.

Two years later, after a season away from football while studying dentistry, Horvath capitalized on war-time rules that permitted players who had been ineligible as freshman to return to the sport and made off with the 1944 Heisman Trophy.

He rushed for 669 yards that season and accumulated 953 yards total offense, doing virtually everything for head coach Carroll Widdoes's offense.

Horvath played quarterback when the Buckeyes operated from the T-formation and halfback when Widdoes put them in the single wing, while also playing safety on defense.

Widdoes's squad that year looked to be in for more of the same difficulty Brown's 1943 Buckeyes experienced when they went 3-6 thanks to a squad depleted by OSU's affiliation with the U.S. Army.

Other Big Ten schools in those days chose the U.S. Navy as their military affiliate, and the navy allowed players to participate in football while they remained on campus for ROTC training.

Such was not the case with the army, hence the Buckeyes sagged under .500 in 1943 and had no better prospects for 1944 with a squad populated by four seniors, three juniors, five sophomores and 31 freshmen.

One month before the season, however, the specialized army training program in which Horvath was enrolled disbanded, so he was free to return to the field if he desired.

"At first, I wasn't sure I wanted to play," Horvath said in 1994, a year before his death. "Dental school was quite taxing, but Coach Widdoes said I wouldn't have to practice all the time and agreed to fly me to the games, both of which gave me more time to study."

Horvath's presence helped the Buckeyes far exceed the modest expectations they entertained before he agreed to rejoin the squad.

OSU rolled through its first eight games without an opponent coming within a touchdown, then archrival Michigan and legendary coach Fritz Crisler came to town for Homecoming on the final Saturday of the season.

The lead see-sawed from 6-0 OSU to 7-6 Michigan before Horvath scored from the one-yard line to put the Buckeyes in front, 12-7.

Again, Michigan came back and reached the end zone to reclaim a 14-12 advantage, but Horvath had another one-yard touchdown in him, and the Buckeyes were 18-14 victors.

Horvath played all 60 minutes in that game, but he wouldn't get the chance to play in the Rose Bowl because the conference did not permit postseason competition in those days.

The closest it came to allowing such games arose during what Horvath thought at the time would be his last season of eligibility in 1942.

The Buckeyes won the Big Ten title that year with an 8-1 overall mark spoiled only by a loss at Wisconsin, a defeat that was traced to a case of dysentery players caught on the train ride to Madison.

Horvath threw a touchdown pass and teammate Paul Sarringhaus threw a pair in the 21-7 victory over Michigan that gave OSU the league title, after which a game against powerful Iowa Pre-Flight was added to the schedule.

The Seahawks were a collection of former collegiate All-Americans and professionals training at a military academy under the tutelage of legendary Minnesota coach Bernie Bierman, so Ohio State was expected to absorb a thorough beating.

Instead, the Buckeyes administered one, winning 41-12 to ascend to the national championship thanks to losses by No. 1 Georgia and No. 2 Boston College on the same day.

OSU retired Horvath's No. 22 jersey in 2001.

Les Horvath was OSU's first Heisman Trophy winner.

Andy
KATZENMOYER

As Good As Advertised

He came along well after Joni Mitchell's popular 1970s tune, "Big Yellow Taxi," but the lyrics from that hit perfectly summarize the Ohio State football career of 1997 Butkus Award-winner Andy Katzenmoyer.

"Don't it always seem to go, that you don't know what you've got 'til it's gone . . ."

Those words could be Katzenmoyer's epitaph at OSU, where he burst onto the scene as a true freshman in 1996 and did something few recruits ever manage—he played better than the hype that preceded him to campus.

Having played at nearby Westerville South, Katzenmoyer was familiar to Buckeye fans by the time he was a sophomore in high school. At 6 foot-4, 250 pounds, he seemed a natural to step into the middle linebacker spot at OSU and further a tradition of excellence that stretched from Randy Gradishar to Tom Cousineau to Marcus Marek to Chris Spielman.

Katzenmoyer did just that, but was so successful so soon that it became difficult for him to keep pace with the performance expectations that multiplied with his every tackle.

By the time he left school after his junior year to become a first-round NFL draft pick, his role on the Buckeyes' defense had changed such that he wasn't making the spectacular plays with the same regularity he did early in his career.

Coaches and teammates said Katzenmoyer was playing just as well, if not better than ever, but it wasn't until the season after he departed that those opinions gained credibility.

With Katzenmoyer from 1996-98, the Buckeyes finished in the top ten nationally in total defense each season, and were among the country's stingiest units against the run.

Without Katzenmoyer in 1999, but with its entire first- and second-team defensive line returning, Ohio State slipped to sixth in the Big Ten in total

defense and seventh against the run in a 6-6 finish that broke a streak of 10 straight bowl appearances.

"People didn't realize how much Andy meant to us until he was gone," OSU coach John Cooper said. "It was impossible for teams to run wide with Andy in the middle. He had so much speed, he could get from sideline to sideline, and he didn't miss many tackles."

Katzenmoyer's impact with the Buckeyes was immediate.

Even before he became the first player in school history to start at linebacker as a true freshman, he captured considerable attention by requesting to wear his high school jersey, No. 45. That desire clashed with some traditionalists, who believed no one should ever wear No. 45 after two-time Heisman trophy-winner Archie Griffin distinguished himself with that number during his storied career.

Griffin, however, didn't object, asking only that Katzenmoyer perform in such a manner to do the number proud.

That he did, winning All-Big Ten and second-team All-America honors as a freshman when he led the Buckeyes in both sacks and tackles for a loss with 12 apiece.

He stripped the quarterback of possession at Indiana in the next-to-last game that season to allow teammate Matt Finkes to return the football 45 yards for the go-ahead touchdown in the victory that clinched the Rose Bowl berth.

Then in Pasadena, Katzenmoyer tied a school record with five sacks and also had an interception in the thrilling victory over Arizona State.

"The word that comes to mind when I think of Andy was just domination," former teammate Ahmed Plummer said. "Early in his career, he just made so many plays that by the time he was a junior, teams were using two and three guys to block him and that opened things up so other guys could make plays. He was a pure athlete. I don't think I've ever seen a man that size who could move like he could."

Katzenmoyer was at his best in 1997, when he won the Butkus Award (given to the nation's most outstanding linebacker) and was a consensus All-American, becoming the first OSU linebacker to be so honored as a sophomore.

His thunderous hit on Missouri quarterback Corby Jones was a finalist for ESPN's college football play of the year and typified the ferocity with which Katzenmoyer played.

"Andy was a great player who just had no physical weaknesses," said his position coach and defensive coordinator Fred Pagac. "He had everything you wanted in a linebacker. He had speed, strength, and a desire to get better every day."

Katzenmoyer's junior season was fraught with off-field criticism after a drunken driving conviction, an August flirtation with academic ineligibility, and fans' demands for him to increase the production he offered his two previous seasons.

He again made first-team all-conference and was a Lombardi Award

finalist and Maxwell Football Club defensive player of the year finalist.

"I thought I played the best I played in my three years at Ohio State," Katzenmoyer said. "I did everything I was asked. I made fewer mistakes. I didn't have the same numbers, but we had an excellent defense."

His legacy secure at OSU, Katzenmoyer bypassed his final season of eligibility to enter the NFL draft, where he was picked up by the New England Patriots.

"I have lifelong friends (from playing at Ohio State)," he said. "Overall, it was a great experience.

"I always knew when I was young that when I grew up, I wanted to play football. I believe everybody is blessed with one special talent in this world, whether it be in business or education or law. I was blessed with athleticism and the gift to play football."

Katzenmoyer started at middle linebacker for three seasons.

Rex KERN

Follow the Leader

Being the leader is a distinction earned, not endowed, so it typically takes time for a first-year starting quarterback to command the respect necessary to be acknowledged as the heart and soul of a successful team.

It was no different with Rex Kern, the quarterback of Ohio State's undefeated 1968 national championship team.

He needed awhile to settle into his role as the Buckeyes' on-field leader. It took him almost two complete quarters before he had it down.

"We wouldn't have been the team that we were without Rex," said Jan White, the tight end and Kern's teammate on the Super Sophomores and the 1969 and 1970 Buckeyes that also won the Big Ten championship. "Certainly, he made his contributions on the field, but aside from the tangibles, there were so many things he did in the locker room and everywhere else that you couldn't find in the stats. He had an intuitive-

ness that everyone recognized and respected."

Kern was in a tough spot when he took over as a starter in 1968. Not only was he just two months removed from back surgery, he was also replacing popular senior Bill Long, who had been a two-year starter.

Any potential for grumbling vanished by halftime of OSU's opener, for what transpired in the second quarter permanently branded Kern as the gutsy leader the Buckeyes would need to become a powerhouse.

Leading only 7-0, facing a fourth-and-10 near midfield, Kern waved punter Mike Sensibaugh off the field and quickly called a play before head coach Woody Hayes could take a timeout to ask his sophomore starter whether he'd suffered a concussion.

"I don't know if Woody really meant what I took him to mean when he told me something before the season," Kern said. "He told me, 'Rex, there are going to be times when you'll see things I

won't see, and the coaches won't see and you'll have to go with your gut.'

"That situation against SMU was one of those times. There were three minutes left in the first half and we had them on the run. I felt we were one play away from breaking the game open. There was anticipation in the huddle that we could make this thing work.

"I saw the punt team coming on and I looked at my teammates. To me, they seemed to be saying, 'Rex, you're not going to let him punt, are you?' So, I just waved Sensibaugh off, huddled us up real quick, and called a play."

Had Kern not made the first down, he might have gone to the bench, never to be heard from again. But destiny was on his side, even if brilliant play-calling wasn't.

SMU blitzed and triple-covered fullback Jim Otis, the only receiver in the pattern, so Kern scrambled. Sixteen yards later, he had his first down, the Buckeyes had their leader, and college football was about to get a dose of Ohio State dominance.

The Buckeyes went 10-0 that season, defeating then No. 1 Purdue in week three, 13-0, and ending the regular season with a 50-14 dismantling of Michigan.

Then it was on to the Rose Bowl, where Kern directed OSU to another upset of the nation's No. 1 team, making Heisman Trophy winner O.J. Simpson and USC the victim of a 27-16 defeat.

"I was very confident in our team and our ability to win that game until we went to Disneyland," Kern said. "They had this deal where both teams went to Disneyland for some sort of a promotional appearance. That was the first time I got a look at the USC players.

"My goodness, I thought they were the San Diego Chargers when they showed up. They were huge. It was unbelievable to me the size that they had. I thought, 'Holy, Toledo, what are we in for?'"

The Rose Bowl's first quarter did nothing to remove Kern's fears, for USC jumped to a 10-0 lead thanks to Simpson's 80-yard touchdown run.

Kern, though, brought the Buckeyes back to a tie by halftime and directed their getaway to an easy victory with two touchdown passes in the second half.

He was voted the game's MVP, but in the locker room after going 9-of-15 for 101 yards and rushing for 35 more yards, said to his teammates, "Every part of this belongs to you guys."

"That's the way I felt then and the way I still feel now," Kern

said. "We were the epitome of a team. We had a lot of great players on that team, but none were bigger than the team as a whole."

OSU would go on to win 27 of 29 games during Kern's career, losing only the Michigan game when ranked No. 1 in 1969 and the Rose Bowl when ranked No. 1 at the end of the 1970 season.

Had the Buckeyes not lost those games, they would have claimed an unprecedented three consecutive national championships.

That still stings Kern somewhat, but not enough to tarnish the distinction of being part of perhaps the most beloved Ohio State team of all time.

"Not winning it all in 1969 and 1970 lingers a bit for all of us, but then we look back and say, 'Wait a minute,'" Kern said. "We didn't really know at the time what kind of history we were making when we were 18 and 19 years old. To win one national championship and come close to two others was a wonderful, wonderful accomplishment. It was a time in my life I'll never forget."

Rex Kern was the 1969 Rose Bowl MVP.

Jim LACHEY

A Gentleman Until the Whistle Blew

Earle Bruce shakes his head and furrows his brow in disagreement until the veracity of what he's been told sinks in.

The intervening years since Bruce coached his 1984 Big Ten champions at Ohio State have dulled the realization that Jim Lachey, the right guard on that Rose Bowl team and the fulcrum on which the Buckeyes' powerful ground game relied, started only that one full season during his college football career.

"Well then," Bruce says, "that was a real bad mistake."

Although Lachey indeed only started full-time his final season and in just 16 games in his career, his inclusion among the greatest linemen ever to play for Ohio State is unquestioned.

He made All-American as a senior and was one of three Buckeyes up front—the others being center Kirk Lowdermilk and tackle Mark Krerowicz—who made first-team All-Big blocking for the nation's leading rusher, Keith Byars.

"We had a pretty good group of guys," Lachey said. "We could really run the football. Back then, we'd throw it only about 18 or 20 times a game, because we could run it so well. We trapped a lot and we pulled a lot. That's all we ever did."

There is one thing that never changed about Jim Lachey, and that's the friendliness and down-to-earth nature instilled in him by his small-town upbringing in St. Henry, Ohio.

Even when he was a three-time Pro Bowl selection during his NFL career, Lachey never got too big to donate money to his high school athletic program or make a visitor from Mercer County feel welcome in the locker room.

"It was important to me that I never forgot my roots," Lachey said. "If someone came all the way to Washington to see me play, the least I could do was go over and shake their hand and thank them for coming."

Such humility comes hard for some successful athletes, but Lachey had it from the day he was

the 12th overall pick in the first round of the 1985 NFL draft and stepped into the San Diego Chargers lineup as their starting left tackle.

"I'll never forget this about Jim," former teammate Chris Spielman said. "It was just after his third year in the pros, after I had finished my senior year at Ohio State. I didn't have a lot of money in those days, and this was back when you weren't allowed to eat with the team at training table once the season was over.

"Jim was in town one day and came over to my apartment. I wanted to make him feel welcome, so I offered him something to eat. The trouble was, back then, I was buying loaves of bread and eating peanut butter sandwiches all the time.

"So I'm making Jim this peanut butter sandwich and the bread is falling apart as I'm putting the peanut butter on. Finally, he says, 'Chris, what are you doing?'

"I told him, 'Hey, Jim, this is it, pal. This is all I've got.'

"Jim says, 'You know what? Meet me tomorrow at my house.'

"Well, I went over there the next day and he took me downtown to Bank One and loaned me $2,000 to open up a checking account. He said, 'Listen, you can't be eating peanut butter if you're getting ready for the draft. You have to start eating right.'

"I never forgot that, and when I got my first check from the Lions, the first thing I did was pay Jim back. I never would have asked him to do that. He took the initiative. That's just the kind of guy Jim is."

On the field, Lachey's chief weapon was his athleticism. Former OSU offensive line coach Bill Myles tells the story of analyzing Lachey on film once to determine how he consistently beat his man so thoroughly.

"I slowed the tape down and you could see that Jim was so quick off the snap he was able to take his first step and get his foot on the ground for leverage while the defensive lineman still had his foot in the air from his first step," Myles said. "He just had such tremendous speed and agility, he was delivering the blow to guys who were still on one foot."

Perhaps the greatest testament to Lachey's speed and agility was the ill-fated trick play it inspired in the Buckeyes' 24-21 loss at Michigan in 1984.

OSU was driving to a go-ahead touchdown when Lachey came off the field to confer with Bruce, who was sending in the plays via messenger guards

"He looked at me and said, 'We're going to run your play,'" Lachey said.

The play, "Lachey Right," called for center Joe Dooley to snap the ball to quarterback Mike Tomczak, but take the ball back and set it on the ground. Lachey would then pick up the football and speed toward the end zone, hoodwinking the Wolverines and crushing their spirit.

At least that's how it was supposed to happen.

"As soon as I went into the game and we called, 'Lachey Right,' I heard (left guard) Scott Zalenski say, 'Oh, no,'" Lachey said. "Well, that didn't give me a lot of confidence.

"Then we lined up and Michigan had its nose tackle cocked (in an off-set alignment). We had never practiced against that with this play. I probably should have called timeout right there, but I didn't."

Dooley snapped the ball, took it back from Tomczak and set it on the ground, but then struck the football with his heel as he stepped to block the nose tackle.

"By the time I turned," Lachey said, "The ball was seven yards away."

Michigan recovered the fumble, captured the three-point victory and went on to the Rose Bowl.

OSU got revenge the following season, however, with a 21-6 win in Lachey's final home game that stood as the Buckeyes biggest margin in the series from 1969-1994.

"The Michigan games are what I remember most about my career. That, the Rose Bowl, and just the memories of playing with the guys I played with. Growing up, I never dreamed about playing in the NFL. I dreamed about playing for Ohio State. So those were some of the greatest years of my life."

Lachey (No. 64) blocks for Mike Tomczak.

Jim OTIS

A Get-Well Cure For Woody

Most people see a doctor hoping for a clean bill of health, but legendary Ohio State football coach Woody Hayes came away from his annual check-up with something more.

During the mid-1960s, Hayes would take time out each summer to visit his physician in Celina, Ohio.

That might seem a long way to travel for something that could have been done in Columbus, but Hayes was loyal to his former Denison University roommate who had gone on the medical school and set up his practice in Mercer County.

It was also a fortuitous piece of luck for Hayes that Dr. James Otis happened to have fathered a namesake who was born for the "Three Yards and a Cloud of Dust" playing style that the football Buckeyes featured.

"My dad and Woody were college roommates, so I'd say it was pretty automatic that I was going to attend Ohio State," said Jim Otis, OSU's leading rusher

from 1967-69. "I had dreamed about going to Ohio State since the time I was around five years old."

Otis doesn't remember the first time he met his future coach because "I pretty much always knew him.

"Woody would bring his family up to Celina for a couple of days every summer," Otis said. "We lived on the lake, so he'd bring his wife and son and he'd get a physical from dad while they were visiting. That's how I knew him then, but our relationship changed once I went to Ohio State.

"Woody was pretty rough on me then, and he needed to be. He didn't want anyone to say that I was playing because he was friends with my father. Of course, Woody would never have allowed anything like that to happen, but he made sure no one thought it by the way he stayed after me."

Otis's performance dismissed any notion of nepotism figuring in his playing time.

He gained a team-best 530

yards as a sophomore, while playing in just seven games.

As a junior, Otis averaged 4.5 yards per carry and accumulated 985 yards, scoring 17 touchdowns to lead the team with 102 points.

His senior season, he became the first 1,000-yard rusher in OSU history with another 4.5-yard per carry average, 1,027 yards, and 16 touchdowns.

"I didn't ever think about gaining 1,000 yards in any one year," Otis said. "I played 10 games my junior year and just missed it, then I played in nine as a senior and just got it.

"The thing that's most gratifying to me is knowing how many yards I got per game, because it meant that I was always involved and always consistent."

Otis's 2,542 career yards made him Ohio State's all-time leader upon his graduation, placing him just ahead of 1954 Heisman Trophy-winner Howard "Hopalong" Cassady's 2,466 yards.

"I had my picture taken with Hop Cassady the year he won the

Heisman," Otis said. "He autographed it and wrote, 'I'll see you play here in 1966. Your friend, Hop Cassady.' That was really a thrill. I still have that picture."

Otis also has another piece of memorabilia that's rather famous in Ohio State lore.

Although he can't be sure he was in the crowd that day—"I saw a lot of games back then, but I don't remember if I was at that one, specifically"—Otis was a close follower of the Buckeyes in 1961 when they closed an unbeaten season with a 50-20 victory at Michigan.

OSU fullback Bob Ferguson plowed his way to four touchdowns that day, prompting a young fan to approach him as he walked off the Michigan Stadium playing field and request a memento.

Ferguson flipped the child his chinstrap, never thinking the item might resurface some day to figure in a future win over the Wolverines.

Seven years later, however, on the eve of OSU's Big Ten championship game against Michigan in Ohio Stadium, Otis attended a pregame bonfire and was approached by an admirer with the very chinstrap that Ferguson wore.

"The snap was busted, so I couldn't wear it, and it was a little bit rusty," Otis said. "It had just the one snap, and by then we had more modern equipment with two snaps. So I taped it under my shoulder pads for luck and wore it that day."

Otis, like Ferguson, wound up the catalyst for another OSU rout by scoring four touchdowns himself, including the last one on a five-yard run in the game's waning stages.

"Coach Hayes had taken all the starters out," Otis said. "We actually had the ball on the 1- or 2-yard line, and then we went backward. I was standing behind him and said, 'Hey, coach, you want that touchdown, don't you?' He looked back at me and said, 'Yeah, why don't you go in and get it?'"

Otis did, then stayed on the field for one of the most famous two-point conversions in school history.

Lou Holtz, an assistant on that Ohio State coaching staff, has joked for years that Hayes had a humorous response when asked why he went for two in that situation.

Otis was OSU's first 1,000-yard rusher.

"Because I couldn't go for three," Holtz has quoted Hayes.

"That's such a great story people would rather believe that than the truth," Otis said. "The truth is, we went for two because our kicker didn't come on the field. We were disciplined enough that we knew how to line up and run a play, even though what we probably should have done in that situation was call a timeout to get the kicker out there."

Otis played nine seasons in the NFL, but never gained the enjoyment from professional football that he did from his years as a Buckeye.

"There was no comparison," he said. "I can remember one time being up at St. John Arena and I asked Coach Hayes, 'Do you think I have a chance to play in the pros?' He laughed and said, 'Are you kidding me?'

"It's not that I was so naive, it was more that my dream as a kid growing up wasn't to play in the pros, it was to play for Ohio State in Ohio Stadium. That's why those years will always be the most special to me."

Orlando PACE

A Star from Day One

There are experiences in everyone's life that make them wonder if their chosen field is indeed the best place to apply themselves.

Sometimes those introspective moments come on birthdays or anniversaries and sometimes on other landmark dates, like New Year's Eve.

For Lee Owens, the offensive line coach at Ohio State in the mid-1990s, it was when his life flashed before him on a recruiting trip.

Picture a small airplane, an icy runway, an unforgiving cross-wind, and you have the scene into which Owens was placed heading for Sandusky, Ohio, and a visit with 330-pound offensive tackle and eventual two-time All-American Orlando Pace.

"I wasn't sure we were going to make it," Owens said. "I thought, is this kid really worth this kind of a risk?"

Those who saw Pace perform for the Buckeyes from 1994-96 would answer affirmatively, as would Owens upon further review.

All Pace did was step into the starting lineup from day one of his freshman season and foster a running game that led OSU to an 11-2 season his sophomore year and an 11-1 season and Rose Bowl title his junior year.

"I stood there that first day and all I could think was, 'Wow,' Owens said. "I mean, wow! He was incredible."

Pace inspired the same reaction in others by clearing a path for tailback Eddie George to win the Heisman Trophy in 1995.

The following season, Pace nearly became the first interior lineman ever to win college football's most coveted award with a fourth-place Heisman finish.

"We had a lot of great players in our program—guys like Eddie George, Bob Hoying, Terry Glenn, Joey Galloway and Shawn Springs—but I'm not sure we ever had a player play his position any better than Orlando Pace," OSU coach John Cooper said. "If the Heisman Trophy goes to the best college football player in America, then Orlando definitely should have won it."

Pace did not, finishing behind Florida's Danny Wuerffel, Iowa Sate's Troy Davis, and Arizona State's Jake Plummer, but the quiet, engaging OSU star still made history before he departed for the NFL with one season of eligibility remaining.

In 1995, Pace became the first sophomore ever to win the Lombardi Trophy, given to the nation's best interior lineman, and after that the Lombardi's first two-time winner, and ultimately only the 10th player ever to win both the Outland Trophy and the Lombardi in the same season.

"The things you wouldn't see from an offensive lineman in a year are the things we came to expect from Orlando every week," said Mike Jacobs, who joined Owens in coaching the offensive line. "He knew where to place his hand to get the maximum out of it in terms of change-of-direction or leverage. Once he got that, no matter who a guy was, he was going down."

Since Pace didn't score any touchdowns or compile any other statistics common to Heisman Trophy candidates, OSU's coaches came up with a way to track his dominance.

The concept of the "pancake block" was born to credit Pace for the times he put opposing defenders on their backsides.

He wound up with 74 such hits his final season.

"As a sophomore, I started to feel pretty confident and pretty dominant with what I was doing," Pace said. "My first year, I was kind of shaky. Not shaky in the sense that I wasn't getting the job done, but just that I wasn't as dominant as I wanted to be. That's the one thing I set out to do as a junior— dominate my man every play, every game. I was pretty successful at doing that."

So successful that Pace didn't give up a quarterback sack either of his last two seasons and left some indelible memories of the uncommon athleticism he possessed for a man his size.

Against both Rice and Iowa his junior year, Pace ran with Ohio State's tailbacks on long breakaway runs and blocked the final defender clear of the play as much as 50 yards downfield.

"Some guys who are great players on the offense line, their technique had to be perfect on every play," said Jim Lachey, an All-American guard at OSU who returned to Columbus after his NFL career to broadcast Buckeye games on the Ohio State radio network. "But Orlando could take a bad step and his feet were good enough that he could recover and still get the job done. He had everything you needed in an offensive tackle."

Pace indeed had both the talent and the publicity campaign to qualify for Heisman consideration, getting a boost from OSU's distribution of refrigerator magnets to voters that showed a stack of pancakes with Pace's name atop the pile.

In the end, though, he fell short of unseating players at more glamorous positions for the top award in college football.

"I think winning the Outland and the Lombardi that year proved that I was the best lineman," said Pace, who following the 1996 season as the No. 1 overall pick in the NFL draft. (He went to the St. Louis Rams.) "The Heisman gave me a chance to see how I stacked up against the guys at the other positions.

"I never expected to win it, because I learned soon after I started playing football that running backs and quarterbacks got all the glory. Linemen just kind of go about their business without anyone noticing. I didn't expect to change that.

"One player might be the best quarterback or the best running back, but it's hard to judge different positions together. That's why the Heisman is such a hard thing to vote on."

Pace was the first sophomore to win the Lombardi Trophy.

Jim
PARKER

Woody Was Right

Jim Parker's legacy is often lost among the names that leap to the forefront of Ohio State All-Americans, which is solely a casualty of the positions he played, not the way in which he played them.

For three years, from 1954-56, Parker was as dominant an offensive and defensive lineman as there was in college football, and probably as has ever performed for the Buckeyes.

He was OSU's first Outland Trophy winner as the nation's top interior lineman and became the standard by which legendary coach Woody Hayes would measure the blockers who followed Parker into the trenches.

"Jim Parker was the greatest offensive lineman I ever coached," Hayes once said. "I'm not sure there has ever been a better offensive guard. He was everything an offensive lineman should be."

Hayes found Parker in Toledo, where his family moved in time

for him to play his junior season of football.

"I remember Woody Hayes came to our school to give a speech that year, and he said to me, 'I'll be back to get you next year,'" Parker said. "He told me once that I had a chance to be the best player he ever coached. I thought he was crazy."

Hayes turned out to be close enough to correct that no one would debate Parker belonging among the greatest players in Buckeye history.

The testament to Parker's excellence shows up in the success OSU enjoyed during his career, when it won 23 of 28 games, starting with a 10-0 national championship season his sophomore year.

Howard "Hopalong" Cassady, Dave Legette, and Bobby Watkins gave OSU a formidable threesome in the backfield that year, and each of them wore a path behind Parker's blocking.

"I laugh now when I hear

people talk about playing against eight- and nine-man fronts on defense," Parker said. "That's all we saw in those days, because Woody always said there were three things that could happen when you passed, and two of them were bad."

Cassady gave the Buckeyes a running back that made passing a needless risk, particularly when he ran behind Parker.

"In those days, we had to keep our hands in," said Frank "Moose" Machinsky, a tackle who played beside Parker. "We couldn't extend our arms away from our body the way players can today. Jim would have been absolutely unstoppable if he could have used his hands. He was a big, powerful man."

Parker played at a listed weight of only 230 pounds, but that made him a giant among the players of the mid-1950s.

"He was an athlete, though," Machinsky said. "Jim wasn't just good because he was big, he was good because he was just a good player."

Defensively, Parker was the anchor of a unit that allowed only 75 points—just more than a touchdown a game—in going through the 1954 schedule without a blemish.

His stop of Michigan's Dave Hill on fourth-and-goal at the one-yard line swung the momentum to the Buckeyes in their Rose Bowl-clinching victory over the Wolverines, and Parker's fumble recovery at the OSU 31-yard line in the Rose Bowl stopped USC's most serious scoring drive.

The Trojans' only points against the Buckeyes that day came on an 88-yard punt return.

Parker was back in 1955, and so was Cassady, teaming to give the Buckeyes a combination that worked for another Big Ten championship, the school's first back-to-back titles since the Chic Harley era prior to 1920.

OSU didn't play in the Rose Bowl that year because of the Big Ten's rule against repeat participants, so it had to settle for the satisfaction of a season-ending 17-0 triumph at Michigan that gave Michigan State the trip to Pasadena.

Hayes termed that victory "the best I've ever had a team play," largely because of Parker's work on defense that held the Wolverines scoreless.

OSU sank to 6-3 Parker's senior season, the only year he played without providing the escort for Cassady.

Still, Parker was so impressive that he won the Outland Trophy, even though that's not where he had his sights.

Parker (No. 62) was OSU's first Outland Trophy winner.

"I used to go home and rehearse the speech I was going to give if I won the Heisman," said Parker, who went on to a Pro Football Hall of Fame career with the Baltimore Colts. "I had it all ready, but I knew I didn't have a chance. Hop Cassady won it the year before, and I knew they weren't going to give it to a pair of Buckeyes right in a row."

Art SCHLICHTER

Golden Arm, Tarnished Legacy

Ohio Stadium has been the backdrop for a myriad of memories throughout its storied history, moments when the foundation of the venerable Horseshoe vibrated from the roar of its enraptured partisans.

Choosing a single signature thrill is impossible, but the drama that bathed Art Schlichter's debut in 1978 ranks favorably with any in terms of anticipation.

Schlichter's arrival out of Miami Trace High School, some 60 miles south of Columbus, gave birth to a wave of expectation unlike any seen previously in OSU history.

Scarlet-and-gray loyalists had often awaited seasons armed with aspirations for Big Ten titles and national championships, but never before had their focus been tied to a freshman whose talents figured to transform the Buckeyes so dramatically.

Schlichter had the running skills common to previous Ohio State quarterbacks who skillfully operated coach Woody Hayes's option attack, but it was his extraordinary passing abilities that were so intriguing.

Would Hayes, whose distaste for throwing the ball was as legendary as his temper, actually be moved to scrap his first love for an 18-year-old who he forecast would be the nation's best quarterback by his second year?

A capacity crowd came to its feet, awaiting an answer, on that sun-splashed September day as Schlichter, Hayes, and senior Rod Gerald huddled on the sideline in advance of Ohio State's first play.

Gerald wasn't just any holdover, but a two-year starter who had been All-Big Ten the season before. Surely, the "Old Man" wouldn't start an untested freshman and put a proven senior on the bench.

Oh, yes, he would.

And he wouldn't.

With a national television audience looking on, Hayes confounded everyone by sending both Schlichter and Gerald onto the field together—the youngster at quarterback and the veteran at wide receiver.

Ohio Stadium throbbed from the ensuing roar that seemingly couldn't get louder, but did when Schlichter faded back with his first collegiate snap and completed a six-yard pass to Doug Donley. A new era of Ohio State football had officially begun.

The years have passed and the Norman Rockwell nature of Schlichter's debut has faded, turning from fairy tale to tragedy, as the farm boy from Bloomingburg became the poster child for the ravages of compulsive gambling. Schlichter spent the turn of the century in prison, his legacy tainted by a long-running inability to resist the temptation to wager on the games of youth.

Before falling victim to those bad choices, Schlichter seemed destined for a different legacy lifted straight from the pages of a Chip Hilton novel.

He started every game of his Ohio State career, becoming the first quarterback in school history to achieve All-American status as a sophomore en route to etching his name all over the OSU record book.

Schlichter set school marks for single-season (1,816) and career (3,066) passing yardage by the end of his second year and went on to extend those numbers and establish an assortment of other standards.

He accumulated 8,122 yards total offense and accounted for 76 touchdowns—44 passing and 32 rushing—while directing the Buckeyes to bowl games each of his four seasons.

The unquestioned highlight was OSU's 11-0 regular season mark in 1979, which gave the Buckeyes an undisputed Big Ten title and No. 1 national ranking entering the Rose Bowl against USC.

That success came as a shock, given Ohio State's 7-4-1 record Schlichter's freshman season, which ended with Hayes's firing after he punched Clemson linebacker Charlie Bauman in the waning seconds of a loss at the Gator Bowl.

Rumors of Schlichter's transfer circulated during that winter, but those proved false once he took a look at the passing game new coach Earle Bruce planned to implement. It paid immediate dividends in the fourth game of the 1979 season, when OSU trailed UCLA, 13-10, with 2:21 remaining and the Buckeyes on their own 20-yard line.

Schlichter masterfully directed the two-minute offense, hitting five different receivers and completing six passes in a span of just 95 seconds.

Schlichter was even better in the Rose Bowl, passing for 279 yards and one score to give the Buckeyes a 16-10 lead until the Trojans drove 83 yards for a one-point win in the final seconds.

A fourth-place finish in the Heisman Trophy voting that year suggested unparalleled future success, but a 9-1 start in 1980 disintegrated with losses to Michigan and Penn State at the finish.

That left Schlichter's senior year for a storybook send-off, but a sprained ankle proved meddlesome to those plans. He played through the injury, but was not at his best until just prior to the regular-season finale at Michigan.

The Buckeyes rolled into Ann Arbor on a five-game winning streak, having bounced back from earlier losses to Florida State and Wisconsin. Michigan needed a victory to clinch a Rose Bowl bid and was an eight-point favorite, but Schlichter wasn't about to go out a loser.

Schlichter led OSU to an undefeated regular season in 1979.

His one-yard run gave OSU a 7-3 halftime lead, only to see the Wolverines use a pair of third-quarter field goals to take a 9-7 margin into the final minutes.

Schlichter and the Buckeyes had been outgained, 352-167, when they took over at the Michigan 20-yard line with eight minutes left.

A third-and-eight dilemma presented itself early in that drive, but Schlichter scrambled away from pressure and found John Frank for 11 yards.

A 17-yard completion to Gary Williams fed a drive that reached the Wolverines' 6-yard line with the clock ticking inside three minutes.

Needing only a field goal to go in front, Schlichter stunned the capacity crowd at The Big House by rolling right behind Vaughn Broadnax's block and ducking into the right front corner of the end zone.

That score sealed OSU's 14-9 victory and knocked Michigan out of the Rose Bowl. Schlichter and the Buckeyes headed for Memphis and a 31-28 victory over Navy in the Liberty Bowl that made his career record 36-11-1.

Don SCOTT

Unique in Life and Death

Don Scott had a secure legacy as an Ohio State athletic legend before he became a war hero who gave his life in the defense of the country and before his name became synonymous with the university airport that bears it.

Throughout the 20th century, while numerous players would distinguish themselves in Ohio Stadium playing football for the scarlet and gray, Don Scott was the only one who gained All American honors as a quarterback.

Toiling in the colorful era that closed the tenure of head coach Francis Schmidt, Scott was a two-time All-American at his position, being selected after helping the Buckeyes win the 1939 Big Ten championship and despite their disappointing 4-4 finish in 1940.

"He was a big strong guy who went about 220, with big legs who could really move," said Sid Gillman, the legendary offensive coach from numerous AFL and NFL teams who was the Buckeyes' receiver's coach when Scott

played. "Don had a great arm. He was a fine player."

Scott played left halfback on Schmidt's 1938 team that lost to Michigan, 18-0, in what would be the first of three straight seasons the Buckeyes spent chasing "Ol' No. 98," Tom Harmon.

Harmon rushed and passed the Wolverines to victory that year to break a four-year string in which Michigan had not only lost to OSU each season, but had been shut out every time.

Realizing his team needed more offense, Schmidt switched Scott from left halfback to quarterback in 1939, and the results paid immediate dividends.

He threw a 15-yard touchdown pass and ran for a 34-yard TD in the opener, a 19-0 victory over Missouri, to convince all doubters of the move's merit.

Scott's one-yard touchdown run in the fourth quarter of the Big Ten opener against Northwestern broke open a scoreless affair and led to a 13-0 victory.

The Buckeyes' biggest victory

that season came at Minnesota, which had won four of the last five conference titles, but hadn't played OSU since 1931.

Scott and his teammates gained a 23-20 victory when a Gophers' field goal attempt hit the crossbar and fell off on the final play. Scott caught a touchdown pass and threw for another in the Buckeyes' victory over Illinois, which supplied a one-game lead in the standings entering the season finale at Michigan.

A victory would give OSU the outright conference title and close Iowa out of a share of the championship, but Harmon and the Wolverines proved too tough.

The game was tied, 14-14, when Michigan lined up for a winning field goal inside the final minute. OSU rushed hard and was caught by the trick play, a fake that resulted in a touchdown and 21-14 Wolverines' victory.

Iowa, however, lost that day at Northwestern, so Ohio State still came away with the outright conference title.

Scott was OSU's first All-American quarterback.

Hopes were high the following season, Scott's senior year, given the return of 22 lettermen and the outstanding season he had the year before. Scott averaged 40.4 yards per punt, completed 30-of-72 passes for 494 yards and six touchdowns, and also ran for a 4.6-yard average on 49 attempts.

The Buckeyes were picked No. 6 in the nation prior to the 1940 season, but those hopes never translated into a serious run at either the conference title or the national championship. A three-game losing streak early in the year—OSU's first since 1924—created dissension on the roster and not even Scott's heroics could overcome that dilemma.

He scored all the team's points in a 14-6 victory over Illinois the week prior to Michigan's annual visit.

Scott and his senior teammates were hoping to end their careers with a victory, but instead, Harmon put the cap on a Heisman Trophy season by rushing for three touchdowns, throwing for two and kicking four extra-points in Michigan's 44-0 triumph.

Despite that loss and OSU's .500 finish, Scott was again selected as the nation's All-American quarterback, completing his career in distinguished fashion before he embarked upon his fateful career as an aviator. He died while in military service in Great Britain.

Tom SKLADANY

A Real Kick in the Pants

His career was laden with enough gaudy numbers to make his legacy sheer statistics, but it's a measure of Tom Skladany's impact at Ohio State that his teammates remember him more for his engaging manner and personality than they do his prodigious talents.

"Tom was just a whacko," said Tim Fox, an All-American safety for the Buckeyes while Skladany was making All-American three times himself from 1973-75. "He talked a mile a minute. He was one of those guys that, if you had a long plane trip, Tom was the guy you wanted to sit beside you."

Skladany is fond of saying, "I should have paid Ohio State for the time I was there. I had such a good time."

From playing his accordion on the team plane, to amazing his teammates with card tricks, to eating jelly doughnuts in the locker room during practice, Skladany milked the most out of his career on the field and off.

"Woody used to make Tom play that accordion in front of the team," two-time Heisman Trophy-winner Archie Griffin said. "He just loved the guy. He kept everybody loose with how crazy he was, but don't ever lose sight of this—Tom was a tremendous punter and a great athlete."

Kickers and punters don't typically engender such affection. After all, specialists are universally loathed for standing on the sidelines while their teammates endure workouts of as long as three hours.

Skladany managed to convince Woody Hayes that he couldn't stand during practice because it tired his legs, so he literally sat out while the other Buckeyes toiled.

By then, Hayes knew how valuable Skladany was, even if it took some convincing in the beginning.

"Woody didn't want to give me a scholarship coming out of high school," Skladany said. "Coach (George) Chaump kept pushing him, trying to convince

him, but I didn't end up signing until April. I had offers from Notre Dame, Michigan, Penn State, Pittsburgh, and Michigan State. They all said, 'We think you can kick here. We'll give you a full ride, but we're also looking at some others, and we're not waiting.'

"I kept putting them off by telling them I needed to take all my visits before I'd make up my mind. But Woody, he wouldn't go for it at first. He kept saying, 'You can come here if you want, but we don't give scholarships to kickers. If you prove yourself, we'll give it to you your sophomore year. But we just don't (give freshman kickers full scholarships) here.

"Coach Chaump kept pushing him and Woody kept getting more and more upset. 'We're not wasting a scholarship on a punter,' he'd say. That went all the way into April until Chaump called me one day and said, 'We got him to go for it.' So I signed."

Hayes was right all along, of course, for by signing Skladany, the Buckeyes definitely weren't wasting a scholarship.

In high school, he once kicked a 43-yard field goal, threw a 20-yard touchdown pass, had a 75-yard run from scrimmage, got off a 54-yard punt, and kicked three balls over a fence 30 yards beyond the playing field.

"I had a natural affinity for punting," Skladany said. "I started playing soccer when I was eight. That was my sport from 8 to 12. I was in Baltimore then, which was a huge soccer town. Then my dad got transferred to Pittsburgh and there wasn't any soccer, so I switched to football.

"My father was a punter at Temple, so he taught me the drop. I was able to kick a spiral early on, and it felt so good I'd just practice it for hours."

Skladany wound up a three-time All-American at OSU and was the first specialist ever named a team captain, but he earned the respect of his teammates as much with his aggressive mentality as his punting.

"Tom was just an exceptional athlete," Griffin said. "He could really boom the ball, not only on punts, but on kickoffs. Woody used to call Tom's kickoffs 'beer cans,' because they were non-returnable. He'd say, 'Tom, I need a beer can.'"

Every time Skladany obliged, he robbed himself of the chance to do what he enjoyed the most-crashing into ballcarriers on coverage units.

"I was a wide receiver and a defensive back in high school," Skladany said. "I never left the field then, but I didn't have the speed for big-time football. It never stopped me from trying to make tackles, though. I loved to hit from being a defensive back. Me and Doug Plank used to knock each other out trying to get Buckeye leaves."

Skladany was too valuable to the Buckeyes as a punting and kicking specialist to risk him in any other role.

In the days when Hayes and Michigan's Bo Schembechler were approaching the end of their Ten Year War, Skladany was the ace up the old man's sleeve that twice contributed greatly to OSU victories.

People remember Tom Klaban as the hero in 1974 because of the four field goals he kicked in OSU's 12-10 victory in Ohio Stadium.

Skladany's punting was also critical, for he kept the Wolverines pinned deep with five punts that averaged 45.2 yards. The next year, Skladany averaged 45 yards on eight punts in Ann Arbor to assist the Buckeyes' 21-14 comeback victory.

In 1976, Michigan finally broke through and ended its frustration with a 22-0 win in Columbus.

Skladany couldn't be blamed for that, for his 52.3-yard average that day on eight punts remains the OSU single-game record for highest punting average. That's only one of two distance marks Skladany holds, for he also boomed an OSU-record 59-yard field goal at Illinois in 1975.

He closed his career with an outstanding Orange Bowl performance in a win over Colorado, booting two field goals and three extra-points in the Buckeyes' 27-10 victory. He turned pro with the Detroit Lions and now owns a printing business in Columbus.

Skladany was a three-time All-American.

Chris SPIELMAN

Put Me in and Get Out of the Way

It made for good theater at the time, but looking back, there was no more appropriate way for Chris Spielman to foreshadow the impact he would have on Ohio State's football program than the manner in which he made his first impression as a Buckeye.

Before any of the jarring tackles or crucial interceptions, before he even stepped on the field for the first time, there was a flash of the unrelenting desire that would typify Spielman's four-year career in scarlet and gray.

It was a sunny September day when OSU opened the 1984 season in Ohio Stadium against Oregon, but the dark clouds were hovering in Spielman's head.

An aggravation of an ankle sprain he had suffered the second week of fall practice hadn't healed sufficiently to allow him to debut in the starting inside linebacker spot he had earned as a true freshman.

This would be the first football game of Spielman's life that he would not start, and he wasn't at peace with the idea at all.

So, while the teams went at it on the field, a better show was taking place on the sideline, where Spielman was stalking back and forth, always in close proximity to head coach Earle Bruce, snorting loudly enough to be heard over the racket of 90,000 fans and whatever clatter was coming over Bruce's headset.

"I just remember saying, 'Put me in. I gotta be in there. I want to be in there,'" Spielman said. "I wasn't really screaming, but I made sure I was close enough that he could hear me."

Bruce gave in before the end of the first quarter, and it took all of one play for Spielman to make his first tackle.

By halftime, Bruce was impressed enough to order linebacker coach Bob Tucker to start Spielman in the second half.

"All he did was go out there and make the first 10 tackles,"

Bruce said. "He played a heck of a game."

It wouldn't be Spielman's last, of course, for he would finish his career in 1987 as OSU's career leader with 283 solo tackles, fed by his single-season record total of 105 as a junior in 1986.

That season ended with Spielman intercepting two of OSU's Cotton Bowl-record five picks in a 28-12 victory over Texas A&M, one of which he returned for the first touchdown of his college career.

"The thing I remember most about Chris is that every game, every play, he gave great effort," Bruce said. "His game was making tackles. It wasn't unusual for him to be in on 20 or 25 a game. He was at the ball, I'll tell you."

Spielman's 205-tackle season as a junior ended with him making 29 stops against Michigan.

As a sophomore, he teamed with Pepper Johnson in the middle to give the Buckeyes a vaunted inside tandem that knocked No. 1 Iowa off its perch atop the polls, 22-13, when it came to Columbus in mid-October.

Pundits suggested Hawkeye's quarterback Chuck Long might throw for 1,000 yards that day against OSU's beleaguered secondary, but Long had none of the success he did the week before when he passed for six touchdowns.

Spielman had two of the Buckeyes four interceptions, but it was his jack-hammer hit on a fourth-down plunge deep in OSU territory that denied Iowa a fourth-quarter first down and preserved the victory.

"Playing at Ohio State was the four greatest years of my life," Spielman said. "I loved being a part of Ohio State. I was a guy who was honored to be a Buckeye. Everything about it meant the world to me. I got choked up at the Captain's Breakfast, taking a walk with the team on game day, eating the pregame meal at the golf course, Senior Tackle, all of it. The traditions that were there before me, that I could be a part of, it made it a very special time."

Spielman had a distinguished postcollegiate

Spielman tracks an opposing ball carrier.

career with the Detroit Lions and Buffalo Bills. He now hosts a sports talk show in Columbus.

Shawn SPRINGS

Sheriff in the No-Passing Zone

The indisputable indicator of a cornerback's effectiveness is when a team changes its game plan to cope with his abilities.

Shawn Springs made teams do that.

Not only the ones he played against, but the one he played for.

Springs's coverage skills were so sharp that new Ohio State defensive coordinator Fred Pagac was convinced the Buckeyes could break from the conservative strategy they employed in 1995 and play man-to-man on the edge in 1996.

That invited opponents to isolate their best receiver on an OSU cornerback, but that risk was no risk at all with Springs playing the role of stopper.

"Shawn had the ability to lock guys down and take them out of the game," Pagac said. "He took away teams' No. 1 option catching the ball, and once he did that, we could attack the quarterback with our blitz packages."

Pagac saw all the evidence he needed to know the new scheme would work in Springs's redshirt freshman season of 1994.

OSU was in a tight game at Michigan State, with the Spartans going repeatedly to wide receiver Mill Coleman throughout the first half.

Desperate to abort Coleman's effectiveness, Ohio State's coaches switched Springs from boundary corner to the wide side of the field, even though he had never played the position before.

Coleman proved no threat thereafter against Springs's one-on-one coverage, and Pagac filed that information away until he was promoted to defensive coordinator two years later.

That's when the Buckeyes surprised the Big Ten by winning a conference co-title, despite losing a host of offensive stars from the 1995 roster.

Not only did OSU bid goodbye to Heisman Trophy-winner Eddie George, but also to Biletnikoff Award-winner Terry

Glenn and record-setting quarterback Bob Hoying.

The Buckeyes' defense, however, more than made up for those departures by stifling opponents on the ground and in the air.

Springs was chiefly responsible for the latter on the heels of making first-team All-Big Ten as a sophomore in 1995.

He led the Buckeyes with five interceptions that season, including a spectacular one-hand grab at Michigan and a pick Springs returned 60 yards for a score against Iowa.

In 1996, although he didn't intercept a single pass, he still was voted the Big Ten's defensive player of the year.

"You don't intercept many passes when you play man coverage, particularly when you play it as well as Shawn," said John Cooper, Springs's head coach. "You intercept passes when you play a lot of zone. But we didn't play much zone that year. We didn't have to, because Shawn was so good at stopping the other team's No. 1 receiver."

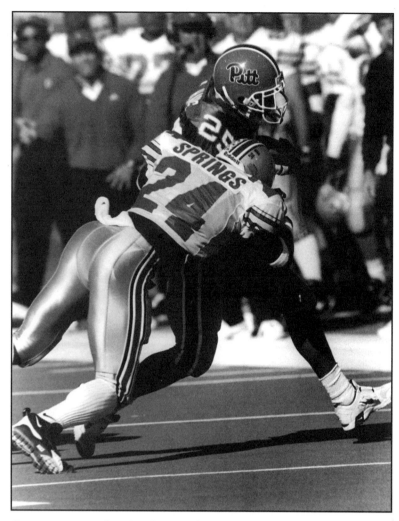

Springs was crucial in OSU's 1997 Rose Bowl victory.

Springs led the Buckeyes with 15 pass break-ups in 1996, but his ability was never more evident than in the Rose Bowl against Arizona State.

The Sun Devils won the Pac 10 largely because of quarterback Jake Plummer's passing artistry.

Springs put a dent in ASU's plans in the Buckeyes' 21-18 win by repeatedly thwarting Plummer's attempts to hook up with his favorite receiver, Keith Poole.

Poole caught only one pass for 10 yards that day, while Springs broke up four passes thrown to him and also made five tackles.

That performance exhibited why Springs made All-American his junior year, and why he went No. 3 overall in the NFL draft to the Seattle Seahawks after leaving OSU with one season of eligibility remaining.

"Shawn may not have had any interceptions, but the guys he was covering didn't have many catches,

either," Pagac said. "He didn't get many chances to make interceptions, because not too many teams threw at him."

The only blemish on Springs's resume his final season came in the Buckeyes' only loss, 13-9, against visiting Michigan.

The Wolverines came back from a 9-0 deficit thanks in part to 69-yard touchdown pass to Tai Streets on the first series of the third quarter.

Springs had coverage on the slant pattern, but slipped as he broke for the ball and watched helplessly as Streets went the distance.

"If Shawn hadn't slipped on that play, he might have made the interception or he certainly would have made the tackle," Cooper said. "It was just one of those things. It's too bad it had to happen that way."

Jim STILLWAGON

West Virginia Missed a Gem

Jim Stillwagon left a legacy the defensive linemen and linebackers who followed him at Ohio State—and throughout college football—would have difficulty duplicating.

"Wagon," as the native of Mount Vernon, Ohio, was known to his Buckeye teammates, became the first player in history to win both the Outland and Lombardi Trophies when he did so after his senior season in 1970.

Not bad for a guy who was kicked off the team midway through his first practice.

It was the fall of 1968, weeks before OSU would begin an improbable run to the national championship, when Stillwagon and his classmates (who would come to be known as the Super Sophomores) suited up for their initial varsity workout.

They had spent the previous year on the scout team in those days of freshman ineligibility, and 15 spring practice sessions that April hadn't done much to straighten out who would be playing where when Southern

Methodist University came to Ohio Stadium that fall for the season-opener.

Stillwagon, clearly, was bent on impressing his coaches, and figured there was no better way than to level the guy with the football.

Trouble was, that player was sophomore quarterback Rex Kern, who only two months before had undergone back surgery, and whose recovery was crucial to OSU's hopes for bettering its 6-3 record from the season before.

"Wagon came through the line and knocked me on my rear end," Kern said. "I mean, he really clobbered me. I thought my world was going to end. I had yellow jersey on, which meant you couldn't hit me, but Wagon, with his intensity, man, he just leveled me."

What followed could accurately be termed an eruption of Mount Woody.

"Oh, Coach Hayes kicked me off the team right on the spot and took my scholarship away," Stillwagon said. "He called the

armed guards over and told them, 'Get this guy out of here.'

"I was mad. I had a few choice words for him as I was leaving. I told (assistant coach) Bill Mallory when he came into the showers, 'That's it. I'm outta here. I'm going to West Virginia.'

"He kept telling me, 'Jim, that's OK. You did the right thing. Woody will cool off.' I didn't care. I wasn't going to cool off. I was leaving."

Hayes smoothed the waters with Stillwagon by impressing upon him how disappointed the players' parents would be if he left campus.

Not to mention, of course, the legions of OSU loyalists who would have been deprived watching the last member of the Super Sophomores to sign a scholarship with the Buckeyes.

"I didn't even think I was going to get a scholarship," Stillwagon said. "I just happened to be up there the day one of the guys who they were going to sign backed out. Woody asked me if I wanted the scholarship and I took it."

Good thing, for Stillwagon became the anchor of an OSU defense that shut down Purdue's vaunted offense early in the 1968 season and stuffed Heisman Trophy winner O.J. Simpson in the second half of the Rose Bowl victory that gave the Buckeyes the national championship.

As a junior and senior, Stillwagon was a consensus All-American and the force in the middle of an OSU defense that allowed just 93 points in 10 games during the 1969 season and held five of 10 opponents in 1970 to 10 points or less.

"Wagon was the consummate, go-to-work-every-day player," Kern said. "He'd just work as hard as he could and make things happen. We overuse the term, giving 100 percent, but Wagon would give you every ounce of energy he had in his body. He was a guy you loved to go to battle with."

"Jim Stillwagon was just an awesome athlete," said Jan White, the tight end on the 1968-70 Buckeyes. "Even today, when I see Jim, I'm just in awe of him. He was not a very big guy (at 6-0, 220 pounds). In fact, he was relatively small for a nose guard. But he had such quickness and field sense, and such a presence about him on the field. He was just a tremendous player."

OSU went 27-2 during Stillwagon's varsity career, winning or sharing the Big Ten title every season after going six years without a conference title prior to that.

"I am amazed by all the attention people still pay to what those teams I played on accomplished at

Stillwagon won both the Outland and Lombardi Trophies in 1970.

Ohio State," said Stillwagon, who eventually played in the Canadian Football League.

"I think it's because we did the unexpected. We were a team on the heels of an average team the year before.

"People didn't know what to expect from us. Every Saturday was like Homecoming. We just kept winning and winning, and the million-dollar question became, 'What's going to happen next?' I think that's why we're remembered so well."

Jack TATUM
Thank Goodness it Was "Heads"

There are those who believe the turning point in Ohio State's unbeaten 1968 national championship season came with an upset of No. 1 ranked Purdue in the year's third game.

Others would cite the fourth-quarter rally that backup quarterback Ron Maciejowski led at Illinois, or the way the defense stiffened when Michigan State threatened an upset in week six.

But the circumstance that made the biggest difference in the Buckeyes' transformation from a 6-3 team in 1967 to an unbeaten national champion the following season might have taken place during a fortuitous spring coin flip.

That's when a bit of trickery by the OSU defensive coaches stole Jack Tatum away from the offensive staff to foster one of the greatest careers by a collegiate defensive back in college football history.

Even now, well-removed from the days when he roamed the secondary for the Buckeyes and the Oakland Raiders of the NFL, Tatum's name is synonymous with ferocity and utter domination.

Those who watched Tatum star for the scarlet and gray will never forget the veritable shutout he threw at Purdue's Leroy Keyes in OSU's 13-0 win that season.

Others remember Tatum for running down Michigan's Ron Johnson from behind on a breakaway, foreshadowing the manner in which Ohio State would rule in its 50-14 annihilation of the Wolverines.

Still others can't shake the image of Tatum coming out of nowhere in the Rose Bowl to plow Heisman Trophy winner O.J. Simpson out of bounds at the three-yard line on an early USC drive, forcing the Trojans to settle for a field goal.

Had Simpson scored on that play, which he could have done if not for the hustling Tatum, the 10-0 lead the Trojans built would have been 14-0, and perhaps the Buckeyes would not have found the spirit to come back.

"People used to ask me, 'How fast was Jack Tatum?'" said Rex Kern, the quarterback of the 1968 Buckeyes. "I'd always say, 'Jack Tatum was as fast as he needed to be.' I used to pinch myself, wondering where the guy got the ability to explode on people and hit them the way he did. He was just a great, great athlete."

That fact was not lost upon defensive coaches Bill Mallory, Lou McCullough, and Lou Holtz, who saw enough of Tatum as a fullback on the freshman team to make him the object of their desires from among all the soon-to-be-Super Sophomores the following season.

"We knew we had to get some of that talent spread around to our side, but we also knew Woody would want to hoard all those guys over on offense," said Mallory, who coached the defensive line in those days, before his career as the head coach at Miami of Ohio, Colorado, and Indiana. "He always wanted us to stop people, but he never wanted to give us anybody to do it with.

"So, that spring, we got together as a defensive staff and came up with the idea of a lottery. We sent Lou in there to really pound the table on that one. He convinced Woody we had to have a draft to determine which guys would play offense and which ones would play defense.

"Of course, the guy we wanted all along was Jack Tatum, who had played fullback as a freshman and probably would have been one of the best fullbacks Woody ever had. Woody didn't need him at fullback, because he already had Jim Otis and John Brockington, and we really needed Tatum on defense.

"Well, fortunately, we won the flip and said, 'OK, we take Tatum.' Right away, Woody just went bananas. He said, 'I knew you'd do that.' I thought, 'Oh, boy, this one's going down the tubes.' But, he let us have Tatum and that really made a difference."

It certainly did when Keyes and his fellow All-American, quarterback Mike Phipps, came to Ohio Stadium to face the fifth-ranked Buckeyes.

Purdue was touting Keyes for the Heisman Trophy, but his campaign was over after Tatum limited him to 19 rushing yards on seven carries and four catches for 44 yards.

"When he was in the backfield, I kind of moved in and either blitzed or made sure they didn't get around the outside on the run," Tatum said. "When Keyes split out, I just covered him man-on-man."

The performance made Tatum a household name, contradicting something McCullough told him in the immediate aftermath of the fateful coin flip.

"He comes to me and he says, 'Well, we're going to switch you to defense. You're not going to get your name in the paper very much, and if you do it's going to be on the bottom line,'" Tatum said. "He was trying to sell me on playing defense, but I always liked defense better anyway."

The move will go down as one of the great position shifts of all time, for no matter how Tatum would have excelled on offense—and everyone agrees he would have been a standout—his importance to the Buckeyes in 1968 and to their 27-2 success during his career was immeasurable.

"I personally think Jack Tatum's best position would have been offensive back, but we couldn't have done what we did without him," said Holtz, who coached the OSU secondary in 1968. "He's one of the greatest players I've ever been around.

"It didn't take you very long to see that he was going to be special. I remember a drill we used to run where everybody was a ballcarrier, then you switched lines and became a tackler. Well, the guys in the other line, they'd start fighting and pushing, because they didn't want to go against Tatum. That told me he was going to be something."

Tatum was a first-round draft pick for Oakland in 1971. He went to three Pro Bowls and helped the Raiders win the 1976 Super Bowl over the Minnesota Vikings.

Tatum was a welcome addition to OSU's defense.

Tom TUPA

A Cannon in His Shoe

It is a day that observers who turned out for Ohio State's football practice will never forget.

Tex Schramm of the Dallas Cowboys, a legendary evaluator of talent, was walking the sidelines that afternoon on a scouting mission in search of players to restock America's Team and keep it among the elite of the NFL.

Schramm had his eyes on the Buckeyes' offense and defense as head coach Earle Bruce put them through a grueling workout, when suddenly a sound intruded that caught Schramm's attention.

"BOOM."

Schramm looked around to see where the sound was coming from.

"BOOM."

Again, he looked, this time pinpointing the general vicinity of the source.

It was coming from a nearby practice field, one occupied by only a few kickers and punters.

Suddenly, what 98 percent of the Buckeyes were doing in practice made no difference to Schramm, who took out his stopwatch and began staring in disbelief as he clocked the hang time on freshman Tom Tupa's punts.

"It was a sound," Schramm told reporters, "I'd never heard before."

It was the sound of Tupa's foot sending the football into orbit.

For four seasons, from 1984-87, his punts more frequently resembled satellite launches than they did special teams plays, resulting in distances as prodigious for their height as they were for their length.

"Boy, he could really put that ball up there," said Earle Bruce, who coached Tupa during his OSU career. "He'd hit that thing and it was like a shotgun going off. He was something else. He had an exceptional leg and timing. I'll tell you, when he hit that ball, it went."

Tupa was an instant success as a Buckeye, leading the nation with a 44.3 net punting average his first season, when he averaged 47.1 yards per kick.

He made All-Big Ten that year and twice more during his career, which ended with a 46.5 yards per-punt average as a senior that helped him make first-team All-American.

"We were supposed to have a pretty good team in 1984 when he was a freshman, but a lot of us were worried about what we were going to do for a punter," said Jim Lachey, an All-American guard on the Buckeyes Rose Bowl team of that season. "We'd had Karl Edwards do our punting for most of the previous three years, so a lot of us were worried about who was going to step in.

"Earle told us he had a freshman who was going to be great and we're thinking, 'Yeah, right. A freshman.' But sure, enough, Earle knew what he was talking about. Tupa was just unbelievable. You didn't have to see him punt. You could hear him punt.

"You'd be practicing and just hear this unbelievable noise when he hit one. He'd boom those things 45, 46 yards every time."

Tupa came to OSU from Brecksville High School, near Cleveland.

He was an accomplished option quarterback, who led his team to the state championship, and a talented basketball player, scoring nearly 21 points per game and averaging 12 rebounds his senior season.

Tupa served as the Buckeyes' backup quarterback as both a sophomore and junior and stepped into the starter's role in 1987, when he finished third in the Big Ten in total offense with a 173-yard per-game average.

"Tom was a much better quarterback than people gave him credit for," said Chris Spielman, a two-time All-American at OSU during that era and Tupa's roommate. "He would have been a great quarterback his senior year, except we lost Cris Carter in that agent scandal and our other wide-out was academically ineligible. That didn't leave Tom anyone to throw to."

Tupa was still a weapon with his right leg, however, putting 19 of his 63 punts that season out of bounds inside the 20-yard line.

The final three years of his career, the only years such statistics were kept, he killed 54 of his 163 punts inside the 20-yard line.

Tupa's OSU career record 44.7-yard punting average could have been even higher were he not so concerned with stopping the ball short of a touchback.

He had five games as a freshman where his longest punt traveled at least 60 yards, with a long of 70 that season against Wisconsin.

Tupa's career long was a 75-yarder as a junior, a length he nearly surpassed with a 72-yard punt his senior season.

"I never worried about him at all," Bruce said. "Well, I'll take that

back. The first punt he ever had was against Oregon his freshman year. I turned around when he ran out there and said, 'Watch this,' because I just knew he was going to kill it. I was just so proud of that kid.

"Well, he must have taken his eye off of it or something, because when I turned around, he's laying on the ball right there in the backfield. I'm asking, 'What happened? What happened?' Then I see Tupa walking off the field, way down the sideline.

"I walked over to him and said, 'Hey, what happened out there?' He says, 'Coach, they were bringing 10 guys at me and I just took my eye off the snap for a second. It went right through my hands.' That's the pressure of the Horseshoe, I guess.

"But you know what? He never dropped another one."

Tupa prepares to launch another booming punt.

Paul
WARFIELD

Poetry in Motion

It was viewed as one of the most bitter defeats ever for an Ohio State football team, made more so by the fact that the opponent came from within the university rather than from without.

The decision by OSU's Faculty Council not to permit the 1961 Big Ten champion Buckeyes to participate in the Rose Bowl kept coach Woody Hayes's team from playing in Pasadena and also cut into the legacy rightfully due several players on that team.

Few mention the 1961 backfield of Paul Warfield, Bob Ferguson, and Matt Snell among the greatest in school history, most likely because the three have no postseason history to go with their considerable regular season achievements.

Warfield was doubly hexed, for his wondrous skills as a pass receiver—later exhibited regularly during an NFL Hall of Fame career—were prisoner to the conservative offensive philosophy the Buckeyes employed during his career.

Despite that, Warfield has nothing but glowing memories of his time at OSU and his football playing days under Woody Hayes.

"Playing for Woody gave a player the full collegiate experience," Warfield said. "Yes, there were victories in football and a dedication to winning championships, but more than that he was a teacher in every respect. I had profound respect for him, because he was truly committed to making you the best you could be on the field and in the classroom."

Warfield was a multi-talented player for the Buckeyes, leading them in minutes played in both 1962 and 1963.

He was a first-team All-Big Ten selection both seasons-OSU's only such pick in 1963-and led the team in receiving both years.

Warfield's athletic excellence wasn't limited to the football field. In both 1962 and 1963, he won Big Ten championships in the long jump.

He is, however, best remembered for his achievements as a football Buckeye, none of which

left a more lasting memory than the 69-yard touchdown run Warfield offered in the 1961 Michigan game in Ann Arbor.

OSU began that season with a tie against Texas Christian and then ran off eight straight victories, needing a win over the Wolverines to secure the league title.

The game was a typical tightly-contested affair into the third quarter, when Michigan pulled within 14-7 of the Buckeyes.

Less than two minutes later, however, Warfield broke the game open on a counter play that caught the Wolverines by surprise.

"That play was a little contrary to what Ohio State did at that time," Warfield said. "It was a misdirection play, where we sent Bob Ferguson, our fullback, one way. Michigan was looking to stop him on every play, so when he went to the left, the defensive flow went in that direction.

"I took a false step in that direction, too, then took the handoff and could see that there was a huge opening. Our guard, Rod Foster, led me into the open field, and I could see it was going to be a huge gain, so I took off at a dead sprint."

Warfield believed he would score until he saw a Michigan defender angling toward him along the sideline. That's when Warfield made a move to cut back inside, until his pursuer slipped and fell, allowing him to reverse back to his original path and go in for the score.

Winfield broke open the 1961 Michigan game.

"After the game, everyone thought I made such a wonderful fake, but it was totally accidental more than anything else," Warfield said.

Minnesota lost at Wisconsin that same day to give the Buckeyes an undisputed Big Ten championship, but a rift between Hayes and the Faculty Council caused the unprecedented vote that kept the Buckeyes at home from Pasadena.

"While disappointed, I was not disheartened," Warfield said. "It was something that we learned to get over. I never had any bitterness about it."

OSU debuted as the nation's No. 1 team in 1962, but despite having 22 returning lettermen, couldn't make its potential pay off.

The Buckeyes lost a 9-7 affair at UCLA in the season's second week when they were stopped from scoring on three separate possessions inside the five-yard line.

"We just could not find a way to get into the end zone," Warfield said. "Had we won that game, I'm sure we would have had a better season. But that taught me something that would later serve me well in professional football. The success we had enjoyed in 1961 made teams play us harder in 1962. So once I was fortunate enough to win a Super Bowl in the NFL, I realized that the following year, teams would play us as if it was the Super Bowl every Sunday."

Warfield helped the Buckeyes post a 28-0 win over Michigan in 1962 and caught the winning touchdown pass the following year in Ann Arbor to culminate a 76-yard drive that provided a 14-10 victory.

Time magazine then picked Warfield to its All-America team, terming with remarkable accuracy that he was "the complete pro player with the instinctive savvy to do the right things and be in the right places."

Merle WENDT

The Stars Lined Up Just Right

Merle Wendt didn't know how good his sense of timing was when he decided to leave his home in Middletown in 1933 and play football for Ohio State.

Of course, it wasn't all that good until a year later.

Wendt's arrival at OSU coincided with the final season for head coach Sam Willaman, whose offensive style wasn't exactly suited to feature a two-way end like Wendt.

But when Willaman resigned after the 1933 season and Ohio State brought in Francis Schmidt from Texas Christian, Wendt suddenly couldn't have been in a better place to become eligible for the varsity as a sophomore.

He wound up making All-American three straight years, joining an elite group of OSU players with that distinction that includes only Chic Harley (1916-17, 1919), Wes Fesler (1928-30), Lew Hinchman (1930-32), Archie Griffin (1973-75), and Tom Skladany (1974-76).

Willaman's teams didn't display enough offense to get an end noticed when the Buckeyes were in possession of the football, as evidenced by the fact that OSU scored a touchdown or less in 10 of the 41 games he coached.

Scoring wasn't a concern with Schmidt's razzle-dazzle brand of football, and he wasn't just a wizard at devising plays.

In six years at TCU, he went 46-6-5 with a defense that registered 34 shutouts.

Wendt gave Schmidt an end to build both of his units around, and the collaboration was one the player thoroughly enjoyed.

"He's the best offensive coach I've ever seen," Wendt told *Buckeye Sports Bulletin* in 1995, several years before his death. "He wouldn't have cared about defense if he didn't have to. He'd always say, 'You have to beat them by making more points.' If (an opponent) got 20, he'd say, 'That's all right. We'll get 25.'"

Wendt said Schmidt was devising new plays every week,

and often lost patience with those who couldn't keep up with his innovative tactics.

"You couldn't count them all," Wendt said. "He was really something. He was a very eager man and gosh, did he have a loud voice. He had a good side. He told you when you did well. But you better believe you were going to hear it if you did wrong."

OSU hadn't won a Big Ten championship since 1920 and had lost nine of its last 12 games against Michigan when Schmidt arrived and immediately began turning those fortunes around.

Wendt scored on a 66-yard pass in the Buckeyes' 34-0 victory over the visiting Wolverines in 1934, prompting the Ohio Stadium crowd to tear down the goal posts for the first time in the history of the Horseshoe.

If not for a 14-13 loss at Illinois in game two, Ohio State would have ended its conference championship skid that year. But the Buckeyes' 7-1 finish, and the fact they outscored their opponents by a whopping 267-34 margin, created plenty of excitement for 1935.

Wendt helped OSU secure a league co-championship that season by catching a 30-yard pass from Stan Pincura to erase what was a 13-0 deficit in a key league game at Chicago.

The Buckeyes went into that affair nursing bruised egos because of an 18-13 loss to visiting Notre Dame the week before. That was a crippling defeat because OSU owned a 13-0 lead entering the fourth quarter, only to allow three Fighting Irish touchdowns, including two in the final two minutes.

Still, the Big Ten title was there for the taking, but Ohio State had to keep pace with Minnesota, which it did not play that season.

It looked like the Buckeyes would fail when they fell behind at Chicago by two scores, one of which was a breathtaking run by Jay Berwanger that many credit for winning him the inaugural Heisman Trophy. Wendt's touchdown catch forged a 13-13 tie and OSU completed its comeback to claim a 20-13 victory.

It then avenged its 1934 loss against Illinois the following week to set up the first-ever meeting with archrival Michigan on the season's final day.

The Wolverines and All-American center (and future President) Gerald R. Ford were no match for the visiting Buckeyes, who breezed to a 38-0 victory that remains OSU's largest margin of victory in the series.

Wendt earned All-American honors again in 1936 when Ohio State brightened a 5-3 finish with a 21-0 victory over Michigan.

That means Wendt played on teams that not only never lost to the Wolverines, but also never allowed a point in pounding out three wins by a collective 93-0 margin.

Seven of the existing eight NFL teams made offers to Wendt following his graduation from OSU, but he turned those down and instead married his wife, Jane, just six days after receiving his degree in chemical engineering.

Merle Wendt and his wife, Jane.

She had opportunities in modeling and acting on the West Coast at the same time professional football wanted her husband, but the Wendts chose to begin their life together.

He served for many years as director of chemical engineering for Goodyear Tire and Rubber Co. in Akron.

"We gave up some opportunities that other people might not have had, but we didn't want to live apart from each other," Wendt told *Buckeye Sports Bulletin*. "I was happy with my education and did what I said I always wanted to do, so you'll never hear me complain. We had just a wonderful life."

Among their memories were three special years together at Ohio State when Wendt was among the nation's finest collegiate players.

"We really had a good strong team that liked the game and enjoyed playing it," he said. "All the players were close then. We made ourselves best friends, and we always left the field knowing we did the best we could."

Jan WHITE

Sacrifice for the Good of the Team

The memories of his accomplished Ohio State football career have faded since those glorious days when Jan White was an oft-overlooked force on the Buckeyes' 1968 national championship team and the 1969 and 1970 Big Ten championship squads.

The passage of time might well have worn away all thoughts of going 10-0 as a sophomore, 8-1 as a junior, and 9-1 as a senior, if not for the constant reminders of those days that keep White connected to his youth.

What brings him back to Columbus, to Ohio Stadium, to the autumns when OSU dominated the Big Ten and the national rankings, isn't some trophy on a mantle or scrapbook full of photographs.

White's refresher course comes in living, breathing form so frequently that it amazes him still.

"I've never gotten over how many people will say, 'Are you the Jan White that played for Ohio State?'" White said. "It just amazes me. I mean, it's been more than 30 years. You'd think people would have forgotten that by now, but they haven't.

"I've had people come up to me and say, 'I remember watching you on TV when I was five years old.' On one hand, I'm thinking, 'Oh, Lord, am I that old?' But on the other hand, it's very special and very touching that our team struck a chord with so many people."

White's name may not be the first that leaps to mind when visions of the Super Sophomores arise.

Rex Kern, Jim Stillwagon and Jack Tatum were bigger names, but perhaps no one exemplified the spirit of that team more than White.

He came to Ohio State as a wide receiver and was about to start at that position his sophomore year when tight end Dick Kuhn got hurt.

"They moved me over there strictly as a fill-in until Dick came back, or so I thought," White said. "I was starting ahead of Bruce Jankowski at wide receiver, but once they got a look at Bruce, I never got back out there, and the rest is history.

"To be honest, I didn't really like it at first and complained a little bit. But I came to believe that I was helping the team at tight end, so I didn't really mind it."

Kern remembers White having a work ethic second to none on the Buckeyes throughout his career.

"Jan and Jim Stillwagon from a work standpoint were just amazing," Kern said. "They just worked the heck out of every practice. Jan was so conscientious, and ability-wise, he had all the talent in the world. He had speed, size, quickness and great hands.

"He was probably the first tight end at Ohio State to possess all those qualities. Jan could have easily been our wide out, but he moved over to tight end for the good of the team and was a tremendous player there."

White could have been a tremendous player at any school, since more than 150 recruited him.

Joe Paterno of Penn State made a strong pitch for White, whose high school teams in Harrisburg, Pa., didn't lose a game during his three seasons.

White didn't just appeal to coaches within his state, however.

John McKay at Southern California thought White would be the perfect wide receiver to balance a powerful running game he figured to have in 1967 and 1968 with a junior college transfer named O.J. Simpson.

Out of all the offers, though, White took Ohio State's-much to the consternation of his friends.

"I took a lot of flak from my buddies, because at the time, Ohio State wasn't really up there in terms of national standing," White said. "I think they were something like .500 or under .500 (actually 4-5) the season before I signed.

"But as I was traveling around the country being recruited, I kept running into the same guys, and a lot of them were going to Ohio State. The Big Ten was my favorite conference, even though I was from Pennsylvania, and Ohio State was the closest Big Ten school at the time, so I decided to play there.

"My friends told me I was crazy. They said, 'Woody Hayes? Man, he's three yards and a cloud of dust. You'll never catch the ball there.'"

White didn't figure as prominently in the passing game as Jankowski, but he does have one long

White was a three-year starter at tight end.

touchdown pass to look back on-a 70-yarder from Rex Kern that opened the scoring in OSU's 45-21 Homecoming victory over Northwestern in 1968.

"That one, I won't forget," said White, who eventually played in the NFl with the Buffalo Bills. "I caught that ball and I was scared to death. I remember thinking, 'Don't get caught from behind.' I was running scared all the way."

Bill
WILLIS

You'll Find Him in the Hall

The hat trick is an achievement that's common to ice hockey, accorded to a player that scores three goals in a single game.

There is no term for what Bill Willis attained during his football career, perhaps because it's so rare that devising an appropriate name would be as impossible as it would be inadequate.

Willis made not just one or two, but three separate halls of fame for his performance on the field as a two-way lineman of unprecedented ability during his era.

He is a member of the Ohio High School, College Football, and NFL Halls of Fame, and was the pioneer of a defensive scheme that is so common today no one even thinks to track down the innovator who made it possible.

Willis' quickness and speed as an Ohio State Buckeye and a Cleveland Brown convinced his coach, Paul Brown, to employ him as a stand-up defender in the middle of the defensive line.

That made him the forerunner of the modern middle linebacker and the force behind football's switch from the exclusive use of the five-man front to the 4-3 look that has been prevalent since the 1950s.

That's when Willis was starring for the Browns as a two-way tackle, making the All-NFL team from 1950-53 on teams that played for the championship of professional football every season.

He and Brown's relationship began, of course, at Ohio State, where Willis was a three-year starter between 1942-44 after nearly going to the University of Illinois once graduating from Columbus East High School.

"My coach had gotten me a scholarship at Illinois, but when Paul Brown came to Ohio State (in 1941), he was the one who suggested it would be the better part of wisdom to attend Ohio State and stay close to home," Willis said. "Paul Brown was such a fair and outstanding individual that I decided he was right."

Brown once described Willis as "quick as a snake's fang," and he put that skill to use on the Buckeyes' first national championship team in 1942.

"We had a remarkable group of individuals," Willis said. "The fact that we were the very first to be recognized as national champions, I love to think that we were the very beginning of the Ohio State tradition. We were the reason that Ohio State was known nationally for the very first time as a great football power."

Willis made All-American in both 1943 and 1944 and then began a coaching career at Kentucky State until Brown, who had left OSU for an assignment at Great Lakes Naval Academy, called again.

This time, the legendary coach had taken over the Cleveland franchise in the new All-American Football Conference and was loading up with ex-Buckeyes and former Big Ten standouts he knew would turn his team into a powerhouse.

Willis was one of the players Brown targeted, but again it seemed he was too late.

Montreal had an agreement with Willis to lure him north of the border, where black players were more welcome than they were in the NFL.

Brown, however, prevailed upon Willis to change his plans and worked behind the scenes to make the arrangements for him to play in the AAFC.

"It just wasn't done in those days, a black man being pursued openly to play in professional football," Willis said. "In a roundabout way, Paul got things started. He worked it out so it appeared as if I just walked into camp and requested a job, when in reality that was all arranged."

Willis was the first black starter in professional football and helped the Browns win the AAFC championship all four years of the league's existence from 1946-49.

Willis was "quick as a snake's fang."

"Paul was a great teacher," Willis said. "He used to coach by the rote system. Write it down, review it, then you do it again until you get it right. He felt that if you wrote it down, if you did it, then you'd learn it. He always said, 'Practice makes perfect, so long as you practice the right things.'"

The AAFC and the NFL merged in 1950, and the Browns won the championship again, then lost in the title game each of the next three years before Willis retired.

He was elected to the College Football Hall of Fame in 1971 and the Pro Football Hall of Fame in 1977.

"That means a great deal to me," Willis said. "Being in the Hall of Fame is something every football player aspires to, even the High School Hall of Fame. When I look back at some of the players I played with and against at every level, it's a tremendous feeling to think that I was among those who were considered the cream of the crop."

Antoine
WINFIELD

Good Things Come in Small Packages

The annual arrival of Ohio State's football recruits always brings a collection of fans to the Woody Hayes Athletic Center, peering through the chain-link fence to lay eyes on the players they've heard the most about and hope will become the next Buckeyes' All-American.

Back in 1995, anybody who eyeballed the incoming freshman and picked Antoine Winfield as the guy most likely to distinguish himself would have inspired a unanimous reaction.

Laughter.

At only 5-foot-9, 170 pounds, Winfield looked more like a manager among the hulking teammates he joined that August.

But by the time his career was over, Winfield had earned the respect of every player in uniform and every coach on staff.

"Antoine Winfield is the most instinctive football player I've ever been around," said John Cooper, Winfield's head coach at OSU. "You've probably heard the old

saying that you need to find guys who can play better than you can coach. Well, Antoine Winfield was one of those guys."

What made Winfield a force wasn't what elevates most football players to star status.

He wasn't born with the size to be an outstanding cornerback, nor did he have speed or quickness that set him apart from other players at his position.

What made Winfield special was something buried inside his No. 11 jersey.

What made him special was his heart.

"It never bothered me that I was smaller than other guys," said Winfield, who capped his career by winning the Thorpe Award, given to the nation's outstanding defensive back, as a senior in 1998. "I got used to that growing up in Pee-Wee football and in junior high and high schol.

"If anything, that made me more determined to succeed, because at every level, people always thought I was going to be too small to play."

"Sure, Antoine was five or six inches shorter than a lot of guys he covered, but you could never tell that when he went up for the ball," said Damon Moore, who played beside Winfield in the defensive backfield for three seasons. "He never let that stop him from smacking running backs, tight ends, linemen, you name it. I saw him run through offensive tackles and get the better of them."

Winfield's cumbersome coverage of opposing receivers allowed OSU to stick with the same defensive strategy in 1997 and 1998 that it used so successfully to win the Big Ten championship and the Rose Bowl his sophomore year.

All-American Shawn Springs had just graduated, and the Buckeyes wanted to stick with the man-to-man coverage that allowed them to blitz relentlessly and play the run with nine defenders the year before.

Winfield and Ahmed Plummer were new cornerbacks for OSU in the fall of 1997, however, and opponents figured to challenge them extensively.

Winfield, having started occasionally because of injuries to Ty Howard the previous two seasons, was the most experienced OSU cornerback in 1997 and consequently drew the toughest receiver an opponent had to offer.

"I think Shawn was probably a little better cover corner than Antoine, but Antoine turned out to be a better all-around cornerback than Shawn," Cooper said. "Antoine just made play after play after play for us.

"He'd lock people up outside and he'd fight off blocks and make tackles for a loss. He was all over the field. The guy was just amazing."

Winfield's play-making ability was never demonstrated better than in the 1997 Michigan game in Ann Arbor.

The No. 1 ranked Wolverines played host to the No. 4 Buckeyes with a share of the Big Ten championship and a Rose Bowl berth on the line.

OSU's defense permitted only one touchdown, and no one played bigger than the smallest Buckeye on the field.

Winfield's 10 tackles included nine unassisted stops, several of which were highlight-reel material.

None were better than the play on which Winfield corralled eventual Heisman Trophy winner Charles Woodson on a 29-yard pass in the second quarter.

Woodson lined up on the left sideline and caught the crossing route in stride at the left hash.

His path to the end zone was clear. . .was, until Winfield came off his spot covering a receiver along the right sideline to run down Woodson and stop him with a diving ankle tackle at the Wolverines' 16 yard-line.

Woodson emerged with the spotlight that day because of his interception in the end zone that prevented an OSU touchdown and his 78-yard punt return for a touchdown.

But while Michigan's defensive back/wide receiver probably won the Heisman that afternoon, even those with maize-and-blue allegiances acknowledged that Winfield held up well by comparison.

"That's what separated him from the rest of the corners in the country," OSU defensive coordinator Fred Pagac said. "Most safeties will hit you. Some safeties can cover you. Most corners are pretty good cover people, or at least should be good cover people.

"But Antoine had the ability to do both. Not only did he have the ability to do both, he did both."

Winfield wound up the first cornerback in OSU history to lead the team in tackles that season, making 100 stops, even though teams designed their offenses to run away from him.

"Anybody that saw him play fell in love with him," Cooper said. "Antoine was always around the ball. He may not have made every tackle, but I'll tell you what, he was in the picture. You didn't have to look for him."

After his collegiate career, Winfield was a first-round draft pick for the Buffalo Bills.

Winfield is the first cornerback to lead OSU in tackles.

Clark
BURROUGHS

Never a Dull Moment

They hung the nick-name, "Bulldog," on Clark Burroughs soon after he arrived on the Ohio State campus, and it fit him as stylishly as an Armani suit for the duration of his golfing career.

Few could, or would, grind like Burroughs, the irrepressible native of Shawnee Mission, Kansas, who made All-Big Ten four times from 1982-85 and finished his time as a Buckeye with the ultimate flourish for a competitor in his sport.

Two shots off the lead going into the final round of the NCAA Championship his senior year, and then six strokes back at the turn, Burroughs continued to plug and wound up becoming the first OSU player since Jack Nicklaus in 1961 to win medalist honors.

In true Burroughs fashion, he then quipped, "I have my team-mates and coach (Jim) Brown to thank for this and for putting up with me for four years."

Putting up with Burroughs required some effort, but not to stay awake.

"He had me on my toes all four years he was here," Brown said of Burroughs with a laugh. "I spent a lot of nights with him on road trips, that's for sure."

One thing Burroughs never did was cause Brown any sleepless nights with his play on the course.

Nothing seemed to bother the lanky player, not even his own absent-mindedness.

"I remember one year we were going over to Purdue for the Big Ten championships and we packed everything into the van and got ready to go," Brown said. "I asked, 'Are we sure we have everything?' Oh, yeah, they were sure, so off we went.

"Well, we got over there and were unpacking the van and all of the sudden Clark goes, 'Oh, no, I forgot my golf shoes.'

"So, I say, 'We're going to have to get up there to the pro shop and get you another pair.'

"Without batting an eye, he looks at me and says, 'Ah, don't worry about it coach. I'm good enough to whip these guys in my sneakers.'"

Burroughs was, too, winning seven tournaments his senior year.

One of them came after Burroughs shot an 80 in the opening round, but came back with a 66 the next day to lap the field.

Brown remembers that well: "He comes up to me and says, 'Don't worry about me coach. I'm going to shoot low. Just keep your eye on these other guys. I'm going to shoot a low number for you.' I came in and saw the scoreboard and doggone if he wasn't right."

Burroughs's 66 that day remains the competitive course record at Scarlet.

Such success wasn't hard to spot when he arrived as a fresh-man, for he joined the Buckeyes' varsity immediately and became an instant contributor.

Burroughs advanced to the semifinals of the U.S. Amateur in the summer of 1982, losing to eventual champion Jay Sigel, who also defeated OSU's Chris Perry in the finals.

That top four finish earned both Buckeyes a berth in the 1983 Masters.

Burroughs not only made the cut, he helped another former Buckeye do the same by missing an eight-foot putt on the 18th hole on Friday.

"If I would have known that, I would have missed that putt on purpose, just to let Mr. Nicklaus in," Burroughs said.

Burroughs made third-team All-American as a sophomore, second-team as a junior and first-team as a senior, winning medalist honors at the NCAA with a 2 1/2-foot par putt on the first hole of sudden death.

USC's Sam Randolph appeared in command at the turn on the final day, but shot 40 on the back side to Burroughs's 34 to force the playoff.

"I was just playing for second at the turn, but I was always the type to grind things out and keep trying," Burroughs said.

Just like a Bulldog.

There was never a dull moment during Burroughs's career.

John COOK

Performance Beyond His Years

There's an adage in college athletics that the best thing about a freshman is that one year later he becomes a sophomore.

In the case of three-time All-American golfer John Cook, that bromide required amending to: The best thing about John Cook was that he played like a senior when he was a freshman.

Learning how to stand up to the rigors of collegiate competition wasn't among the things Cook needed to learn when he arrived at OSU in the fall of 1977.

His amateur career in California was without peer, including victories in the State Amateur at age 17 on the heels of wins in the California Juniors, Los Angeles Juniors and California State High School Championships.

While most players who come to OSU aspire to some day rub elbows with golfers on the PGA Tour, that goal didn't phase Cook one bit, since he had been working with former Masters champion Ken Venturi since the age of 13.

The only thing no one could quite put their finger on when Cook agreed to come and play for coach Jim Brown was, "What is a California kid doing coming to Ohio State to play golf?"

"Growing up in Southern California, one might think my decision to go to Ohio State was questionable at best," Cook said. "I had played golf in California all my life and felt that, if I wanted to further develop my skills as a golfer, I had to learn to play in all kinds of conditions."

Cook's decision to play nearly 3,000 miles from home wasn't as off-the-wall as it appeared.

His father, Jim, was the former director at Akron's Firestone Country Club, and had moved the family to California when John was 10.

Cook's grandparents lived in the Columbus area, and, after all, what high school golfer's head wouldn't be turned by a phone call from Jack Nicklaus telling him there would be no better place to play college golf than Ohio State?

Cook took all of that into consideration and spurned the interest of every major golf program in the South and West to join an accomplished group of players at OSU that included Rod Spittle, Rick Borg, and Mark Balen.

During Cook's freshman year, the Buckeyes not only won the Big Ten championship, they did so by 29 shots, and had six players finish among the top 12 individuals.

"We were young, but we were loaded," head coach Jim Brown said. "We were just killing people. John was so far advanced even at that age. He had a tremendous all-around game. He was a great putter, a great driver of the golf ball . . . just a great all-around player."

Cook finished second in the medalist standings at the Big Ten Championships as a freshman and was awarded the first of three Les Bohlstad Awards for lowest stroke average in conference play.

He topped off his first season by making first-team All-American via a 10th-place finish in the NCAA championships, an event that served as a primer for the leader boards Cook would face on the professional tour.

Among those to finish ahead of him that year were Scott Hoch, David Edwards, Scott Simpson and Dan Pohl, with Chip Beck and Ed Fiori sniffing Cook's exhaust.

Cook's return that fall gave OSU a No. 1 player capable of leading them to victory in any tournament, and 10 of the top 11 Buckeyes from the season before provided ample depth to go with him.

That wide-ranging talent at Brown's disposal led to the Buckeyes' Big Ten win by a ridiculous 59-shot margin.

Cook was the medalist for what he termed at the time, "my biggest thrill in golf," thanks to a second-round 68 in a wind that unnerved the first-round leader enough that he shot an 84 that day.

Cook would soon get a bigger thrill, winning the U.S. Amateur championship that summer after leading the U.S. Open at Southern Hills through 12 holes of the first round.

That success on a national level, and the disappointment of the team's 20th-place finish among 21 teams at the 1978 NCAAs, served to steel the Buckeyes for the following year.

Cook and Borg not only tied for medalist honors at the Big Ten, they came through at the finish to hand OSU its first NCAA championship since 1945.

Borg birdied the last two holes and Cook birdied the 18th at Bermuda Dunes to give the Buckeyes the title by two shots over Oklahoma State.

Cook won the Ohio Amateur that summer and finished runner-up in the U.S. Open, after which he embarked on a professional career that saw him end the 1990s with more than $5 million in career earnings.

He was inducted into the Ohio State Athletic Hall of Fame in 1986.

Cook was the leader of OSU's 1979 NCAA champions.

Cathy Kratzert GERRING

Better Late Than Never

Cathy Kratzert Gerring has one big regret in her Ohio State golf career.

One nagging, 365-day regret.

"I enjoyed every minute of the three years I played for Ohio State," Gerring said. "I just wish it would have been four."

The culprit for that looks back at Gerring in the mirror every morning, for it was her choice to attend Marshall University as a freshman.

That trip to Huntington, West Virginia, seemed like a good idea until Gerring made it and realized she was six long hours from home in Fort Wayne, Indiana.

"I was unbelievably homesick," she said. "I just didn't feel like I fit in there. I was driving home every chance I got, 12 hours round trip. That got old fast."

So old that Gerring had no intention of returning to school-Marshall or anywhere—until she accepted an offer from her brother, PGA Tour pro Bill

Kratzert, in the spring of her freshman year.

"He asked me to come to Greensboro and pick up their daughter the week they were going to the Master's," Gerring said. "I ended up staying with them for three weeks. I just fell in love with pro golf and knew that's what I wanted to do."

Not prepared to join the LPGA quite yet, Gerring began looking for a new college closer to home.

OSU coach Steve Groves was friends with Kratzert from their collegiate days and pounced on the opportunity to add his sister to the Buckeyes' roster.

"Cathy was the type of player that the bigger the event, the better she played," Groves said. "She was a real gamer. She wasn't without injuries during the course of her college career. She battled a hand injury for a while, but you could just tell, nothing was going to get in her way.

"She was one of those players

who, whenever she stepped on the tee in competition, you knew you were going to get a good score out of her. Very rarely did she not produce. She might not be at the top of her game, but she was still going to battle and score."

Gerring finished fifth in the Big Ten championship as a sophomore in 1981, helping the Buckeyes win their third straight league title.

She won medalist honors at the conference meet as both a junior and a senior, dropping her stroke average from 79.7 to 77.3 and then to 74.5 in 1983.

"By the time I got to Ohio State, I was tunneled in toward the goal of becoming a professional," Gerring said. "I played so many sports in high school, I never really focused on just one until I got to college.

"I never thought about joining the LPGA Tour, because it just wasn't that popular then, and I never really watched it. I always thought I was going to be an attorney, a doctor, or something other than a pro golfer until I went out there and stayed with my brother for a while. That gave me the bug and the incentive to work toward that goal."

OSU benefited from Gerring's drive with a spring season in 1981 unlike any experienced before or since by a Buckeyes' player.

She won four tournaments and finished second in another that she lost in a four-hole playoff.

Gerring lapped the field at the Big Ten, winning by nine shots to help the Buckeyes claim the team title by 41 strokes over Indiana.

"Cathy was one of the best shotmakers that I saw in the time that I coached," said Groves, who also coached Rosie Jones and Meg Mallon at OSU. "When we played in the Big Ten, she was just head and shoulders above everybody else when it came to hitting the ball."

Gerring attributes that ability to a natural athleticism she was favored with by her father, Bill Kratzert Sr., the head professional at Fort Wayne Country Club for more than 40 years.

Before that, Gerring's father was a three-sport star at Florida State in football, basketball, and tennis after twice making all-state in four different sports as a Florida high school phenom.

"I got great genes from my parents," Gerring said. "My dad was a great athlete. He was the one who got me started when I was 11 or 12 years old. He taught me to hit it hard, then we'd go find it.

"He gave me the OK to play fearlessly, and it wasn't too long afterward that golf started to come fairly easily. I'll never forget when I was 12, we were playing his course one day on the 18th hole, a par five, and I was playing from the ladies' tees.

"That was the first time I hit the green in two. He looked at me and said, 'OK, no more ladies' tees.' He never let me play them again. That probably helped me more than anything."

Gerring joined the LPGA Tour in 1984 and lost in a playoff four times before recording her first victory in 1990.

She won twice more that year and finished fourth on the money list, but her rise to prominence was derailed two years later when a food-warmer exploded in a catering tent and severely burned Gerring's face and hands.

She and her husband, Jim, the former head professional at Muirfield Village Golf Club, live with their children in Charlotte, N.C.

Kratzert won four tournaments in 1981.

Jack NICKLAUS

The Best There Ever Was

The scope of athletic excellence at Ohio State throughout the 20th century was so broad that a spirited debate will almost always ensue if one particular athlete in any one specific sport is tagged with the label as the best ever to compete in his or her chosen endeavor.

Football, basketball, baseball, and track and field have each had their share of talent-laden performers, making the selection of a king or queen of the mountain in their respective sport nearly impossible. Such, however, is not the case in golf.

The engraved inscription on the clubhouse at The Ohio State University Scarlet and Gray course has long since proclaimed the venue "collegiate home of Jack Nicklaus, the greatest golfer who ever lived," and no one has or will dare dispute it.

Nicklaus's 18 major championships and 19 second-place finishes in golf's premier events have made him the consensus

choice as the best ever at his sport.

The foundation for that incomparable career was laid both on and near the OSU campus.

"He always reminded me of a young fellow who was in a hurry to get to the top, who was in a hurry to win, in a hurry to be a champion," said long-time Scioto Country Club pro Jack Grout, Nicklaus's first golf teacher, in the book, *Columbus Unforgettables*.

Graf remembered Nicklaus as the first boy to show up on the first day of the first junior class he gave at Scioto upon being hired in 1950.

"He was the first one on the tee," Grout said. "He couldn't wait to start . . . He was there at Scioto every day. He'd play anywhere from 18 to 36 holes every day and practice in between, morning, noon, sometimes until almost dark."

Not surprisingly, then, Nicklaus was already established as one of the best amateur players in the country by the time he began

playing competitively for the Buckeyes in 1960.

He had his pick of colleges to attend, but the choice was easy.

"I had a lot of schools across the country talking to me about playing golf," Nicklaus said. "I just told them not to bother with it. I was going to Ohio State."

Before Nicklaus chose OSU, he had to choose golf over a host of other sports at which he excelled as a youngster.

"I think baseball was probably my best sport growing up," Nicklaus said. "I was a catcher and a switch hitter. Could I have played (professional) basketball? Yeah, I think I could have.

"I played all sports, but I think I chose the right one for me. The reason I say that is I don't have the height for basketball . . . and I was probably too small to play football.

"I was the kind of kid that I think was better suited for an individual sport. Golf was the kind of thing I could really get my teeth into.

"So I don't have any regrets about giving up any other sports, even though I loved those other sports and still love them."

Nicklaus was such an accomplished all-around athlete that he caught the attention of the folk in his suburb of Upper Arlington.

One of those was OSU head football coach Woody Hayes, who lived just two blocks over from the drug store operated by Nicklaus's father, Charlie.

"I was a pretty decent quarterback, because I had a strong arm," Nicklaus said. "Well, the coach at Upper Arlington came into the store one day and told my dad he wanted me to play when I got to high school. My dad had played pro football, so he was a proponent of football, but one day Woody came into the store and so dad asked him about it.

"He said, 'Woody, you know Jackie?'

"Woody said, 'Yeah, he's got a great arm. He's a great talent.'

"So my dad asked him, 'What do you think about (him) playing football?'

"Woody said, 'Charlie, I've seen Jack play golf and I've seen him play football. He's a good football player, but you keep him as far away from that game as possible with the talent he has for golf.'"

Nicklaus didn't compete for the Buckeyes in 1959 because he made the United States Walker Cup team and therefore was committed to playing in that match.

The two years the Buckeyes did get out of him, however, were enough to foreshadow the dominance the Golden Bear would enjoy once he turned professional.

Before playing his first season at OSU, Nicklaus won the U.S. Amateur championship on his fifth try, claiming his first national title with a one-up victory in the finals.

He had also played in three U.S. Opens and one Masters before teeing it up for the Buckeyes.

Nicklaus advanced to the NCAA championship both years he played at OSU, falling in the third round in 1960 and then winning the title in a walkover the following year with a 5 and 3 victory over teammate Mike Podolski.

Earlier that season, Nicklaus won the Big Ten individual championship by a whopping 16 shots.

"I remember when I won the Big Ten and (Coach) Bob Kepler came to me and said, 'Jack, the only way we're going to get this team to the NCAA is for you to spread-eagle the field.' We were playing at

Indiana, and I won it by 16 shots. We also won the team title by one shot, which allowed us to go to the NCAA."

Years later, Hayes would play a key role in getting Nicklaus's son, Gary, to play golf for the Buckeyes.

"He always told me he was going to get one of my sons to Ohio State," Nicklaus said. "Well, he tried with Jack and Steve, but they both went to other schools. Finally, Gary came along and Woody told me, 'I'm going to get this young man to Ohio State.'

"He talked to Gary on a Wednesday and was supposed to have lunch with him on Friday, but Woody died on Thursday. Up to the day he died, he was still recruiting for Ohio State. And, of course, Gary wound up there, I think because of how well and how nice Woody had treated him."

Nicklaus's many achievements in golf, both as an amateur and a professional, are on display in the Jack Nicklaus Museum on the OSU campus, near The Jerome Schottenstein Center and Bill Davis Stadium.

"I can't think of any place that better encompasses my life than the site they have set aside for us," Nicklaus said.

Nicklaus: The Golden Bear

Chris PERRY

He Made the Right Choice

Ohio State golf coach Jim Brown learned all he needed to know about the competitive drive of Chris Perry, one of only two three-time, first-team All-Americans to play for the Buckeyes, before he ever saw him pick up a club.

"I went up there on a recruiting visit and saw him play hockey," Brown said of Perry, who was the captain of his high school team in Minnesota and an accomplished skater. "He was sicker than a dog, but the game went two overtimes and they couldn't get him off the ice. He played his butt off."

The same zest for competition came to typify Perry throughout his Ohio State career, one in which he won the Big Ten individual title twice and missed a third by one stroke.

The love for competition came to him honestly, given that both his father, Jim, and uncle, Gaylord, were accomplished Major League pitchers.

Perry therefore grew up around professional athletes. While he didn't choose to follow in his father's footsteps, he did learn from his dad the desire necessary to succeed at whatever athletic endeavor he chose.

"My dad was always behind me 100 percent, no matter what I did," Perry said. "When I was young, he said to choose between baseball and golf and stick with my decision. He told me there was no way I could play both."

Perry's father, of course, chose baseball, but he was enough of a recreational golfer that he first exposed Chris to the game.

"My dad played golf during spring training and I watched him," Perry said. "Then I got curious about the game and by the time I was 14, got serious about it.

"It came natural to me, because I was a good athlete. Golf is a hand-eye coordination sport. It was just a matter of getting the proper fundamentals down and improving on them."

Perry had them down enough to win three Minnesota state high school championships, delivering on the expectations that accompanied him as the son of a pitcher for the Minnesota Twins.

"I felt some pressure," Perry said. "I felt if I wasn't as good as (his father and uncle) in baseball, it would bring my name down. I liked golf more, because I was more of an individual achiever."

Perry immediately fortified an already formidable OSU golf team that included, among others, Joey Sindelar.

The two played only one season, after which Sindelar left to join the PGA Tour with a then-record 10 tournament victories while a Buckeye.

Perry set about taking aim at that mark and surpassed it early in his senior year, winning 14 events—before he left OSU.

He reached the finals of the 1983 U.S. Amateur, losing to Jay Sigel, and therefore played in the 1984 Masters.

Perry also won three Les Bohlstad awards as the golfer with the lowest stroke average in Big Ten play.

"Chris was really a competitor," Brown said. "He always played to win. He didn't care if it was his mother, he'd beat her brains out to win. Every practice round, every qualifier, every tournament, he wanted to win it.

"We called him 'Incredible' because he had this uncanny ability to make shots. He'd do the incredible to win tournaments. He'd birdie the last two holes, knock in a 50-footer or chip in at the last hole. He always wanted to know what was going on and where he stood.

"The first thing he'd ask was, 'How's the team doing?' Then it was back to killing people. 'What's the low score? What do I have to shoot?' It was always fun to watch him play in, because you knew he was going to do something amazing."

Perry was a three-time All-American.

Joey
SINDELAR
The Obvious Choice

Jim Brown was struggling with a decision in the spring of 1978.

Brown, the Ohio State golf coach, had four strong players in whom he had confidence, but needed help deciding on who would play fifth for the Buckeyes.

As luck would have it, Brown's college roommate was in town at the time, so the OSU coach decided to bounce the issue off him.

After all, the roommate knew a little something about golf.

His name was Tom Weiskopf.

"I told Tom, 'I've got this kid I want you to play with and see what you think,'" Brown said.

So, the coach, Weiskopf and the prospect teed it up one day at OSU Scarlet.

Before too long, the birdies began to fall.

Not for Weiskopf.

Not for Brown.

But for the prospect.

His name was Joey Sindelar.

"Joey ends up shooting a 65," Brown said. "Weiskopf looks at

me and says, 'If I were you, I'd play that kid.'"

Sindelar indeed joined the Buckeyes' lineup that spring and became a fixture from that point on, helping them gain a berth in four straight NCAA Championships and win the title in 1979.

During that span, Sindelar would make first-team All-American twice, second-team All-American once, and first-team All-Big Ten three times.

"My reasons for attending Ohio State were many," Sindelar said. "I set forth several criteria I felt necessary for my college choice.

"Number one, a strong competitive golf program from coaching to scheduling.

"Number two, a fine facility, and Ohio State's was the best.

"And number three, a high-quality university academically."

Sindelar was a big part of OSU's domination of conference golf during the last half of the 1970s, during which the Buckeyes won five straight league titles by margins as large as 59 strokes.

Sindelar was groomed to participate in that success from the first time he picked up a club under the tutelage of his father and teacher, Joe Sindelar.

"My relatives got on him for pushing me so hard," Sindelar said of his father. "They would say, 'Let him be a kid.' But you can't be successful if you start too late. You can't be good at a sport unless you live the sport."

Sindelar did so, taking his practice regimen as serious as any player Brown ever had.

"He used to make himself hit 100 three-footers before he left every night," Brown said. "He was so disciplined. He knew that to get to the Tour it took work, so we worked very hard on his short game."

Sindelar's dedication was never more in evidence than after the first round of the NCAA Championship in 1979.

He had finished in the top ten in nine of 11 tournaments so far that year, and went to Bermuda Dunes hopeful of helping the

Buckeyes atone for a disappointing 20th-place finish among 21 teams at the NCAA the year before.

OSU was in better position, but far from where it wanted to be after round one, sitting in 13th place.

Sindelar wasn't happy with his contribution, either, so he headed to the range to work on his swing.

Seven buckets of balls and four hours later, he had his game in shape to shoot 68 in the third round and wound up leading OSU's championship effort with a tie for fifth in the medalist standings.

"Joey was just a very consistent player," Brown said. "You could always count on him to be right there in contention somewhere. He was always going to come out and give you a solid effort."

Sindelar left OSU with a then-record 10 tournament victories, including three wins in the Kepler Invitational and the individual title at the Big Ten Championships his senior year.

A tournament-record 64 in the second round helped Sindelar capture a five-shot victory over future PGA Tour rival Tom Lehman on Lehman's home course at the University of Minnesota.

That win typified the consistency that defined Sindelar's career, during which he finished among the

Sindelar won 10 tournaments while at OSU.

top ten in 10 of 12 tournaments as a sophomore, eight of 11 as a junior, and 10 of 12 as a senior. He has since had multiple wins on the PGA Tour.

Jamie NATALIE

Going Out in Style

Jamie Natalie wound up where he never expected to be because a friend never reached the destination Natalie thought he should.

Growing up in Hockessin, Del., in a family of Penn State fanatics, Natalie always figured his gymnastics talents would lead him to Happy Valley and a storied career as a Nittany Lion.

Lucky for Ohio State, a friend of Natalie's made the trip first.

"Everybody in my family was a huge Penn State fan, so if they had their way, I would have wound up a Nittany Lion," Natalie said. "But I knew a guy at my gymnastics club who went there and just didn't have the kind of success I thought that he should. It wasn't the fault of the program, but he didn't do very well at Penn State, and that hurt them in my opinion."

The Lions' bad fortune was a break for the Buckeyes, who in the late 1990s were facing the loss of perhaps the best one-two combination in program history.

Blaine Wilson and Drew Durbin led OSU to the NCAA championship in 1996 and had the team No. 1 in the nation for almost all of 1997.

As if their departure that spring wasn't damaging enough, Ohio State also lost long-time coach Peter Kormann when he decided to retire.

That left the job to Kormann's assistant, Miles Avery, who found the perfect gymnast in Natalie to lead another drive to the top of collegiate gymnastics.

"Jamie was a very well-rounded competitor," Avery said. "He really didn't have a weakness. He was probably best on floor exercise, the parallel bars, and the high bar, but he was very consistent in every event."

Natalie's career legitimizes that assessment.

He won the NCAA all-around title as both a junior in 2000 and a senior in 2001, but his finishes in the individual events display the wide-ranging talents that Avery lauded.

As a sophomore, Natalie made All-American on the pommel horse with a second-place finish at the NCAA.

He made All-American in the all-around, floor exercise, and still rings as a junior. As a senior, he made All-American in the all-around and on the parallel bars. That's four different apparatuses on which Natalie made All-American.

In the two events he didn't achieve that status, vault and high bar, Natalie placed first and third, respectively, in the team competition his senior year to help OSU win its second national championship in five years.

That meet took place at St. John Arena and capped a week in which Natalie was also awarded the Nissan-Emery Award as the nation's top senior gymnast.

"I couldn't have asked for a better ending," Natalie said. "We wound up the team champions, and I got the Nissan. We had high expectations all season long, but we just couldn't put together the perfect meet until the NCAAs.

"We knew we were peaking at the right time, though. Everything we had done was geared toward us winning that national championship."

OSU prevailed with a score of 218.125 to upset heavily favored Oklahoma, which finished at 217.775.

Natalie was at his best in the team competition, not only winning the all-around with a 55.700, but finishing fifth on the pommel

Natalie went out on top as an OSU senior.

horse (9.300), first in the vault (9.375), second on the parallel bars (9.225), and third on the high bar (9.400).

"We had the support of the home crowd behind us and we fed off its energy," Natalie said. "There was nothing like competing in St. John Arena."

Natalie and his fellow seniors never lost a meet at home, and that NCAA title proved his last as a competitive gymnast.

A four-time scholar athlete, and an alternate on the 2000 U.S. Olympic team, Natalie decided to bypass seeking a berth on the 2004 squad to begin his studies in the OSU medical school.

"I decided I wanted to go to med school around end of sophomore or middle of my junior year," he said. "After going to Sydney in 2000, I was trying to decide what I was going to do. I either had to put off med school and train, or try to do both at the same

time.

"I didn't see myself putting off med school and then going back to it some day, and after talking to some of the gymnasts who had gone to med school, doing both at the same time didn't appeal to me. I didn't think I could have achieved at the level I wanted in both."

Natalie was OSU's male athlete of the year in 2001 and also won the Big Ten's medal of honor that year for attaining the greatest proficiency in both academics and athletics of any conference athlete.

Those honors allow him to look back without regret on his choice to retire from gymnastics.

"So many great things happened to me at Ohio State," he said. "I couldn't have picked a better place to go to school. My uncles, who are Penn State fans, still give me a hard time about it, but even they've conceded now to root for Ohio State gymnastics."

Mike RACANELLI

Not to be Denied

The images are burned into sports history of athletes who toiled for years to achieve a certain goal, only to have fate intervene and deal a cruel blow to their aspirations.

American miler Mary Decker Slaney writhing on the infield at the Los Angeles Olympics, her gold medal hopes dashed by a collision with another runner and subsequent injury, comes to mind.

So does speed-skater Dan Jansen, falling in his bid to win the gold at the 1988 Winter Games on the day of his sister's death.

Mike Racanelli could have been a victim of similar bad luck, but instead he conquered the challenge fate threw in his path to write a storybook ending to his final season as an OSU gymnast in 1990.

Racanelli prepped for the NCAA Championships that year with his eye on completing a stellar career by championing the all-around competition and

winning the Nissen Award, the equivalent of the Heisman Trophy for gymnastics.

As luck–bad luck–would have it, however, a stomach virus struck Racanelli in advance of the meet and forced him to miss practice for five days prior to the event.

Things began turning in Racanelli's favor on the eve of the championships, when he became the first OSU gymnast ever to win the Nissen.

Now however, the pressure on him to produce, to deliver on his brand as the nation's best gymnast, had intensified, and Racanelli figured to be rusty after his virus-induced layoff.

Head coach Peter Kormann's description of Racanelli should have foretold the outcome.

"Mike was a street-fighting kind of guy," said Kormann, who after coaching the Buckeyes moved on to coach the U.S. Olympic team in 1996. "He was a great competitor. That's something that's hard to coach."

Racanelli's competition in the all-around was familiar to him, since Minnesota's John Roethlesberger had beaten him just two weeks before at the Big Ten championships.

Racanelli, though, pulled ahead in the optionals and hung on in the compulsories for the victory.

"It's hard when you are in first, knowing there are so many good guys behind you," said Racanelli, who after competing for OSU became an assistant coach for the Buckeyes. "All you have to do is miss in one event."

Racanelli not only didn't miss a set, he performed so well he made the individual event finals in five of six events.

He failed to finish among the top six in only one of those, thus winning All-American honors in five events, including his second national championship with a win in the floor exercise.

"Every routine prior to mine was a hit," Racanelli said of the floor exercise competition. "I

Not even illness kept Racanelli down as a senior.

knew I had to hit my best set. I was kind of worried and a little tired from the afternoon program, but I couldn't have asked for a better set. I couldn't have had a better performance."

It was, indeed, quite a way for Mike Racanelli to go out.

Like a champion.

Donna SILBER

Leading The Way To Prominence

Elite gymnasts often exhibit greatness the first time a spotlight falls upon them, marrying the grace and elegance of their sport to an athleticism that portends success from that moment forward.

Donna Silber had that kind of career for Ohio State from 1978-81, but not that kind of debut.

There was more pain than promise and more frustration than fulfillment when Silber first took center stage at the Big Ten championships in 1978.

In her initial event-the balance beam—Silber suffered a fall that took her out of the competition on that apparatus.

Just a freshman, but already the headliner on a woefully overmatched OSU team, Silber could have collapsed in panic or folded from embarrassment.

Instead, she rose to win both the floor exercise and the all-around that season and serve notice that one fall wasn't about to foil Donna Silber.

Before graduating from OSU, she would acquire a school-record 10 individual conference titles, including an unprecedented sweep of the five-event competition in 1979.

More impressive than that resume, Silber proved the spark for a gymnastics renaissance at OSU, giving the Buckeyes a proven performer on which they could count to build a program that changed from the laughing-stock to the envy of the Big Ten.

OSU hadn't won either a conference championship or competed in the nationals as a team until Silber arrived after an achievement-laden junior career in Mount Prospect, Ill.

"I remember flipping through the program my first year when we got to the Big Ten meet," Silber said. "The thing that stuck with me was a comment about how Ohio State had no place to go but up. I was just mortified by that. It was horrible to have that image of our team being that bad, but it eventually came back to

haunt them with the way we developed and eventually ended up winning the championship."

That team title started an avalanche of titles for the Buckeyes, who followed their win in 1981 with five consecutive first-place finishes in the conference from 1983-87.

All of that success started with Silber, who made the nationals after winning two Big Ten events as a freshman, only to hyperextend her knee while dismounting the uneven parallel bars the night before the competition.

That kept Silber from competing, but she came back strong as a sophomore and entered the conference championships having won six of seven all-arounds in dual meets during the season.

Her enthusiasm took a hit, however, when she saw that the balance beam would once again be the first event.

"I'd fallen off the beam my first year, so I knew going into the Big Tens my sophomore year that I really needed a good start,"

Silber said. "Well, as luck would have it, I had to start on the beam again. I was thinking, 'Oh, no,' but I managed to start off with a great score and that really got me going."

Silber's 9.4 on the beam won that apparatus and proved the first domino in her sweep of every event. She won the floor exercise with a 9.0, the vault with an OSU-record 9.5 in the compulsory and a 9.15 on her optional, and then took the uneven bars with scores of 8.8 and 8.7.

The all-around competition wasn't close, with Silber's 35.1 easily surpassing the second-place mark of 33.5.

From there, she advanced to the AIAW Regionals (the forerunner of the NCAA staging women's competition).

Silber won the all-around and three individual events–the uneven bars, vault and balance beam–but had to withdraw from the floor exercise because of a nasty fall.

"I caught my foot on a dismount from the uneven bars and fell right on my head," Silber said. "I wouldn't say I was injury-prone, but the injuries that I had always seemed to happen at the wrong time. Nothing was extremely devastating. It's just that my timing was bad."

A broken bone in her foot kept Silber from defending her three titles at the Big Ten meet her junior year, but she returned as a senior to anchor OSU's strongest team in school history.

The Buckeyes–who in Silber's freshman season had been labeled a program with "no place to go but up"–won 12 of 14 dual meets that season to capture the top seed in the conference meet.

Michigan State foiled Ohio State's bid to win the title at Larkins Hall, even though Silber won her third all-around title in the league and her tenth overall title with wins in both the vault and floor exercise.

One month later, however, OSU got its revenge by defeating the

Spartans in East Lansing to win the AIAW Midwest Regional and claim a team berth in the national championships.

Silber anchored that effort with her third regional all-around victory and another win on the balance beam.

"Winning that team championship, for me, was more special than anything I accomplished individually," Silber said. "Ohio State had been so down in gymnastics when I got there that my goal was more to get the team where it needed to be.

"It was just a wonderful experience to achieve a goal together with the other girls. We were so excited to win that, because it really showed that we had arrived and that all of our hard work had paid off."

Today, Silber resides in Marysville, Ohio and is a school teacher.

Silber led OSU's rise in women's gymnastics.

Kip SIMONS

A Simple Plan for Success

The legacy Kip Simons carved as an Ohio State gymnast stands out because he transformed himself from simply an accomplished competitor to the best in the nation by sheer hard work and determination.

OSU's only four-time all-conference performer, Simons won the 1994 Nissen Award, the gymnastic equivalent of the Heisman Trophy, after finishing fourth in the NCAA all-around the season before.

What made the difference for Simons?

Nothing more than a shift of the USA Gymnastics calendar and a willful choice to make the most of his final season as a Buckeye.

The first three years of his career at OSU, Simons used the summer months to recuperate after the national championships in June.

But prior to his senior year, that meet was moved to August.

The choice was simple–

Simons could stay at Ohio State that summer and train like he never had. Or, he could give into his body's need for rest and let the skills he had shown that spring taper off a bit before retooling in time to compete in the national championships.

"I decided I would go ahead and give it my best shot," said Simons, a member of the U.S. Olympic team in 1996. "Always before, I had competed in the nationals and then taken the rest of the summer off to give myself a break. When I heard that the meet was going to be in August that year, I thought, 'This is going to be a long, dreadful summer.'

"But I said to myself, 'If I'm going to stay here and train all summer, I'm going to train hard.' I knew, unless I was totally motivated, the people who were going to the USAs weren't going to do well. I knew if I really buckled down, I could leap over some people, and that's kind of what happened. Some of the guys

who had been ahead of me didn't seem to have the same drive I had.'"

Don't believe for one second that Simons came out of nowhere his senior year.

He had, after all, been voted the Big Ten's freshman of the year in 1991, and he'd finished 10th in the all-around at the NCAA Championships that season.

The following year, he won the Big Ten championship on the still rings and the parallel bars, while also winning the floor exercise at the East Regionals.

Simons also had a solid junior year, winning the Big Ten high bar and finishing second in the league's all-around. His leap into the upper echelon came after his intense summer between his junior and senior years.

"Kip stayed here all summer working for the national championships that were in August," then-OSU coach Peter Kormann said. "He learned difficulty in every event and really put himself into the next level.

Simons was four times all-Big Ten

"He was very strong physically. He could make the difficult move look easy. But the best thing about him was he always wanted to get better."

Simons's freshmen teammates, Drew Durbin and Blaine Wilson, stole some headlines with their eye-opening performances late in the year.

Durbin won three individual titles at the Big Ten meet and Wilson edged Simons in the all-around at the regionals.

Nevertheless, on the eve of the NCAA Championships, voters rewarded Simons for his consistency by voting him the Nissen winner.

"Winning that meant more to me than any individual title," Simons said. "It represented excellence both in and out of the sport and how other people saw my performance. It meant a lot to know that other people looked at my gymnastics as something they enjoyed, because I always enjoyed performing."

Blaine WILSON

The Team Is the Thing

The individual honors Blaine Wilson won as an Ohio State gymnast would likely tower over him if all the awards were stacked atop each other.

Picking one and only one favorite would perplex most athletes awash in such honors, particularly when Wilson had a habit of collecting trophies in bunches.

He was the Big Ten's gymnast of the year three times and won a conference-record 14 individual titles, but none of those honors ranks as Wilson's personal highlight.

He was also a two-time NCAA all-around champion, a two-time winner in the still rings competition, and a two-time selection as Ohio State's male athlete-of-the-year.

He also won one NCAA title in both the vault and the parallel bars and was the Big Ten's choice as its male athlete of the year for 1996-97.

None of those rank atop Wilson's list, either.

Surely, it must be the Nissen Award as the nation's top senior gymnast that Wilson claimed in 1997.

Good guess, but no.

Instead, the top individual achievement of Wilson's career isn't an individual achievement at all—except to his way of thinking.

"Without a doubt, the highlight of my college career was winning the NCAA team championship in 1996," Wilson said. "That's the fondest memory I have, because it's something I was able to share with the guys I spent so much time with every single day at practice.

"So much of gymnastics is looked at individually, but when you think about it, every time you walk out there, you walk out as a member of a team. You're by yourself when you're competing, but, really, you've trained with your teammates four hours a day, six days a week."

"To be able to look in those guys' faces after we won that national championship, nothing tops that in my mind."

OSU's national title in 1996 wouldn't have happened had Wilson not posted a 9.90 on the high bar on the Buckeyes' final performance on that apparatus in the preliminary competition.

That effort pushed Ohio State into third place by one-tenth of a point and allowed it to compete the following night for the team title, when Wilson once again delivered under pressure.

Again, the final standings came down to the high bar, and again it was Wilson in the spotlight.

Another 9.90 made the difference, lifting OSU over second-place and host team Stanford to give the Buckeyes their first national championship in 11 years in any sport.

"My most painful memory of college was in my freshman year," Wilson said. "We had a sweet team. We won the Big Ten title by 6 1/2 points and we walked into the national finals thinking we were going to win and then we lost. We didn't even make the finals. I was devastated. I think that's what started my whole, 'I want to win,' philosophy, because I hated losing.

"The following year we had the NCAAs at Ohio State and we lost. We didn't even make the team finals. I remember walking back from St. John Arena to my apartment. I didn't stop for anybody. Everybody was like, 'Let me give you a ride.' And I said, 'I don't want a ride. I want to walk.'"

Those frustrations only made the 1996 team title all the sweeter, rewarding Wilson for a dream he had held since his childhood.

Back then, growing up in Bexley, he devoted himself to gymnastics from the age of 3 and stuck with the sport in his formative years when his friends were focusing on soccer, baseball, and other team sports.

At Columbus DeSales High School, Wilson began thinking he might have made a mistake when many of his friends were part of a state championship team in soccer.

He later came to know that same thrill at OSU, although Wilson wasn't the Buckeyes' main recruit as a freshman and didn't take over as head coach Peter Kormann's headliner until his sophomore season.

Teammate Drew Durbin, who went to DeSales with Wilson, was the Big Ten's gymnast of the year their freshman year and came in more highly touted.

"I was recruited by only one other school besides Ohio State," Wilson said. "Peter told us he had two scholarships, one for Drew and one for me, so we decided to take them and stay together.

"Most of the schools in the country were recruiting just Drew. That kind of fueled my fire to get better."

Wilson wound up the more decorated college gymnast and continued his success after concluding his OSU career.

He won five straight U.S. national championships and was the top competitor on Team USA's Olympic squad in both the 1996 and 2000 Summer Games.

He finished 10th in the all-around at Atlanta in 1996 and sixth in the all-around and sixth in the vault at Sydney in 2000.

Wilson's sixth-place finish in the all-around was the highest ever by a United States male in a non-boycotted Olympics.

Competing in the high-pressure world of international gymnastics never unnerved Wilson, chiefly because of lessons he learned at OSU.

"I was pretty good when I came to Ohio State, but I wasn't great," Wilson said. "Peter Kormann and (assistant coach) Miles Avery turned that around for me. They made me stronger mentally and taught me a lot about the things I needed to do to win.

"They really helped me relax and trust my training. I was able to learn how to turn my brain off and let my body do the work. They got me to relax in competition to the point where everything just happened involuntarily.

"You just stop thinking and let your body do the work. That's what it felt like. It was sort of an out-of-body experience. They taught me how to relax and just sort of watch myself do gymnastics."

Wilson was crucial to OSU's '96 national title.

Arnold CHONKO

Just What the Doctor Ordered

Many an agreement between a coach and a high school recruit has been sealed with a handshake.

In the case of Arnie Chonko, who would become an All-American in both football and baseball at Ohio State, his career nearly expired before it started from too arduous a handshake.

"I'll never forget when Woody (Hayes) came to recruit me," said Chonko, who played at Parma High School in suburban Cleveland. "My dad worked in a slaughterhouse in those days and had forearms like Popeye the Sailor Man.

"When Woody stuck his hand out to shake my father's hand, my dad put his grip on there and Woody said, 'Gee, I should be recruiting YOU!' I thought we'd blown it right there. Woody comes all the way from Columbus to meet us and gets his hand squashed."

Hayes proved too resilient in his desire to recruit Chonko for a squeezed hand to deter him, and that determination paid dividends for OSU not only on the football field but on the baseball diamond, as well.

Chonko was the glue that held the 1965 Buckeyes of coach Marty Karow together, playing stellar defense at first base and providing solid hitting near the top of the order.

The Buckeyes won their first Big Ten championship in 10 years that season and advanced to the College World Series.

Chonko hit .329, with 27 RBI in 39 games.

His three-run home run in the first inning of a second-round game against Washington State put OSU on top and allowed it to breeze to a 14-1 victory and berth in the winner's bracket finals.

Ohio State lost that game to Arizona State, 9-4, but eked out a 15-inning, 1-0 victory over Washington State in the loser's bracket to stay alive.

Chonko had the only RBI in that game.

A 7-3 victory over Arizona State brought on a winner-take-all final between the two teams, which ASU won 2-1.

Chonko was an all-tournament team selection, pairing that honor with the second-team All-America mention he also received that year.

"That was one of those magical years," Chonko said. "We actually had better teams my sophomore and junior years, but that season we just got our hits in bunches and were able to score runs when we needed them. That team meant so much to me."

Chonko wouldn't have those memories if he hadn't held Hayes's feet to the fire on the promise the coach made to him on his trip to Parma.

"I remember going down to Ohio State for a visit one time and seeing that John Havlicek was playing baseball in the spring," Chonko said. "That's what gave me the idea. I thought, 'Well, if he can do it, maybe I can too.'

"So I asked Woody about it, and he said I could after my freshman year. I had to go through spring practice my freshman year, but after that I could play baseball if I wanted to. He tried to talk me out of it, but he had written it right into our agreement and I reminded him of that."

Hayes still got his money's worth out of Chonko, even though the Buckeyes of 1962-64 came up short in their attempt to win the Big Ten championship and get to the Rose Bowl.

They came tantilizingly close in 1964, finishing 7-2 overall, but losing a 10-0 struggle at No. 3 Michigan in the season finale with the conference title and Rose Bowl berth on the line.

"They had a great team that year, but we bottled them up pretty good," Chonko said. "We just didn't have enough offense to score on them."

Chonko was voted an All-American defensive back after that season, putting a flourish on a career that saw him help the Buckeyes claim some memorable victories.

One of those came early in his senior season when USC and Heisman Trophy winner Mike Garrett came into Ohio Stadium and left a 17-0 loser.

That victory came on the heels of a 26-0 victory at Illinois, the Rose Bowl participant from the previous year, which targeted the Buckeyes as their homecoming opponent that year.

"They had Dick Butkus and they were really planning on beating us bad," Chonko said. "We ended up giving them a pretty good beating in their own back yard. I enjoyed that tremendously."

No amount of athletic success could turn Chonko's head away from his desire to be a doctor, however.

He toyed with the idea of pursuing a professional career in baseball, believing it would afford him greater longevity than a career in the NFL, but ultimately settled on a path which was true to a philosophy his brothers imparted.

"It became clear to me that if I was going to become a doctor, it was going to take years," Chonko said. "Who knows, if I had gone to play profession-

Chonko made All-American in two sports.

ally some where, I might never have gotten back into school. I finally decided, 'Nah, if you're going to do this, you better do it right now.' So, I went to school.

"I had two older brothers that had a great impact on me, along with my mother and father. They always emphasized giving back more to society than one takes. That was sort of a philosophy that was imbued in me. I adopted it, and I felt the best way to do that was in medicine."

Chonko not only became a doctor, he was among the top graduates in his medical school class at OSU.

He relocated to Kansas City and became in instructor at the University of Kansas College of Medicine.

Paul EBERT

Nothing to be Nervous About

It's unfathomable to imagine a university placing such pressure on an athlete today, however well intentioned.

Officials at Ohio State knew what they were doing, however, in the spring of 1954 when they held Paul Ebert Day to coincide with a crucial double-header against the University of Minnesota.

To be sure, letting Ebert complete his star-studded, two-sport Ohio State career without some sort of commemorative celebration would have been an oversight.

But on the afternoon Ebert was to be honored, he had quite enough on his mind—pitching the first game of a doubleheader, a game the Buckeyes needed to win to maintain their hopes of claiming the conference championship.

The mayor of the City of Columbus, OSU president Howard Bevis, and even the legendary Jesse Owens turned out for Ebert's tribute.

A lesser man might have folded under that pressure, but not Ebert.

As one his teammates told the *Columbus Dispatch*, "Everyone was tied up in knots but Paul, the guy who carried all the pressure."

Sure enough, Ebert delivered, just as he had throughout three achievement-laden baseball and basketball seasons as a Buckeye.

He pitched OSU to a 3-1 victory that day, his fourth win in as many starts in the conference and his seventh win in nine decisions overall.

Such clutch performances typified Ebert's athletic career, which at the time of his graduation was unsurpassed in OSU history for excellence in separate sports.

As a baseball pitcher, he led the Buckeyes in victories, strikeouts and innings pitched all three seasons he played from 1952-54.

Ebert's career record of 21 victories was second in school history when his eligibility expired and remains among the top 20 by Ohio State pitchers, as do his career marks for innings pitched, fewest bases on balls, and won-loss percentage (.724).

The 79 runs he allowed are the second-fewest in OSU history among pitchers to throw at least 175 innings.

That alone would have earned Ebert induction into the Ohio State Athletic Hall of Fame, but the Columbus South graduate was just as big a force for the Buckeyes on the basketball court.

He made All-American in that sport, as well, finishing his career as the leading scorer in school history with 1,436 points.

Ebert set single-game school records with 15 field goals, 40 points, and 20 free throws in separate games during his career, while also setting a career mark with 243 free throws. His 516 points as a senior was the OSU single-season record at the time, and never in his career did he offer a single-season scoring average under 20 points per game.

Ebert had his best games

Ebert set a single-game scoring record for the Ohio State Coliseum.

against the opponent all Buckeyes most want to defeat, the University of Michigan.

He had games of 34 and 35 points against the Wolverines, setting an Ohio State Coliseum scoring record with the former total.

Ebert followed his graduation from OSU by enrolling in the School of Medicine, where he obtained his degree and set out on an accomplished career.

He became a renowned heart surgeon and chairman of the Department of Surgery at the University of California, San Francisco, before later relocating to Chicago upon being named executive director of the 49,000-member American College of Surgeons.

Alice "Lefty" HOHLMAYER

In a League of Her Own

They didn't give Varsity O awards in Alice Hohlmayer's era for one simple reason—there were no varsity sports for women at Ohio State in the 1940s.

That gives Hohlmayer a unique distinction among honorees in the OSU Athletic Hall of Fame, since she doesn't have a sweater, a jacket, or any other official university award to commemorate her performance as a Buckeye athlete.

Hohlmayer, though, has a leg up on her Hall of Fame counterparts, all of whom would be humbled if forced to match the sum total of their varsity letters against the number of sports Hohlmayer played for OSU during her days as a student.

She starred at field hockey, volleyball, basketball, softball, soccer, fencing, badminton, archery, and mixed tennis, exhibiting an all-around athleticism that drew her away from school starting in the spring of her junior year when the call came beckoning from the All-American Girls Professional Baseball League.

"I was a physical education and health major at Ohio State," said Hohlmayer, who started her studies at OSU in 1943 after growing up in Springfield, Ohio. "We had gas rationing in those days, so we would play teams like Ohio Wesleyan, Oberlin, and others in the area. Mostly, it was the girls, like myself, who were in physical education classes.

"We would go to the other campuses or they would come to ours. We would play more than one sport. We might play hockey one day and then basketball the next. Sometimes, we'd stay over night on their campus. Other times, they'd come to Columbus and stay over night there.

"I was really into all sports, and I was able to do them well. I guess I was a tomboy growing up. I just enjoyed playing just about everything."

Hohlmayer's talent at softball got her noticed at a tournament in Cleveland when organizers were scouting the nation for players in the Girls Professional Baseball League.

"I was at school in the spring of 1946 when I got a call one day from Max Carey, the president of the league," Hohlmayer said. "He asked me if I wanted to try out that weekend. I told him if I did, I'd have to get back right away, because in those days, if you missed more than three classes, you flunked."

Carey sent a train ticket, and Hohlmayer was off to the tryout camp in Pascagoula, Miss.

"I was kind of scared, going down there on the train alone," Hohlmayer said. "In those days, a young lady just didn't do that. Her mother and father looked after her. I was afraid no one would be there to pick me up when I arrived."

Those fears were groundless, for league officials were so intent on scrutinizing Hohlmayer that she tried out the next day in front of all eight managers of the league's teams.

"They knew I was only going to be there a short time, so I guess they each wanted to get a look at me," she said. "I hit the ball hard and played really well. I guess being scared brought out the best in me."

Before returning to Columbus, Hohlmayer spent the night in a local hotel, which wasn't the best advertisement for the league's off-field care of its players.

"I was ready to go to sleep that night, and I noticed that my roommate, Audrey Wagner, was sitting in a straight-backed chair," Hohlmayer said. "I asked her, 'Why are you doing that?' She said, 'Cockroaches.' So, I got the other straight-backed chair and sat with her all night. We sure didn't get much sleep."

That experience didn't sour Hohlmayer on a baseball career, however, but she did hold out for more money when Carey called three days later and asked her to drop out of school and join the league.

"He said they would pay me $80 a week," Hohlmayer said. "Rookies were supposed to make only $55 a week, but they knew I didn't want to quit school."

Her father gave his blessing, and Hohlmayer was off to Wisconsin to play for the Kenosha Comets.

She played three seasons there before deciding to sit out spring training in 1949 to finish her degree at OSU.

Hohlmayer was then traded to the Muskegon Lassies, which later moved to Kalamazoo.

Her final season was with Peoria in 1951, where Hohlmayer batted .267 and compiled a 17-11 pitching record with an earned run average of 2.02.

Hohlmayer (back row, second from left) with the OSU championship team.

Hohlmayer settled in California, where she became a widow seven years into her marriage. She taught school and worked with youth recreation leagues for 17 years before retiring and beginning a second career at memorabilia shows.

She has appeared with numerous baseball legends, trading off her years in the AAGPBL and a famous encounter with Hall-of-Famer Satchel Paige at a 1947 exhibition.

"Max Carey called me when I was in school at Ohio State and asked me if I wanted to make $100," Hohlmayer said. "I said, 'Heck, yeah, who wouldn't?' He told me all I had to do was play in this exhibition game against the Kansas City Monarchs.

"Of course, I had to get up and bat against Satchel Paige. Well, he struck me out the first time, throwing all this crazy stuff, so the second time I came up to bat I just walked out to the mound first. I said, 'Hey, Satch, I'm part of the exhibition, too. How 'bout you throw me a straight ball I can hit?'

"So, he threw me a straight pitch, and I got a base hit into right field. I think that makes me the only woman ever to get a hit off of him."

Vic JANOWICZ

A Man Ahead of His Time

Others would come after him and get more publicity for the same parlay, but whatever notoriety Deon Sanders and Bo Jackson received for being two-sport athletes professional athletes was due–make that overdue–Vic Janowicz.

Those who saw the native of Elyria play for the Buckeyes from 1949-51 marveled at his ability to achieve in all phases on the football field, and that's not even the sport in which Janowicz first made it professionally.

He was the seventh overall selection in the 1951 NFL draft, but fulfilled a two-year commitment in the National Guard and then shocked everyone by accepting a $25,000 bonus contract with the Pittsburgh Pirates.

Janowicz hadn't played baseball since high school, but played two seasons before Washington Redskins owner George Preston Marshall convinced him to jump to the NFL.

Despite missing all of the Redskins' preseason practices while finishing the 1954 season in Pittsburgh, Janowicz became an immediate starter at halfback and in his second season lost the NFL scoring title to Detroit's Doak Walker the final week.

"Vic had to be one of the finest athletes ever to play at Ohio State," said Walt Klevay, a teammate of Janowicz's all three years at OSU. "He could do everything-punt, kick field goals and extra-points, play defense, and play offense. He played halfback, linebacker, and quarterback. You name it–basketball, football, golf–he could do anything."

In 1950, Janowicz became just the third junior to win the Heisman Trophy, getting more than twice as many votes (633) as runner-up Kyle Rote (280) of Southern Methodist.

"Basically, he was our man," said Henry Bill Trautwein, the captain of the Buckeyes that season in Wes Fesler's final year as head coach. "He could do everything. He's the only player I've ever seen at Ohio State who could do it all.

"That year, he played both ways. He played defensive back and on offense he ran and he passed and he caught passes. He kicked and he punted. I don't think they've ever had another like him since."

Janowicz accounted for 16 touchdowns and 875 yards of offense in 1950 and led the Buckeyes in scoring with 65 points.

He was at his most spectacular in OSU's 83-21 victory over Iowa, a game in which Janowicz ran for two touchdowns, passed for four scores on six attempts and kicked a Big Ten-record 10 extra-points.

"The first half, it seemed like every time he touched the ball, Ohio State scored," said Marv Homan, Ohio State's retired sports information director, who began calling games on radio in 1949. "People forget, but that was not a bad Iowa team. I've never seen such a demonstration. He did it so many different ways."

Janowicz was also responsible for what is acknowledged as the most amazing field goal in Ohio Stadium history, his 27-yarder into the teeth of a driving snow storm in the famous 1950 Snow Bowl loss to Michigan.

Janowicz also punted a school-record 21 times for 685 yards in that game.

"That Iowa game is the one everyone remembers, but every game I played, I had a great game that season," Janowicz said in a 1995 interview shortly before his death after a five and one-half year battle with prostate cancer. "If it wasn't on defense, it was passing the ball. If it wasn't passing, it was running. If it wasn't running, it was blocking. I don't think I ever had a bad game my junior year."

Homan supports that view.

"I just can't imagine Ohio State ever having a more versatile player," Homan said of Janowicz. "I don't see how anyone could have been more versatile. He was the epitome of the single-wing halfback. He could quick-kick. He was an efficient runner and he could pass. There's your triple-threat, right there.

"He also kicked off and kicked field goals and extra-points. On top of that, he was an outstanding defensive player."

Janowicz's involvement in the OSU offense dwindled when Woody Hayes came on as the Buckeyes head coach in 1951 and brought the new Split-T formation with him.

Even so, he and Hayes formed a close friendship in later years when the coach helped organize medical care for Janowicz after a serious automobile accident in August of 1956 cut short his NFL career.

"He was well on his way to the football hall of fame when he had his accident," Klevay said. "I'm sure he would have ended up as one of the all-time greats if not for that."

Versatility was Janowicz's trademark.

Bo REIN

A Promising Career Cut Short

In an athletic program as diverse as Ohio State's, with a century of competition in the history books, there's bound to be an assortment of athletes whose legacy endures as much for their eccentricity as their ability.

Such is the case with Robert E. "Bo" Rein, who flashed across the OSU landscape in the mid-1960s as a two-sport star and then rose through the ranks as an up-and-coming football coaching coach until his life tragically ended at age 34.

Bo Rein, like all of Woody Hayes's players, had character.

But more than that, Bo Rein was a character, an unforgettable sort whose teammates remember him as a loveable scatterbrain with a white-hot competitive streak.

"Bo wasn't a bar-room brawler, but he was one of those kids who, if you knocked him down, he'd get back up in a hurry and always wanted more," said Arnold Chonko, Rein's teammate on the OSU football and baseball teams in 1964 and 1965. "He was a supremely confident individual who thought he could take on anyone at any time. That, and, I'd have to say, he was a bit of a hairbrain."

Steve Arlin, the ace pitcher on OSU's 1966 College World Series champions, recalls Rein's goofy side.

"The thing I remember about Bo was that he forgot his shoes on a road trip one time," Arlin said. "In football, they had guys to handle their equipment for them. But in baseball, we had to do that stuff for ourselves, and Bo just lost track of his things sometimes.

"He used to drive our coach, Marty Karow, absolutely crazy. That time Bo forgot his shoes, he took infield practice in his socks and then borrowed some (spikes) from somebody else for the game."

Rein came to OSU out of Niles, Ohio, and immediately showed what he was about when football practice began that fall.

"We scrimmaged the freshmen when I was a junior and Bo was really determined to show the varsity who he was," Chonko said. "We'd pound on him and he'd just get up and laugh. He'd say, 'You can't hurt me.'

"He was a tough kid and a good athlete. He could really run and he was very agile. He could do a little bit of everything, including catch the ball . . . not that Woody threw that much. Bo was kind of wirey. He could bounce off people, spin around, and keep on running."

Rein led Ohio State in receiving with 22 catches for 320 yards as a sophomore on a team that finished 7-2 and No. 9 in the nation in 1964.

The next year, Rein was again used primarily as a receiver out of the backfield, catching 29 passes for 328 yards on another 7-2 finisher that placed second in the league.

The Buckeyes weren't as

successful in 1966, going 4-5. Rein led the team in rushing with 456 yards on 139 carries.

But while OSU didn't reach the Rose Bowl during Rein's football career, it certainly reached the pinnacle in baseball with him starting at shortstop.

Rein batted .282 and led the Buckeyes with 16 steals as a junior on the team that lost in the championship game at the College World Series.

Chonko played first base for OSU that season, and got his exercise tracking Rein's throws from across the infield.

"Bo could really go in the hole, but he had a scatter arm," Chonko said. "I was a good-fielding first baseman, but he really made me earn my keep. He'd get to the ball, but you never knew where it was going to go."

While Chonko had graduated and gone on to medical school by 1966, Rein and Arlin were back to help the Buckeyes once again reach the College World Series.

OSU's toughest game there was a 1-0 win over USC in the semifinals, with Rein providing the only run when he tripled and scored in the fourth inning.

Arlin made that stand up for the victory and the Buckeyes cruised thereafter.

After concluding his OSU athletic career, Rein became a graduate assistant coach on Hayes's football staff in 1967 and two years later was named receivers coach.

He remained in that capacity only one season before moving on to William & Mary, where he joined up with Lou Holtz, who had been on Hayes's staff as the secondary coach in 1968.

That association with Holtz helped Rein land his first head coaching job just eight years after leaving OSU, getting hired at North Carolina State in 1976 at the age of 30.

He went 3-7-1 that first year, but followed with an 8-4 record in 1977 and a victory over Iowa State in the Peach Bowl.

The next season, Rein's Wolfpack went 9-3 and dumped Pittsburgh in the Tangerine Bowl.

North Carolina State won the Atlantic Coast Conference in Rein's fourth and final season, but was not invited to a bowl game despite a 7-4 record.

That success landed Rein the head coaching job at LSU in December of 1979, prompting Hayes to tell reporters who covered the Tigers, "Bo's really a dandy and has proven it. He studies football all the time and is just a heck of a recruiter. He's probably the best young coach in the country."

Alas, Rein would never get to prove his mentor correct, for fate conspired to keep him from ever coaching a game at LSU.

On Jan. 10, 1980, just six weeks after his hiring, he and a pilot departed from Shreveport at 9:10 p.m. for what was supposed to be a one-hour flight back to Baton Rouge following a recruiting trip.

Shortly after takeoff, the pilot radioed for clearance to change course in hopes of avoiding bad weather.

Permission was granted, but air traffic controllers soon noticed the plane climbing above its allowed ceiling of 25,000 feet.

Attempts were made to contact the pilot, but no radio contact could be established as the plane veered wildly off course.

An Air Force pilot whose jet attempted to intercept Rein's plane and hopefully re-establish communication watched helplessly as it crashed from 41,000 feet into the Atlantic Ocean, 120 miles from Cape Charles, Va.

No firm cause for the crash has ever been established, although cabin depressurization is the safest assumption.

That would have caused Rein and his pilot to pass out from lack of oxygen and never know their plane was in peril.

Rein led OSU in rushing his senior year.

Dick
SCHNITTKER

Football's Loss, Basketball's Gain

Before he wound up being the marquee player on Ohio State's only Big Ten championship basketball team in a 13-year span, and before he wound up an instrumental addition to the Buckeyes' first Rose Bowl football championship team in 1949, Dick Schnittker nearly wound up something else.

He nearly wound up a student at Bowling Green.

An All-Ohio selection in three sports at Sandusky High School, Schnittker might never have become an OSU legend had he not taken a telephone call in the fall of 1946 after he had already decided to favor the Falcons with his wide-ranging athletic skills.

"I had a brother who was going to Ohio State at the time," said Schnittker, whose brother Max played for the Buckeyes' football teams in 1945 and 1946. "He played with Les Horvath and Ollie Cline, so I guess Ohio State figured that when I wound up All-

Ohio in football, basketball and track, I would join Max down there in Columbus.

"The problem was, nobody from Ohio Sate ever said anything to me about wanting me to come. I waited around and nothing ever happened, so I decided to go to Bowling Green, where Andy Anderson was the coach and he really acted like he wanted me."

OSU didn't move to correct its oversight until Schnittker failed to show up that fall for classes.

"One day, I was out on the basketball court at Bowling Green, shooting buckets, and this call came in to the coaches' office," Schnittker said. "Somebody came and told me, 'Hey, there's someone on the phone who wants to talk to you.'

"Well, I got on the line and it was Ernie Godfrey, who was a recruiter at Ohio State. He says to me, 'Where are you?' I told him, 'You must know where I am, you called here, didn't you?'"

Godfrey's call resulted in

Schnittker changing his plans and enrolling at OSU, but his rise to prominence as a two-time All-American in basketball wouldn't have happened without some considerable frustration occurring first.

"In 1946, there were about 240 guys or so who were coming back from the service," Schnittker said. "These were all good guys, All-Americans and such, who were going back to school after the war on the GI bill.

"I wound up on the JV team and had a pretty good season, but I felt I should have gotten to play more. That's why I went out for basketball after football ended. I made the varsity by the end of the year, so I dropped football for the next three years."

Schnittker's development on the court caught the attention of OSU head coach Tippy Dye, who was struggling with a roster of unruly upperclassmen.

Dye's solution was to dump that group, barring them from the team in 1947-48, and casting his lot with Schnittker and a group of sophomores that also included future Boston Celtic Bob Donham.

"Deadeye Dick," as Schnittker was called, wound up the Buckeyes' leading scorer that season with a total of 322 points that broke the school's single season record previously set by All-American Jimmy Hull.

Schnittker's 16.1 scoring average and 204 points in Big Nine competition also established OSU marks and set the stage for a junior year in which he would exceed those numbers.

The team improved from 10-10 that 1948 season to 14-7 in 1949, with the highlight easily being the Buckeyes' 68-60 victory over No. 2-ranked St. Louis University on its home court at Kiel Auditorium.

The 6-foot-5 Schnittker boosted his production to 17.8 points per game and a new single-season mark of 336 points as a junior, earning his first set of All-American credentials.

Quite surprisingly, Dye risked the success Ohio State was on the threshold of experiencing in 1950 by offering his star player to the football Buckeyes that fall when head coach Wes Fesler ran short on wide receivers.

Schnittker grabbed his helmet and lent a hand, starting for OSU on a team that wound up defeating California, 14-7, at the Rose Bowl.

"I called my dad and asked him advice when Tip told me they needed me on the football team," Schnittker said. "My dad told me, 'Well, you went down there to play football, so why don't you go do it?'

"That's what I did, and it was kind of a nice feeling. I got to be reunited with all the freshman guys I started out with . . . guys like Pandel Savic, Curly Morrison . . . and we had a super year.

"I've always thought Tip was pretty generous to let me play football that year. I could have gotten hurt and it would have really hurt us in basketball."

Instead, Schnittker emerged from his football adventure unscathed and rejoined the basketball team after a January 2 loss at Bradley had lowered the Buckeyes' record to 5-2.

OSU ran off victories in 16 of its next 17 games, including an 11-1 mark, to easily win the Big Ten title and earn a berth in the NCAA Tournament.

Unfortunately for the Buckeyes, their first game was against City College of New York at Madison Square Garden, where the gambling influences that

would be exposed the following season were already afoot.

"My dad was out in the lobby before that game and the odds were 5-to-1 that I would foul out," Schnittker said. "They were actually taking bets on it, and don't you know, sure enough I fouled out."

Donham was the first Buckeye to suffer the officials' wrath, getting banished with five personals with four minutes remaining in the game.

Schnittker tried to bring OSU back, tightening the score to 55-54 at the two-minute mark, before he was handed his fifth foul just 15 seconds later.

CCNY wound up a 56-55 winner en route to claiming that NCAA title, but would be disgraced the following season when its players' ties to gamblers were exposed.

"That's my only regret in college, losing that game to the fixers," Schnittker said. "There was at least one official and three players who served time for shaving points in that deal. We had the better team. For the longest time, we couldn't figure out why we couldn't win that game.

"Of course, later, it all made sense. The films show what happened. It was all rigged from the start. That was the only dark side to my athletic career."

Schnittker was known as "Deadeye Dick."

Robert SMITH

No Nonsense, But Plenty of Ability

We do not know the name of the great philosopher who said, "It ain't bragging if you can back it up."

We can, however, be reasonably certain the person was somehow related to Robert Smith.

Perhaps no figure in Ohio State athletic history is more controversial than the gazelle-like tailback who graced the Buckeyes' lineup for two eventful seasons in 1990 and 1992.

Smith came to OSU from a storied career at Euclid High School near Cleveland, where he was a two-time Mr. Football after rushing for 5,038 yards and 68 touchdowns.

His decision to play for the Buckeyes was trumpeted as the bridge that would return the Buckeyes to the Rose Bowl under John Cooper, a destination they had yet to reach early in his tenure as Earle Bruce's successor.

Ohio State would most assuredly get there, but not during Smith's career, for he was too young as a freshman in 1990 to carry the team on his back and too bothered by nagging injuries as a sophomore to lift OSU above a second-place finish in the conference in 1992.

He was, however, never too young or too injured to boldly express confidence in his abilities.

Nor was Smith ever unable to back up his words with a worthy performance.

"Robert was a confident player, but he wasn't cocky," OSU coach John Cooper said. "Anything he said he could do, he did it. My only regret with Robert is that we never really got to see what Robert could do, because he was here and gone so fast

"He played two seasons and then he went to the NFL. I've told Robert ever since that if he would have stayed in school, he would have joined Archie Griffin as the only two-time Heisman Trophy winner in college football history. I really believe he could have done that."

Those words might seem strange coming from Cooper, who was the coach Smith left in a lurch in 1991 when he stunned the college football world by quitting the team to concentrate on his academics during fall practice.

But during the year Smith spent away from the field, Cooper worked tirelessly behind the scenes to convince the player to rejoin the team.

"I never had anything against Robert," Cooper said. "I wanted Robert on our football team because I knew he could help us win and because I knew we could help Robert Smith get where he wanted to go.'

Smith got there sooner than OSU loyalists desired, opting to forfeit his final two seasons of eligibility to enter the NFL draft in 1992, when he was the 21st pick of the first round by the Minnesota Vikings.

Before leaving Ohio State, however, Smith left a fleeting legacy as one of the most talented rushers ever to wear the scarlet and gray.

"When he was a freshman, everyone was watching Robert and we thought, 'He looks like a good back. He's pretty decent,'" former OSU quarterback Kirk Herbstreit said. "All of the sudden, he got in that first game and, 'Bang.'"

Stardom was forecast for Smith based on his high school exploits, but few believed it would be as immediate and as all-encompassing as it proved when he burst into the spotlight on an overcast September Saturday in the 1990 season-opener.

OSU trailed Texas Tech, 10-3, at halftime until Smith came off the bench to rush for 87 yards and one touchdown and provide a 17-10 victory.

By the time that year ended, Smith had obliterated two-time Heisman Trophy-winner Archie Griffin's freshman rushing record of 867 yards set in 1972 by accumulating 1,126 yards.

That earned him accolades as the national freshman-of-the-year, a title that only intensified the furor the following fall when Smith suddenly dropped off the roster after a dispute with an assistant coach.

"I never liked having people think about me as the type of person who was always doing things right," Smith said. "I never saw myself as a knight in shining armor to begin with. That was an image that was created.

"There were parts of it that were true, but I never felt any extreme pressure to be perfect, because I knew that was impossible."

Smith was far from inactive during his season away from the Buckeyes, joining the track team as a scholarship athlete and more than earning his keep.

His personal best of 45.73 in the 400 meters met the qualifying standard for the U.S. Olympic Trials, and he finished second in that event at the Big Ten championships.

Smith also helped the Buckeyes winning 4x400-meter relay team achieve All-American status in the spring of 1991.

By then, he had announced his impending return to football, and there were a segment of OSU loyalists who hoped Smith would be rusty enough not to start the first game that season.

Instead, he quickly reestablished himself as the Buckeyes' best ballcarrier and, if anything, looked better than he had before.

"Robert was just a phenomenal athlete," Cooper said. "He had a great work ethic and a great attitude. I don't think he won every gasser we ran in practice that year. But, looking back, he did that as a freshman, too."

Fate wouldn't allow Smith to have the kind of sophomore year his talents were capable of achieving.

He broke his ribs early in the year, but still played in an upset victory at ninth-ranked Syracuse, scoring the clinching touchdown on a breakaway run, and then excusing himself to the sideline to throw up from the pain of his injury.

Later on, Smith sprained an ankle that kept him out of one game and limited him in two others.

But, when fully healthy the final five games of that year, he had four 100-yard games and accumulated 596 of his 819 rushing yards and eight of his 10 touchdowns.

"If I was a fan watching him practice, I would think Robert looked like a pretty good back," Herbstreit said. "On game day, I don't know what happened, but he turned it up a notch. It was incredible. I've never seen anything like it."

Smith made the most of his two seasons.

Fred TAYLOR

The Right Man in an Emergency

His record as the most distinguished head basketball coach in Ohio State history proved Fred Taylor artfully capable of filling a void cast upon him without warning.

That shouldn't have surprised anyone, though, given Taylor's history as a two-sport OSU athlete of distinction.

A decade before he would coach the Buckeyes to the 1960 NCAA Championship, Taylor became Ohio State's first baseball All-American with a 1950 season in which he led the team with three home runs and 25 RBIs.

That followed Taylor's performance as the starting center on the Buckeyes' 1950 Big Ten championship basketball team, when he stepped into a breach thrust upon the team by tragic circumstances the previous spring.

It was then that Bob Raidiger, OSU's starting center in 1949, was struck and killed by an automobile.

Raidiger had been the team's second-leading scorer the year before at 13.6 points per game, giving Coach Tippy Dye's team a viable alternative when opponents chose to concentrate on stopping All-American Dick Schnittker and guard Bob Donham.

Those three had provided the Buckeyes their first trio of double-figure scorers in school history, and their expected return for the 1950 season had championship hopes running high in Columbus.

Raidiger's death left the center spot to Taylor, and he came through with a 10-point average that preserved the team's diversity and helped it post a 22-4 record, including an 11-1 mark that earned the Big Ten title.

"Fred stepped right in and played well for us," Schnittker said. "He wasn't fast. In fact, he was slow. There were some detriments to his game, but he overcame that by being smart. He really fit in with us and he could rebound. He knew just what to

do. He sure had the smarts to be a good player."

Those in Taylor's hometown of Zanesville would likely have scoffed at such a scenario given Taylor's success–or lack of it–on the basketball court growing up.

He was cut from his high school team three times before coming to OSU in the fall of 1942 without any of the fanfare accorded promising high school prospects.

Taylor left school in 1943 to enter the military and gained invaluable strength and experience during his three-year tour of duty.

"Fred was quite a bit older than the rest of us," Schnittker said. "We used to rib him about that and about getting cut from his high school team. It was all in good fun, of course. Fred was good-natured about it and I'm glad he was, because he was a strong as a bull after being in the service all those years."

Taylor once joked that his career wasn't bad for someone who never earned a varsity letter.

"I guess I always kind of enjoyed making the club at Ohio State, because I was told for three years in high school that I wasn't good enough to play," Taylor told Bob Hunter in his book, *Buckeye Basketball.*

Marv Homan, Ohio State's sports information director from 1949-87, remembers Taylor as "the consummate team player on the basketball court."

"He fit in ideally on the basketball team," Homan said. "Of course, it was at baseball that Fred really excelled. He had good power and was very good defensively as a first-baseman."

Taylor and his wife Eileen married in 1947, and he took his bride with him to Chattanooga for the start of his professional baseball career in 1950.

The following year, Taylor batted .296 and drove in 102 runs for the Washington Senators' minor league affiliate, which would have made him one of the woebegone team's best prospects if not for a bit of bad fortune.

"They weren't very good in those days," Homan said. "But the irony of it was that their best player happened to be a first-baseman, Mickey Vernon. I think Fred was somewhat frustrated by that."

Indeed, Taylor was growing increasingly disenchanted with baseball and more and more focused on his love of coaching basketball. During his winters, he had been lending aid to OSU coach Floyd Stahl. That continued until February of 1958, when Stahl surprised Taylor by asking him if he would like a full-time job as the Buckeyes' head freshman coach.

The next spring, Stahl retired and a committee was formed to find his successor.

"I remember getting a letter in the mail asking for my recommendation," Schnittker said. "I recommended Fred. He had all the qualities that Tippy Dye had instilled in all of us. Fred was up front, honest, a good teacher, and very communicative. He was one of my closest friends, and probably the most loyal person I have ever known."

Taylor's character and integrity were cited as often as his technical expertise when his former players remembered him upon his death in January of 2002.

"He was very important to how I evolved as a person and a player. I can truly say I never would have achieved the things I did without him." said John Havlicek, a member of Taylor's 1960 NCAA

championship team at OSU before winning eight NBA championships with the Boston Celtics.

Taylor's teams compiled a 297-158 record in 18 seasons, winning seven Big Ten championships and reaching four Final Fours in an 11-year span from 1960-71.

The Buckeyes went 78-6 from 1960-62 with a lineup featuring Havlicek, Jerry Lucas and Mel Nowell.

Those teams won 47 straight regular season games, 27 straight Big Ten games and 50 consecutive home games, following their 1960 NCAA title with runner-up finishes in 1961 and 1962.

"Fred Taylor almost single-handedly transformed the Big Ten Conference from almost an exclusively football-playing conference to a conference that was one of the very best, year after year, in basketball," said Texas Tech coach Bob Knight, a substitute for the Buckeyes on those Havlicek- and Lucas-led teams.

"He had an awful lot to do with all of our lives- not only on the floor, but off the floor, in the classroom, whatever we did. He made all of us much more than basketball players. He made us people who could contribute to society in whatever way we chose to do so."

Taylor in his days coaching the Buckeyes.

Steve ARLIN

The Man With the Golden Arm

The conventional thinking had always been that to contend for a College World Series championship, a worthy team required a rotation with at least three talented starting pitchers.

Then Steve Arlin came along and offered a twist on that formula, proving a title could also be won if a team had one starting pitcher three times as talented as anyone else.

What Arlin did in carrying Ohio State to a runner-up finish in the 1965 World Series and the championship of that event in 1966 is a tale that transcends the typical one-upmanship of his sport.

Baseball, after all, has a way of treating its records roughly, as evidenced by Babe Ruth yielding to Roger Maris, who yielded to Mark McGuire, who yielded to Barry Bonds.

It is, however, impossible even now to inspect Arlin's statistics from 1965 and 1966 and not be awed.

His 24-3 career record included marks of 11-1 as a junior and 13-2 as a sophomore-seasons in which he was a two-time All-American and led OSU to Big Ten championships and the pinnacle of collegiate baseball.

"Steve was our horse," said Arnie Chonko, a first-baseman for the Buckeyes. "He was absolutely tenacious and fearless. We knew that if he was pitching and we could score a run, we were going to win."

In two years at the College World Series, Arlin went 4-1 with an 0.96 earned run average, but those numbers–brilliant as they are–don't begin to tell the story.

Consider that as a junior, Arlin won complete games in Omaha by scores of 2-1 and 1-0 in 15 innings.

That's right, a 15-inning complete game.

Of course, what's a 15-inning game when you've already pitched a 16-inning, route-going effort in a must-win over Michigan to help give the Buckeyes their first conference title in a decade?

That's what Arlin did late in the 1965 regular season, retiring 19 of the final 21 Wolverines he faced, while surrendering just four hits over the final nine innings.

"It was the greatest pitching I've ever seen in college," OSU coach Marty Karow said at the time.

Of course, Karow couldn't have known what he'd see out of Arlin the remainder of that year or in the season to follow.

"I was able to pitch a lot of innings because I didn't throw any pitches that really stressed my arm," Arlin said. "I was a fastball-curveball pitcher and I came straight over the top. I didn't have a slider, so I could throw all day. In fact, a lot of times, the longer I was out there, the better I got."

Such was the case against Washington State, when Arlin struck out a College World Series-record 20 batters and pitched out of a bases-loaded, no-out jam in the 13th.

"Dale Ford, who led the nation in home runs that year, led

off with a triple," Arlin said. "They were the home team, so if he scored, we would lose and we were going home. So Marty came to the mound and said, 'Let's load the bases and see if you can get out of this.'"

Arlin walked two hitters intentionally, then induced the next to hit a weak come-backer that worked for a catcher-to-first double play. A strikeout got him out of the inning and set the stage for Chonko's RBI single in the 15th that put the Buckeyes in front.

Arlin then struck out the side in the 15th to advance his team to the title game against unbeaten Arizona State.

Needing two wins over the Sun Devils, OSU got the first when John Durant pitched a complete-game, 7-3 triumph.

Arlin, though, was too spent from his 15-inning effort two nights earlier and couldn't go until the seventh inning, by which time Ohio State faced the 2-1 deficit that would prevail.

"After coming so close that year, we all had the attitude, 'Hey, we're going to get back here and win this thing next season,'" Arlin said.

Sure enough, the Buckeyes made it back to Omaha in 1966 and Arlin was even more spectacular than he had been the year before.

He came on to get the save in the opener, protecting a 4-3 victory over Oklahoma State, then struck out 12 and scattered three hits in a 6-2, complete-game victory over USC the next day.

Karow sent four different pitchers to the mound against St. John's the next afternoon, but none of them could close out the win until Arlin came on in the ninth to save the 8-7 triumph.

That pitted OSU against USC once again, and this time, with Arlin sitting out, the Trojans claimed a 5-1 win to stay alive and force a third game against the Buckeyes in four days.

SC coach Rod Dedeaux tried everything to unnerve Arlin in the soggy conditions that prevailed, stalling and hoping for a rainout when the Buckeyes broke through with a run in the fourth inning.

A two-hour delay was all Dedeaux got until the skies brightened and Arlin, still fresh after his teammates spent the delay rubbing his shoulder, returned to the mound and pitched even more brilliantly than he had three days before.

His two-hit, 12-strikeout effort put the Buckeyes into the title game against Oklahoma State.

A three-run first inning staked OSU to an early lead that grew to 6-0 before the Cowboys could answer, and any thought they had of a comeback went away when Arlin came on to pitch a scoreless ninth and preserve the 8-2 triumph.

Arlin pitched five years in the Major Leagues for the San Diego Padres before an arm injury ended his career.

"Professional baseball was a lot of fun, but we were an expansion team," Arlin said. "I missed the winning attitude of the guys I played with at Ohio State. Those were some really great times."

Arlin was OSU's ace in 1965 and 1966.

Mark
COLEMAN

Making the Most of His Time

College coaching contracts didn't come with signing bonuses when Russ Hellickson agreed to take over the Ohio State wrestling program in 1986.

Hellickson didn't think so, at least, until a couple of weeks into his employment.

That's when he began getting whiffs of a rumor that Mark Coleman was interested in swapping his Miami of Ohio singlet for one in scarlet and gray.

"I'd only been here a short time when I got the indication Mark was interested in transferring here," Hellickson said. "I talked to him and he said, 'I want to be a national champion.' Sometimes when you hear that, the person saying it has no idea what that really entails.

"Mark, though, knew exactly how much work that entailed. He brought a dedication to his training and practice that not only served him, but helped instill that same attitude in our other guys."

Although he had only one season of eligibility remaining when he arrived on campus, Coleman made the most of it in 1988.

His 50-2 record at 190 pounds gave him Ohio State's school record for single-season victories and career winning percentage (.962) and culminated in him winning the 190-pound NCAA championship.

"My goal was always to wrestle at a bigger school," Coleman said. "Coming out of high school, I didn't attract any offers and so I wound up at Miami. Ohio State or Iowa is where I always wanted to be, so when I got the chance to be a Buckeye, I jumped at it, and it's the best thing I ever did."

Coleman was an All-Ohio selection in both football and wrestling at Fremont St. Joseph High School, winning two wrestling titles and finishing second another year.

St. Joe, however, was a tiny Class A school dwarfed by the Class AA and Class AAA competition in the Toledo area, and Coleman fell through the recruiting cracks and remained an undiscovered athletic gem in search of a college.

He wound up at Miami, where he finished 35-5 as a sophomore and then finished fourth in the nation as a junior to raise his profile and gain the chance to pursue bigger dreams.

"Once I made All-American, I was able to make the move," Coleman said. "I had just been biding my time at Miami, waiting to get out of there. Once I got to Ohio State, I was raring to go."

Coleman had to wait a year to satisfy NCAA transfer procedures, which only heightened his hunger for when he could finally take the mat in 1988.

"After he redshirted, Mark was like a man wrestling boys," Hellickson said. "He was very mature as a college senior. There were very few people who could match him physically at 190 pounds.

"He was just a complete wrestler. He's the first guy I've ever had to lead the team in back points, pins, team points, and takedowns. He won every single statistical category. He just dominated everyone."

As far as Coleman had come, he still had one last nemesis from the past to vanquish.

"When I was in high school, the wrestler who got all the notoriety was Mike Davies from Chardon," Coleman said. "Nobody even saw me wrestle at the state meet because they were all watching his match.

"He got all the accolades and wound up at Arizona State. I always wanted to face him, but we never got to wrestle until our senior year in college."

Coleman easily dispatched Davies, 15-1, early in the season at the Midlands Invitational, but the pressure of their NCAA final introduced a new dynamic.

"That's a totally different ballgame when there's a championship on the line," Coleman said. "You have to be able to deal with that pressure. Fortunately I did."

After two scoreless periods, Coleman pulled out a 5-0 decision to take the title he still calls "one of my most memorable athletic experiences."

Coleman's 50 wins in 1988 set an OSU record.

That's saying something, because Coleman went on to win the silver medal at the 1991 world championships, losing a 1-0 heart-breaker in the final.

A year later, Coleman made the United States Olympic team and finished seventh in his weight class at Sarajevo.

After that, he turned to competing in the Ultimate Fighting Championships and was world champion in both 1996 and 2001.

"Those days at Ohio State are still some of my fondest memories," Coleman said. "Winning a national championship was something I had been shooting for all my life. To finally achieve that was the ultimate satisfaction."

Laura DAVIS

An Immediate and Lasting Impact

There was unmistakable symmetry to the Ohio State volleyball career of Laura Davis, which is no surprise considering the grace and balance with which she directed the Buckeyes' two Final Four teams during the early 1990s.

The first of those extended NCAA Tournament runs came in 1991, when Davis was one of three freshman starters for the Buckeyes.

The second Final Four finish came in 1994, when Davis was one of three seniors guiding a lineup that included three freshmen.

"My career definitely had bookends to it," Davis said. "I was the inexperienced freshman starting out and I ended up the senior helping to lead the way, so in that sense it was pretty unique."

Nothing less than the mirrored achievements that marked Davis's era as OSU's setter would have befitted her, for to watch Davis orchestrate the Buckeyes' fast-passing, quick-thinking system was to watch an artist at work.

Her canvas was the court, and her brushstrokes were the unerring passes that totaled an Ohio State-record 5,483 assists en route to crowning Davis the nation's Honda Award-winner as the best collegiate player in America her senior season.

"Laura was a special case," OSU coach Jim Stone said. "She came out of a training program in high school that prepared her for competition much sooner than most college freshmen, and she just got more and more refined with her skills as she matured, until, finally, there was simply no one who was better."

Davis was a hands-down selection as Big Ten freshman of the year in 1991, when she meshed with the Buckeyes' veterans on a team that breezed through the conference with a 20-0 mark.

That, though, wasn't OSU's primary goal.

"I remember after we were 10-0 and halfway through the league, Jim came in and said, 'OK, we've beaten everybody in the Big Ten once, so I expect nothing less from here on.'

"He told us that for the rest of the year, we were going to prepare to play Nebraska, which we knew would be hosting the regional later that season. I thought that was the greatest thing, because we had beaten everybody handily and needed a new focus."

Stone's strategy worked, for Ohio State indeed wound up opposite Nebraska in the Mideast Regional Championship before 11,000 screaming Cornhusker partisans in Lincoln.

Davis and fellow freshmen Carrie Leonard and Gabrielle Jobst were seasoned by then, and didn't crack surrounded by the strong leadership of seniors Leisa Wissler, Julie Chellevold, and Dawn McDougall.

They teamed for a four-game victory over Nebraska, which only earned OSU a duplicate challenge the next week at Final Four host UCLA.

The Bruins swept Ohio State in three games, delaying Davis's national championship dream until the Buckeyes could make another run at the title.

That didn't come immediately, for a third-place finish in the Big Ten and NCAA first-round loss followed the next season and a second-place conference finish and NCAA regional semifinal loss ended Davis's junior year.

"That loss to Long Beach in the tournament really put a bad taste in our mouths," Davis said. "We all felt we should have beaten them and we worked really hard in the off-season to get another shot at them the next year."

That chance indeed came OSU's way after a 19-1, Big Ten championship season in which Davis earned league MVP honors.

The Buckeyes exacted their revenge with a four-game victory over Long Beach on its home floor for the West Regional title, earning another trip to the Final Four.

It was there that Davis was walking down the hall when an opposing player passed her and said, "Congratulations."

"I didn't know what she was talking about," Davis said. "I thought she was saying, 'Nice job for reaching the Final Four.' Then I got back to my room and the phone rang. I answered it and found out I had been selected national player of the year. I couldn't believe it."

Only one setter had ever been accorded that honor before, and no player from a school located east of the Mississippi River had ever been chosen.

"All we did was send in the videos of her performance," Stone said. "The committee saw the same things we had seen out of Laura all season. They saw a great player whose team was always winning."

OSU lost its semifinal match to eventual national champion Stanford to finish 29-3, ending Davis's career with a 104-22 record, including a 70-10 record in Big Ten play.

"Even after we lost to Stanford, one of the committee members came up to me and said, 'We made the right choice,'" Stone said. "That felt good, knowing they had seen Laura play only one time, but that it was obvious she was the best player in the country."

Davis graduated with three of the top four single-season assist averages in OSU history, including the top two, led by her 14.64 mark that senior season.

Off the court, Davis was a four-time OSU scholar athlete and a two-time Academic All-Big Ten pick who culminated her career with selection as the conference's female athlete of the year in 1994.

She later played for the U.S. national team on tours of China, Japan, Brazil, Canada, and Europe.

"Those were great memories, but I put my experiences at Ohio State before all of that," Davis said. "I came to school a very raw talent, but I really became a leader and an all-around player at Ohio State.

"On top of that, I made some of the best friendships of my life and I played in some of the best competition of my life. So when I think back on my career, the matches and the memories I have are of my time at Ohio State."

Davis took OSU to two Final Fours.

Ernie
FERNANDEZ

More Than He Bargained For

Collegiate athletic programs annually welcome an influx of eager recruits, most of whom are convinced they're bound for immediate success and eventual professional riches.

There are just a few like Ernie Fernandez, who despite his modest expectations wound up as one of the most successful tennis players in Ohio State history.

Coming out of San Juan, Puerto Rico in 1979, Fernandez had a resume filled with the impressive credentials common to those who expect their youthful achievements to carry over on the NCAA level.

Fernandez, however, saw himself not only as a small fish in a big pond at Ohio State, but a small fish from a small pond in his native land.

"I came from just a small, little island," Fernandez said. "Sure, I was one of the best players in Puerto Rico, but the competition there wasn't that great and so I didn't have any idea how I would

do at a school like Ohio State. I was just hoping to be able to compete."

Fernandez won the national championship of Puerto Rico in the 18-year-old division when he was a mere 15-year-old.

Players of his ability didn't often pay OSU much attention in those days, given the struggling state of the Buckeyes' program under head coach John Daly, who won just one Big Ten team championship in 28 seasons.

Fernandez, however, was drawn to campus because his friend and tennis idol, Francisco Gonzalez, had played at OSU from 1974-76.

"Franciso and I grew up at the same club," Fernandez said. "He was three or four years older than me. I had all the respect in the world for him. So he played a big part in my decision to attend Ohio State."

Gonzalez made All-American twice in his career, but neither he nor anyone in Big Ten history ever did what Fernandez accomplished.

After taking over as the Buckeyes' No. 1 singles player that season, Fernandez entered the conference tournament with a modest 12-10 record.

That was, however, the last time there would be anything modest about his achievements.

He swept through the draw, upsetting Michigan's Jeff Etterbeek in the finals to become the first freshman ever to win the league's singles crown.

"We used to play no-ad tennis," Fernandez said. "It was 3-3, and I was serving when I hit a volley that Jeff called out. I wasn't sure, so I questioned it. (The chair umpire) overruled and Jeff went nuts. I broke him after that, then I held and won the match.

"I still remember that 30 years later. I wonder, was that ball out or not? I really didn't know, so I questioned it. It was a forehand volley into his backhand. If Jeff had gotten that point, he would have broken my serve and served for the match. It's funny the things you remember."

There would be many more memorable moments the next season, when Fernandez won 22 straight matches to break Gonzalez's OSU record of 20. That streak ended in the Big Ten finals in a three-set loss to Michigan's Mike Leach (6-7, 6-4, 6-7).

Fernandez snapped back from that to win four straight matches at the NCAA Championships, upsetting second-seeded Jay Lapidus of Princeton (6-2, 7-5) en route to an eventual loss to top seed Peter Rennert of Stanford (4-6, 4-6) in the semifinals.

"That success at the NCAAs really opened my eyes," said Fernandez, whose 30-10 record in 1980 set an OSU single-season record for victories "It really made me hungry to work harder and see how good I could get."

The answer? Very good.

As a junior, Fernandez got his revenge on Leach by defeating him for the Big Ten singles title and teaming with Reino Jokinen to win the doubles title, too.

Leach was Fernandez's victim again in the Big Ten singles final their senior season, losing, 6-4 and 6-3 as Fernandez joined Illinois' Thomas O'Connoll (1926-28) and Northwestern's Marty Riessen (1962-64) as the only three-time singles champions in Big Ten history.

That victory elevated him to 32-5 and sent Fernandez back to his third NCAA Tournament, where for the second straight year he lost to Harvard's Howard Sands.

"Sometimes in tennis, you run up against a guy whose style is all wrong for you," Fernandez said. "Sands was that kind of guy to me. He took all the

Fernandez surprised even himself as a Buckeye.

speed off my serve and just frustrated me. It's hard to explain. I just hated playing him."

Fernandez's Big Ten competition no doubt felt the same way about him, given that he was an all-conference pick each of his four seasons and had an OSU-record 109 career singles victories.

Fernandez graduated and headed for a five-year professional career with the top three single-season victory totals in school history, 32 as a senior and 30 as both a sophomore and junior.

Sue
MARCELLUS

Paving the Way For Others

The question still sounds silly to Sue Marcellus, even though she knows it's a reasonable inquiry given where women's collegiate athletics has advanced.

Just how Ohio State lured her out of Somerset, Mass., to put the Buckeyes' field hockey program on the map is a matter that appears difficult to explain, but in fact is painfully easy for Marcellus.

"When I was starting out, Title IX was just beginning to take effect," Marcellus said. "I could have gone to a few places, but Ohio State was offering me a full scholarship. I know I was the first there and among the first in the country to get an opportunity like that. That was extremely new and exciting."

Thanks to pioneers like Marcellus, women's athletics has advanced to where it's now unfathomable that a circumstance could occur like that which introduced her to OSU.

Summer camps and AAU events at every level are crawling with recruiters these days, but in the mid-1970s, that concept was so foreign that Marcellus vividly remembers her first contact with then OSU head coach Harriet Reynolds.

"She was coaching at a camp I attended when I was in high school," said Marcellus, whose 111 goals in high school made her Massachusetts' career scoring leader. "She approached me and had this buckeye in her hand. She asked me if I'd ever heard of Ohio State. I said, 'Sure, I've heard of it.' So then she hands me the buckeye and said, 'I'd like you to consider coming to school here.'

"Then she handed me a note with her name and number on it. I hung onto that piece of paper for six hours on the way home. I couldn't wait to show it to my parents."

When Marcellus arrived at OSU in the fall of 1976, the Buckeyes weren't even the dominant field hockey power in Ohio.

That changed immediately thanks to her high-scoring talents honed on the ice hockey rink her father built every winter into the family's back yard.

"My brothers and I played hockey all the time," Marcellus said. "We were on the pond or in the house, playing hockey constantly. It's hard to describe what that's like, but that's how life is (in New England). You just play hockey all the time.

"I played field hockey like I was playing ice hockey. People used to say, 'You look like you're skating out there.' To me, I guess I was. When I first started playing (field hockey), I thought you were supposed to use both sides of the stick like in ice hockey."

Marcellus's shot, learned from an uncle who played professional hockey in Canada, made her an instant sensation with 36 goals as a freshman.

That instantly took OSU to levels it had never reached before, not only as state champion for the first time, but as regional champion and qualifier in the AIAW national tournament.

Marcellus was so dominant that she scored more goals than the rest of her teammates combined. They managed 31, combining with her 36 to give the Buckeyes 67 for the season, which remains the school's single-season record.

"I could put the ball in the net," Marcellus said. "I don't know where I got that talent, probably because of all the shooting my brothers and I did on the ice. I loved to shoot. I played all the time with the boys and then there were a lot of times where I went down to the pond in my figure skates and just shot."

Marcellus's freshman season foreshadowed a stellar OSU career in which she would break her single-season goal record with 40 in 1978 and make first-team All-American each of her final three years.

Her 117 career goals remain the school record, as do her 254 career points, which ranked second in NCAA history when she graduated and still ranks seventh on the all-time Division I list.

Marcellus played for the United States National Team throughout her Ohio State career and was its top offensive threat, leading a climb through various international tournaments that landed Team USA a berth in the 1980 Olympics.

Marcellus still holds most OSU records.

She played before 66,000 in Wembley Stadium in England on one tour, but never got the chance to compete for a gold medal because of the United States' boycott of the 1980 Moscow Games during the Soviet Union's invasion of Afghanistan.

"I think I still carry the disappointment of that every day," Marcellus said. "This past Winter Olympics was the first time I could watch since 1980. Always before, I'd try to sit through it and there would just be a lot of tears and anger. It feels very unfinished to me."

Marcellus has no such regrets about her time at Ohio State.

"I was so grateful to Harriet for giving me the opportunity," Marcellus said. "I had access to so many options that people at other schools didn't have. Even now, when I say I went to Ohio State, people look at me like, 'Wow.' It's an honor to have worn those colors, walked on that campus and to have been in those buildings.

"If you were going to be a jock, there was just no better place to do that than Ohio State. That's something no one can take away from me. I've worn that uniform, and I feel like I was supposed to do that. I would have missed all that if I had gone to an Eastern school."

Paul POOLEY

Brother, Can You Spare a Goal?

Paul and Perry Pooley weren't the type of twins who couldn't wait to get away from each other.

If they were, Ohio State would never have known Paul existed and would only have missed out on the greatest player in the school's hockey history.

The Buckeyes' leader in career points (269), goals (114), and assists (155), Paul was the unknown Pooley to OSU coach Jerry Welsh when he showed up at Perry's game in the Canadian Juniors in 1980.

"They started looking at Perry first," Paul said. "That's when Perry indicated he had a brother playing on a different team that they might want to take a look at. That's how Ohio State got interested in me."

So interested, in fact, that when Welsh got down to only one remaining scholarship, the Pooley brother he offered it to was Paul.

"When I signed my letter-of-intent, I said to Jerry, 'Is it OK if Perry comes, too?'" Paul said.

"That's how it all came together. We never really planned on playing together in college. It wasn't a package deal or anything. It's just how it worked out."

Perry earned a scholarship of his own by his sophomore season, and together the brothers Pooley set about revitalizing the the Buckeyes' fortunes.

Paul had 28 goals and 32 assists as a freshman, made second-team Central Collegiate Hockey Association, and was the CCHA's co-newcomer-of-the-year.

Not bad for a guy who before his first collegiate game looked at a teammate in the locker room and said, "Do you have any idea what to expect out there?"

"I had never seen a college game before," Paul said. "I had no idea what college hockey was all about. I had played at a pretty high level in the Canadian Juniors, but I had no idea how I was going to be able to do at Ohio State."

Paul's path to OSU started as a youth player in Exeter, Ontario,

then he moved away from home while in high school to play at the Major Junior level with the Kitchener Rangers.

"Jerry Welsh actually came to scout me when we were playing a tournament in Providence," Paul said. "I didn't play very well, so I told our general manager to call Ohio State and say I was coming off exams, that we were out of the playoffs, in other words, make a lot of excuses."

Once he became a Buckeye, it was opposing defensemen who found themselves making excuses for his high-scoring success.

Paul totalled 21 goals as a sophomore and 33 as a junior, when the Buckeyes improved from a 16-17-1 season in 1982 to go 26-9-5 and set a single-season school record for victories.

That foreshadowed a surprising rise to No. 1 in the polls early in his senior year.

"We really got off to a great start," Paul said. "We won our first 13 games, then we lost three in a row, but we got it together and wound up having a really nice season. There was a lot of excitement about the program in those days."

Pooley set single-season marks with 96 points and 64 assists in 1984, leading the nation in scoring.

Ironically, he didn't lead the Buckeyes in goals. He had 32, while Perry scored 39.

"That was a really a great way for both of us to go out," Paul said. "There's no doubt about the fact that Ohio State was great to the Pooley family. We never played on the same line in our years at Ohio State, but playing on the same team was great."

Paul earned first-team All-America honors his final season, was the CCHA's player of the year, the Bauer national player of the year, and Hobey Baker Award finalist. Perry earned second-team All-American and second-team CCHA and joined his brother as a first-team Academic All-American.

Paul signed with the NHL's Winnipeg Jets and played two seasons in the American Hockey League, where he played on a Calder Cup Championship team in 1985. In 1986, he moved on to Fort Wayne and the International Hockey League, serving as co-captain and learing the Komets to the regular season title.

Paul played in 15 NHL games before retiring and starting a business with his brother.

He served as a volunteer coach at OSU in the late-1980s, eventually joined the staff full-time, and then took a job as an assistant at Lake Superior State University before becoming the head coach at Providence College in 1994.

Pooley (right) accepts his OSU Hall of Fame award from athletic director Andy Geiger.

Kevin RANDLEMAN

The Eye of the Tiger

Kevin Randleman won 108 matches in his three seasons as an Ohio State wrestler.

Some, after the referee blew his whistle.

Most of the time, even though the scoreboard read, 0-0, Randleman had his opponent at an insurmountable disadvantage before the clock began counting down the first period.

"I never saw anyone intimidate more guys before a match started than Kevin Randleman," said Mark Coleman, an OSU assistant coach and Randleman's training partner during his career. "He absolutely had most guys he wrestled scared out of their minds."

Randleman was the Buckeyes' first two-time national champion, winning titles at 177 pounds in 1992 and 1993 after finishing second at 167 pounds at the NCAA championships as a redshirt freshman in 1991.

No other OSU wrestler had previously reached the national

finals three times, nor had anyone won three Big Ten titles.

Randleman set those standards with an array of skills that, combined with his chiseled features and intimidating warm-up tactics, worked for a career record of 108-7-3.

"Kevin was one of those elite athletes that rarely come along," Ohio State coach Russ Hellickson said. "When you talk about guys who are great in any sport, in some capacity, they are a freak. They are beyond what anybody else brings to the table. That was Kevin.

"Before a match started, he would go out on the mat, squat down, jump up in the air two or three times and kick his legs up behind him. His height off the ground was incredible.

"Then he'd get down in a low squat and put his hands on the mat, like he was an animal ready to pounce. Well, that just totally intimidated most of his opponents. He was plain scary."

Randleman resorted to such tactics not just to loosen up, but to gain an advantage.

"Whatever you're doing in athletics, you're seeking to get an edge on someone," he said. "If there are four or five guys in a weight class and they are even, the winner is going to be the guy who can distinguish himself from the others in some fashion. For me, a way to do that was to use my physical skills to psyche the other guy out.

"If a guy saw me across the mat before we started and I was doing back flips, jumping nine feet in the air, punching the wall, doing the splits, it played with his mind. Sometimes it might have even tired me out to do that stuff, but I know it ultimately worked to my advantage."

Randleman went 42-6 as an OSU freshman after redshirting on the heels of a state champion-ship season his final year at Sandusky High School.

That was his only prep title, causing Randleman to slip beneath the radar screen on some coaches' recruiting lists.

"There were a lot of disbelievers," Hellickson said. "I remember people asked me who we had coming in that year. I told them I had Kevin Randleman of Sandusky. They said, 'What's he done?' I told them, 'It's not a matter of what he's done; it's a matter of what he's going to do.'

". . .Some of the moves we have of him on video are amazing. It seems impossible for a human to do some of the things he did with the thrust and power of his leg drive, but you're talking about a guy who could squat close to 600 or 700 pounds."

Randleman found a mentor in Coleman, who also had modest high school success relative to the 50-2 mark and 190-pound national championship he compiled in his only season with the Buckeyes in 1988.

"It was an honor to coach him," Coleman said. "Kevin Randleman was one of the God-given, blessed athletes I've ever seen. But the thing about him that made him special was, he made the most of those talents by working harder than anyone else.

"He'd psyche you out just to look at him. He was like a Greek god with that body of his, and then the things he could do athletically, well, it was just amazing. People talk about the stuff they saw him do in matches, but I saw him do some incredible things in the practice room to prepare himself to be a two-time national champion and a one-time runner-up."

Randleman's work ethic and determination helped him overcome a series of injuries that would have discouraged lesser competitors.

He won his first national title with a broken wrist suffered in practice, and won his second with a torn knee ligament.

Randleman also broke his jaw as a junior, which brought him to a breaking point.

"Life for me was hard growing up," Randleman said. "Wrestling gave me an identity, but it also brought a lot of pressure. I had to get up to meet that pressure head-on every day.

"I had a kid when I was young and there was a lot of sickness in my family with my mom and my dad. My family and friends always counted on me for strength. When you give so much of yourself like that, you sometimes spread yourself too thin.

"That's what happened to me. I didn't leave anything for myself, and eventually I got to where I just couldn't deal with that pressure any more. I had to walk away from wrestling."

Randleman told Hellickson of those plans after winning a second national championship in 1993, but the coach found it hard to believe.

"He said, 'Oh, you'll be back,'" Randleman said. "But I knew I was done. I couldn't do it any more. Eventually, I just stopped going to class and that's how I wound up ineligible for my senior year."

Despite that, Randleman was still voted Ohio State's wrester of the century by The Columbus Touchdown Club.

"That meant the world to me," said Randleman, who is now one of the top competitors in Ultimate Fighting Championships. "I don't feel I deserved it, because I didn't finish my career. The measure of a man is the one who stays in it until the end. I regret that I didn't do that. I get emotional thinking about it. Being honored like that, in spite of it, that means the world to me."

Randleman is OSU's only two-time NCAA champion.

Janelle BOSSE

Thank Goodness for Ornery Brothers

When they say swimmers are born, not made, the truth in that axiom often has as much to do with the car pool as it does the gene pool.

While heredity no doubt assists in any champion's career, the seeds of their success are often sewn in childhood, when mom packs the kids into the family van for daily trips to the local swim club.

That's how Janelle Bosse began her rise to an Ohio State career in which she achieved All-American honors four times, won an NCAA championship in the 400 individual medley in 1987 and claimed 10 Big Ten individual or relay titles from 1985-1988.

Bosse, though, wasn't a natural who took to her sport without prodding or pleading.

She was–initially, at least–more of a fish out of water. Then her brothers intervened.

"My two oldest brothers were coaching in a summer club meet at the pool where we belonged," Bosse said. "They needed a fourth person for the eight-and-under relay, but I was one of those nightmare little kids who just held onto the wall. I had taken swimming lessons and learned how, but I didn't really like the water. I still remember crying as they came and pulled me off the wall and threw me into that race."

Had Bosse's mother come to her rescue that day, her little girl might never have become one of the most versatile swimmers to compete at OSU.

And had Bosse's mother not come to the rescue years later, Bosse wouldn't have become a Buckeye at all.

"I really owe Janelle's mom for getting her to Ohio State," Ohio State coach Jim Montrella said. "We had seen Janelle swim in high school and wanted her badly, but we couldn't seem to get her interested in coming to OSU. Her mom talked her into making a visit, so every time Janelle won a race for us, I used to think about how I owed her mother a thank you for that."

Montrella would have given himself writer's cramp had he penned notes of gratitude for each victory Bosse gained, starting with an incredible performance at the Big Ten championships her freshman year.

She won the 200 and 400 individual medleys, the 500 freestyle, the 200 butterfly, and anchored the winning 800 freestyle relay team to help the Buckeyes win the conference championship.

"I'd swam the 500 free in high school, but it was never one of my main events," Bosse said. "I was really surprised Jim even put me in the 500 free. I went head-to-head with a girl from Indiana and just out-touched her. When I looked up and saw the time, I said, 'You've got to be kidding me.'"

Bosse's triumph was no joke, but it was a fluke of sorts, since she never again swam the 500 free at the conference level.

She defended her title in the 200 butterfly as a sophomore, got out-touched for first in the 200 IM, won the 400 IM a second time, and led off the winning 400 medley relay to get OSU another conference championship.

"Janelle did everything we ever asked her to do," Montrella said. "She was very talented with all of her strokes at intermediate distances, so she gave us a lot of versatility. We could sit back and assess the field and decide where we needed her the most. The great thing was, she was always willing to do whatever she could to help the team."

A rule change Bosse's junior year limited swimmers to three events, instead of the four individual races she swam as a freshman and sophomore. That hurt OSU in the team standings, but couldn't keep Bosse from sweeping both the 200 and 400 IM titles both of her final two seasons.

As a junior, Bosse won the 400 IM at the NCAA meet to become Ohio State's first national champion in women's swimming.

She finished second in that event as a senior, then retired from her sport following the NCAA's in March of 1988, some six months before the U.S. Olympic Trials for the Summer Games in Seoul.

"At that point, I felt like I had fulfilled all my dreams in swimming," Bosse said. "The trials were still six months away and I didn't really believe I could make it. They took only two in each event, and at that time, Janet Evans was sort of the Michael Jordan of the IM.

"That left basically one spot open, and my lifetime best in each event was the fourth- or fifth-fastest time in the country. If I could turn the clock back now, I probably would give it a shot, but I was happy with my decision at the time, so I don't have any major regrets."

While Bosse doesn't have a gold medal, she does have something as precious in its own way.

"I still have that first blue ribbon from that eight-and-under relay," she said. "I kept it all those years. That's what started it all."

Bosse won OSU's first national title in women's swimming.

Bob
CLOTWORTHY

If You Wanna Beat 'Em, Join 'Em

Robert Clotworthy had enough success as a high school diver to feed a desire to win a gold medal.

That's how the Westfield, N.J., native wound up at Ohio State, figuring that if he some day wanted to make the United States Olympic diving team, he'd be wise to join it as a college freshman.

"If you wanted to be a great diver in those days, the only place to be was Ohio State," Clotworthy said. "I went there in the fall of 1949, and already on the team was Bruce Harlan, who was the defending Olympic champion; Miller Anderson, who had graduated, but had won a silver medal; Joe Marino, who ended up a national champion; Jack Calhoun, who made the Olympic team in 1952; and Hobie Billingsley, who was a national champion. Ohio State was the only place to be."

Clotworthy would soon forge a legacy of his own on par with that illustrious list of OSU champions who performed under the tutelage of the legendary Mike Peppe.

Clotworthy couldn't have done so without a stiff drive to excel, however, because his status on the team as a freshman hardly foretold certain future success.

"I was an OK high school diver," Clotworthy said. "I'd been a state champion and an Eastern champion, but when I got to Ohio State, I was No. 10 on the team my first year.

"I hadn't been able to dive that much in high school because of a lack of opportunity. I could only work out about three hours a week at a YMCA pool.

"When I got to Ohio State, that changed. I could dive three hours a day. I was introduced to the trampoline. I'd never been on a trampoline before, and that's one of the most valuable pieces of equipment there is in a diver's development.

"Now, I was still on a team with nine guys who were better than me, so you either make it or

you don't make it. It just so happened that by the time I was a sophomore, I was pretty good, partly because I improved and partly because of the natural attrition of guys graduating. But pretty soon, I was one of those guys that the other divers were shooting at."

Clotworthy was a three-time All-American from 1951-53, winning the Big Ten championship in the one- and three-meter events as a sophomore.

He placed third in the NCAA in the three-meter that year and second in the AAU national championships to kick-start a career in which he would win five conference titles, five AAU titles, and the 1953 NCAA championship in the three-meter springboard.

Greatness is diving, however, is confirmed in the Olympics, and Clotworthy's resume isn't lacking in that area.

In the 1952 Summer Games in Helsinki, he took the bronze in

Bob Clotworthy (right) with his 1952 bronze medal.

the three-meter behind Skippy Benning of Texas and Anderson, a fellow Buckeye.

"I was absolutely thrilled with third place, because, frankly, I was the third-best guy on our team," Clotworthy said. "That meant we swept the event, which just made me ecstatic."

Four years later in Melbourne, Clotworthy returned to the springboard competition under much different circumstances.

"I was the favorite, and as the favorite, there was much greater pressure," he said. "In the NCAA, if you don't win it one year, you can always do it the next year. The Olympics don't offer that luxury.

"Number one, it's so difficult in this country just to make the team. Once you do that, then you get to the Games, and you know it's your one chance in four years to win a gold medal. The pressure is immense.

"I had gotten to the point in national championship meets where I could be fairly relaxed. The Olympics is another story. It really took a tremen-

dous effort in self control to stay emotionally stable, because you can very easily let your emotions run away with you."

Clotworthy withstood the burden and won the gold to author a fitting climax to his career.

"It was great to have that kind of success in the Olympic Games, just like it was a great thrill to be a part of those teams at Ohio State," he said. "We won the NCAA team championship in 1952, won the Big Ten all three years, that was just a wonderful time in my life.

"I have a picture that someone took in Helsinki, a picture of the Ohio State guys and Mike Peppe, who was the United States' diving coach that year.

"There were nine Ohio State swimmers and divers on that 1952 Olympic team. It was the most incredible experience to go to school there and be involved with all those great athletes. It was just a thrill. I loved it from the day I walked onto the campus until this present day. It was simply wonderful."

Bruce
HARLAN

Tragedy Takes an Artist

Fate can be a cruel author, sometimes scripting numbing finality to a life that's shown no susceptibility to the mortality that stalks us all.

When athletes die before their time, the tragedy is doubly damaging to our perspective, because we see them as more full of life than the average man or woman.

Running faster, jumping higher, moving with more athleticism and elegance than we can muster even in our dreams, the elite athlete who passes this life in his or her prime is a tragic circumstance with which we cannot easily cope.

Hence the shock one awful summer day in 1959 when the news filtered to Columbus from Norwalk, Conn., that 1948 Olympic gold medalist Bruce Harlan was dead from a fall at a diving exhibition.

The news was incomprehensible, for it seemed to those who knew him that there had never

been a more fearless, artful or accomplished man in the air than Harlan.

He swept to Big Ten, NCAA, and national AAU titles at OSU with regularity and ease, and then transferred that success onto the protégés he coached at the University of Michigan with such success that Harlan seemed destined to carve his own lengthy resume in the considerable shadow of his former Ohio State coach, Mike Peppe.

Peppe's OSU teams dominated NCAA swimming and diving during that era, in no small part because of Harlan.

He was a four-time All-American for the Buckeyes from 1947-50 at a time when freshmen were eligible to compete because of the United States' involvement in the Korean Conflict.

Harlan, though, was no ordinary freshman, having already served with the U.S. Navy in World War II, where Columbus native Jack Smith introduced him to diving.

OSU won three NCAA team championships during Harlan's career, and he greatly contributed to that effort with three individual titles in the one-meter from 1948-50 and two in the three-meter in 1949-50.

Harlan also won five Big Ten titles and eight AAU titles amid a career in which the unquestioned highlight was his performance at the 1948 Olympic Games in London, the first Olympics since 1936.

Harlan came home with a gold medal in the springboard ahead of OSU teammate Miller Anderson and a silver in the platform competition behind USA teammate Sammy Lee.

"The amazing thing about Bruce was, he hadn't started diving until he was in the Navy," said Robert Clotworthy, a freshman at OSU during Harlan's senior year and an Olympic gold-medalist in 1956. "He was a wrestler who came out of Lansdowne, Pennsylvania.

"He got started just playing around with diving and ended up the most perfect diver I had ever seen in terms of technique. He really reached a high state of perfection."

Harlan didn't limit his exploits to the pool, however.

He lettered for the Ohio State gymnastics team in 1949 and 1950 and also was a pole-vaulter for the Buckeyes' track team.

"He competed in both diving and gymnastics at the same time in the winter season," Clotworthy said. "There were times he would go upstairs and do a tumbling routine, then come down and do something for our diving team. He was just a marvelous, marvelous athlete."

Harlan was also rare in that he was able to transfer his gifts to those he coached.

Very often, the extremely gifted cannot mine similar perfection from their protégés, but four years after leaving OSU, Harlan gained the job as the diving coach at Michigan and began prodding the Wolverines to excellence on the board.

His prized recruit, Richard Kimball, became the first Michigan diver in 20 years to win both the one- and three-meter events in 1957, the same year the Wolverines won the first of their three team championships under Harlan.

"Our coach was an OSU diver, so it spurred a rivalry," Kimball said. "We stole a lot of recruits from Ohio."

That wasn't all Harlan stole from Ohio. His wife, Francis, was a graduate of Columbus North High School.

They were married in 1948, shortly after his gold-medal performance in London, and had two children, Laura and Freddy.

Both children were with their parents that fateful day in Connecticut, when Harlan and former OSU teammate Hobart Billingsley completed a diving exhibition at the Fairfield Country Club.

Harlan was not only a skillful competitive diver, he also had a flair for the comedic entertainment his art could provide.

He sometimes wore a brightly-colored suit of Gay Nineties vintage and an inside-out sailor's hat while feigning a pratfall into the water, landing smack on the water's surface in apparently-painful fashion.

The crowds' plaintive gasps would turn to sighs of relief and bursts of applause when Harlan sprang from the water, none the worse for wear.

He and Billingsley, who went on to become the diving coach at Indiana University, incorporated a carpenter's scaffolding into their act.

They used that apparatus as a base for a trampoline that added another element of risk to their stunts.

It was in the aftermath of their show, while Harlan was dismantling the scaffolding, that he fell headfirst from the 27-foot-high structure and landed on the pool's edge.

He died the following day, leaving the Michigan program he was in the midst of building to his protégé, Kimball.

Kimball bypassed the remainder of a promising amateur career to take on the task begun by his mentor and remained as the head coach of the Wolverines for the next 43 years, retiring following the 2002 season having coached nine Olympic medalists and won five NCAA and 33 Big Ten championships.

Harlan helped OSU win there NCAA team titles.

Ford KONNO

The Hawaiian Pipeline Strikes Again

He was nine years old on the most famous-make that infamous-day of the 20th century.

Sitting high in a mango tree, peering off into the Sunday morning sunshine, Ford Konno saw black smoke climbing on the Honolulu horizon and began hearing the clatter of artillery shells fall around him.

Life would never be the same after that attack on Pearl Harbor, particularly not for Japanese Americans like Konno.

As a native-born U.S. citizen, he and his family avoided the Japanese internment camps that arose after the onset of World War II, although questions about his heritage often arose.

"I didn't experience much prejudice when I went to school," Konno said. "People probably talked behind my back, but I didn't hear a lot of it. I did get asked a lot—not by swimmers, just regular people—'What are you? Are you Hawaiian?'

"I would say, my nationality is Japanese, but I am an American."

If anyone doubted Konno's allegiance, those doubts faded watching the ardor with which he swam for his country in the 1952 Olympics at the midpoint of his Ohio State athletic career.

Konno won an individual gold medal in the 1,500-meter freestyle at those Helsinki games, won another gold on the United States' 800-meter freestyle relay team and took silver in the 400-meter freestyle.

That success came despite a debilitating sinus infection that struck him in advance of the U.S. Olympic Trials in Flushing Meadow, N.Y.

"I had dropped out of Ohio State for the spring quarter and returned to Hawaii to train," Konno said. "There were only two pools in Honolulu that were 50 meters or longer, and the one closest to me was a salt-water pool in Waikiki.

"I was training there, because the other pool was at an Army base far out in the country.

Everything was going fine until I got a sinus inflammation. I don't know, maybe it was the salt water. But I couldn't swim for a couple of weeks while I got treatment and I lost a lot of strength."

So much that Konno, who would set 10 world and American records in his career from 200-1,500 meters, nearly didn't qualify for Team USA.

"I barely made it by finishing third in the 1,500 and was second in the 400," Konno said. "I was only able to train for a few days and I was very weak. Then we had to leave for Helsinki and the Olympics were starting a week later, so I didn't know how I was going to do. Fortunately, I hit my peak just in time."

Konno's winning 1,500 time of 18:30.3 established a new Olympic record, as did the 800-meter relay team's 8:31.1.

In the 400-meter freestyle, Konno missed the gold by just sixth-tenths of a second, bettering the former Olympic record in the process.

Konno returned to Ohio State following the games and completed a career in which he won 31 major titles, including nine Big Ten championships, 16 AAU championships and six NCAA championships.

"One of the main reasons I chose Ohio State was because of Mike Peppe," Konno said of the Buckeyes' legendary swimming and diving coach. "He had gotten several swimmers from Hawaii to compete there, going all the way back to Keo Nakama in the early 1940s.

"After that, there were many others, like Bill Smith, Halo Hirose, myself, Yoshi Oyakawa—all of them were there in part because of Mike Peppe's reputation as a great coach. I personally did not meet him until I went to Ohio State, but I heard about him enough to know that I wanted to go there instead of the many other places where I had scholarship offers."

Olympic training cost Konno his 1953 collegiate season, but that was the only year from 1952-55 that he didn't win both the 500- and 1,500-meter freestyle at the NCAA meet.

In 1956, Konno returned to Olympic competition and won the silver as a member of the United States' 800-meter freestyle relay team.

That gave him two golds and two silvers for his Olympic career, totals that no doubt would have been greater had the Games in those days staged freestyle competition at 50, 100, and 200 meters, as is now the case.

"Standing on the podium after winning the gold medal, when I heard the national anthem, it sent goose pimples throughout my body," Konno said. "I was very proud to represent the United States. Call it patriotism or whatever, I was just very proud.

"When I came back home, I was interviewed by a reporter from the Honolulu newspaper and he asked me, 'Aren't you proud to have represented Hawaii at the Olympic Games?'

"I said, 'Yes, of course, but I am prouder that I represented the United States.' That is how I looked at it. I represented not just the 500,000 people in Hawaii, but the 200 million in the United States."

Konno's willingness to share his Olympic experience with others has cost him possession of both his gold medals.

"I used to loan them out to high schools and swim clubs," he said. "They kept going from one to another and finally, I don't know where they went. No one returned them to me."

Konno won 31 major titles, including nine Big Ten championships in his career at OSU.

Karen LaFACE

A Natural in Every Way

Karen LaFace's career as an Ohio State diver and scholar athlete left a juicy issue for future generations to debate.

As a two-time Big Ten diver of the year and a three-time All-American, LaFace unquestionably ranks among the finest female competitors in her sport's history at OSU.

As a member of the dean's list every academic quarter of her enrollment, LaFace also rates with the most accomplished student-athletes to compete for the scarlet and gray.

So, was LaFace a better student than she was an athlete or vice versa?

"I never looked at it like one was more important than another," LaFace said. "I just tried to apply myself the best I could when I was at practice and then do the same in the classroom. Things worked out for me pretty well in both areas."

Given a double-major in economics and chemistry, degrees that later led to LaFace completing medical school and becoming a doctor, and given that she also competed on the U.S. Olympic diving team in the Barcelona Summer Games in 1992, LaFace indeed made the most of her years as a Buckeye.

"Winning the female athlete of the year at Ohio State in 1987 was probably the highlight for me at OSU," LaFace said. "To be recognized over all the other great female athletes at the school at that time was very special."

LaFace earned her second Big Ten diver of the year honor that season and followed it with a victory in the NCAA Championships on the three-meter platform.

She had the lead in the one-meter springboard competition until the final dive, but was overtaken by teammate Kim Fugett and wound up finishing third.

"I really did have an absolutely wonderful junior year," LaFace said. "Winning the Big Tens and doing well at the NCAA was such a thrill. That entire season, I just felt like I was 'on' almost the entire time.

"I was doing relaxation drills and visualization drills that really helped me do so well. Standing on the podium as an NCAA champion was just fantastic."

LaFace missed out on that opportunity after winning Big Ten diver-of-the-year honors as a freshman, even though she competed with a painful hand injury.

"I hurt it before the conference meet while competing on the 10-meter platform," she said. "I had my hands together just before hitting the water, but I lost my grip and bent my thumb backward when I hit the pool.

"The doctor taped it up real good before the Big Ten and I wore a rubber cast. After that meet, the surgeon took a look at it and decided things were pretty shredded in there and it might be best if I didn't compete in the NCAAs."

LaFace was disappointed with that development, but she had enough success from the instant she took up diving to be certain that future chances for national recognition would come her way.

"I started doing all sorts of sports when I was really little," said LaFace, who grew up in Pittsburgh. "I had two sisters and a brother, and we were always running around doing something–swimming, ballet, gymnastics.

"When I was eight or nine, we belonged to a summer swim club, and I got to fool around on the diving board. That's when the pool manager told me about a diving team that they had at the University of Pittsburgh.

"I went and tried out and made the team. I remember my first meet, getting second place and being very excited about it. Before too long, I was doing well in regional and national competitions, then I went to my first international meet when I was 13. That's the sort of stuff that really got me hooked."

LaFace moved to Austin, Texas, for her senior year of high school and then chose OSU because of its strong diving program and its pre-med curriculum.

She won the conference title in the one-meter and finished second in the three-meter as a freshman in 1985 to win diver-of-the-year honors and foreshadow the success that would continue throughout her collegiate career.

LaFace also competed internationally while at OSU, winning a bronze medal in the 1987 World University Games.

Four years later, following her graduation, she took home the gold from the Pan-American Games in Havana in advance of making the U.S. Olympic team in 1992.

She placed ninth in the three-meter springboard competition in Barcelona.

"I had been to the Pan-Am Games, the Sports Festival and the World University Games, but the Olympics was on a much grander scale than any of those," LaFace said. "The number of athletes was just amazing. The athletes' village was huge and there was always something going on.

"I think I was just too nervous for my own good that meet. I had always been very relaxed in international competition, but I wasn't able to completely let myself go at the Olympics. I didn't do as well as I would have liked, but the experience was unforgettable."

LaFace retired three weeks after the Games and entered medical school at the University of Pittsburgh.

She graduated three years later and performed her residency at Brown University before settling in Ithaca, N.Y., where she combined her career in family practice with a brief stint as the diving coach at Ithaca College.

LaFace was OSU's 1987 female athlete of the year.

Kelly McCORMICK

Like Falling Off a Log Backwards

She had the pedigree, the talent and every other conceivable advantage to cover herself in diving success.

There was only one thing Kelly McCormick lacked initially.

The desire.

With a four-time Olympic champion for a mother and a father who was the coach behind that dominance, McCormick wasn't born with a silver spoon in her mouth as much as she was born with a gold medal in her future.

And that was exactly the problem.

"Growing up, it was diving, diving, diving, and I got sick of it," she said. "I didn't want anything to do with diving. I liked gymnastics better, and so that's what I wanted to be—an Olympic gymnast."

A little girl's dreams sometimes give way to a young woman's pragmatism. But in McCormick's case, like most 14-year-old Southern California girls, she just wanted to play on the beach.

"I started to just get sick of being in the gym all the time, because I liked to water ski and I really liked different water sports," she said. "So, one day I was at the pool and I started playing around on the board, and I found out it was really, really easy compared to gymnastics.

"It's all the same technique, basically. That's the first time I really tried diving, and I was pretty good at it. Then I was hooked."

It might seem easy to fill in the blanks from there, but McCormick's ascent to Olympic success, election to the International Swimming Hall of Fame, and a two-time All-American career at Ohio State didn't fall into place that easily.

It's one thing to be blessed with natural ability as a little girl, it's quite another to willingly and willfully push the envelope of that ability to its outer reaches and mine worldwide acclaim as an elite athlete.

McCormick found that necessary drive when she found a coach in Vince Panzano.

"I went to Sweden for an international meet and met him there," McCormick said. "I had been to the University of Miami, and that didn't work out. Then I came home and was supposed to go to Long Beach State, but I never really went. Then I met Vince, and I just knew. I was at Ohio State two weeks later and stayed for nine years."

During that span, from 1981 until McCormick's retirement in 1990, she won the Big Ten title in both the one- and three-meter springboard in 1982 and 1983, won gold in the three-meter at the 1983 and 1987 Pan-Am Games, and won nine U.S. championships.

"I just found the right coach to challenge me," she said. "I had a bit of a wild young life. I didn't come from the best of family homes, because my parents were divorced. Vince helped me to really grow up into who I am today. He knew I liked winning. Once he got me to Ohio State, he was able to make me realize that if I put my sweat into diving, I could be good at it."

Panzano's motivation was never more crucial than prior to the XXII Olympiad in Los Angeles in 1984.

Reporters saw a tailor-made story in McCormick coming home to dive for gold in the tradition established by her mother, Pat, who swept the springboard and platform competition in both the 1952 and 1956 Games.

Kelly's father, Glenn–both her first coach and Pat's–was a judge of the diving competition that summer, although not for his daughter.

The script, however, seemed to be coming apart when Kelly was hospitalized six weeks before the Olympic Trials that summer.

"I went to all kinds of doctors and no one could figure out what was wrong," she said. "They finally said it was a dislocated rib and put me in traction for a week. I got really weak from it, and then when I came back and started working out again, I just wasn't making it.

"I wanted to quit. I was giving up . . . actually giving up. I was just sick of being in pain and I was very frustrated. But then Vince came over to my house and said, 'What are you going to say, that you could have or you would have. . .?'

"He got me all pumped up to where I was like, 'To heck with it. I'm going all out.'"

Panzano played his pupil psychologically because he was convinced her only problems were mental.

"We had certain standards on the team, and people who didn't live up to them could either take a walk or shape up," Panzano said. "Kelly wasn't even living up to her own standards. I had talked to the doctors and they said training certainly wouldn't hurt her physically."

Once on the board in Los Angeles, McCormick was clear-headed and pursued the gold medal to the final dive, only to come up 3.24 points shy of Canadian Sylvie Bernier.

Four years later in Seoul, McCormick added a bronze medal in the springboard to her collection, despite training cut short by a spate of pre-Olympic injuries.

"My medals are in a jewelry box upstairs," said McCormick, who today coaches diving in Seattle, where she lives with her husband and three children. "I have some of my national medals in there, too, but not all of them. They all mean something to me, but I don't want my kids thinking that's all there is to life. That's sort of how it was when I was growing up."

McCormick remained at OSU to train for the Olympics.

Yoshi OYAKAWA

A Change That Led To Gold

In a career that landed him 23 major championships as an Ohio State swimmer and an Olympic gold medal at the 1952 Summer Games in Helsinki, Yoshi Oyakawa cut through the water in precision fashion an infinite number of times as the world's premier straight-arm back-stroker.

The best single stroke of his career, however, came as a 16-year-old competitive neophyte on his home island of Hilo in Hawaii.

Having started organized swimming just a year earlier, Oyakawa was already distinguishing himself as a freestyler of note when his coach got wind of another phenom on an adjoining island who was also showing outstanding promise.

Years later, Oyakawa and the rival of his youth would look back fondly on that convergence of their careers, wondering how things might have worked out differently had Oyakawa not flipped over onto his back and left the freestyle to his future Ohio

State and Olympic teammate, Ford Konno.

"Ford and I were the same age," Oyakawa said. "He was doing so well in the freestyle that I thought, well, maybe I ought to try another stroke. That was really a stroke of genius on my part."

Oyakawa's choice wasn't born out of desperation, for he and Konno never raced against each other.

"I started swimming competitively at the end of my freshman year in 1949, but my high school didn't have a swim team until I was a junior," Oyakawa said. "Ford went to school at McKinley High in Honolulu. My junior year, his team came over to our island and that's when my coach suggested I try the backstroke.

"I had been pretty fast in the shorter freestyle races. In fact, I made several of the relays when I was at Ohio State, and I think I had a faster time than Ford in the 100 free."

Konno owned the longer distances like Oyakawa owned

both the 100 and 200 back, giving OSU virtually automatic wins in those races every meet.

The Buckeyes won NCAA team championships three of the Hawaiian duo's four seasons on campus.

Oyakawa won the NCAA 200-yard back all four years and claimed the 100 title as a sopho-more, junior and senior.

As a freshman in 1952, Oyakawa was out-touched in the 100 back by teammate Jack Taylor.

"In the 200 that year, I was in an outside lane," Oyakawa said. "Jack Taylor and Dick Thoman of Yale, who had dominated that event for three years, were in the middle of the pool and were looking at each other. I was able to sneak by them and get the win."

That was the last time Oyakawa would be a secret to anyone, quickly making the transition from hero-worshipper to hero himself.

"I can remember in 1949 when Allan Stack of Yale and

some of the Japanese swimmers who had won at the national championships in L.A. came to Hawaii for a meet," Oyakawa said. "Allan Stack was 6-foot-7 or 6-foot-8. I had never seen a swimmer his size, so I was really impressed with him. He was the Olympic champion in 1948. Little did I know that four years later, I would be his teammate."

Oyakawa made that 1952 Olympic team after some anxious moments in training prior to the U.S. Trials.

He and OSU teammate Gerald Holan were training at a pool on Indianola Avenue and were crushed by the slowness of their times.

"I can remember our final time trial, my time was pretty bad," Oyakawa said. "Gerry and I were hearing reports of some pretty fast times by the swimmers at Yale, so we were worried. We thought that we wouldn't have a chance to make the team, but then in the first race at the trials, Gerry swam the 200 breaststroke in a time that bettered the existing Olympic record.

"He went on to become the No. 1 qualifier in that event, which gave me a lot of confidence. I felt like, if Gerry could do it, I could do it, too, since we had done the same type of workouts."

Oyakawa indeed won the trials and headed to Helsinki full of confidence.

"It sounds strange to say, but making the U.S. team was really the big hurdle," he said. "Americans pretty much dominated swimming in those years, so I knew I could compete evenly with anyone."

Oyakawa won the gold in 1:05.4, breaking the Olympic record of German's Adolph Kiefer by a half-second, while Taylor claimed the bronze.

Oyakawa won seven NCAA titles.

"That was really a great feeling to be on the medal stand with Jack," Oyakawa said. "He had held the world-record in the backstroke and was just a terrific guy. He helped me out quite a bit, both as a swimmer and just by being my good friend."

Oyakawa broke the American record in the 100 back in 1953 and established a new world mark in that event in 1954, but his bid for a repeat gold in 1956 fell victim to a poor start in the Olympic finals in Melbourne.

His record-setting days were far from over, however, for Oyakawa continued swimming in Master's races and set numerous world records in age-group competition into his late 60s.

He was inducted into the International Swimming Hall of Fame in 1973.

Bill SMITH

Unbeatable in Pursuit of a Dream

He was a man with such a generic name it almost seemed an alias—the type thrown out to obscure one's true identity in a fog of anonymity.

There was, however, nothing common or indistinguishable about Bill Smith during an Ohio State swimming career in which he dominated the freestyle events so thoroughly that he never lost a race in Big Ten competition throughout his four seasons of eligibility.

Smith arrived on campus in the fall of 1942 from his native Honolulu and immediately seized upon the newly granted eligibility for collegiate freshmen because of the United States' involvement in World War II.

He won the NCAA title in the 200-yard freestyle that season, joining with fellow-Hawaiian Keo Nakama to power the Buckeyes to the national championship.

"When I graduated from high school, I wasn't sure about where to go to college," Smith said.

"What helped me make up my mind was that Keo Nakama was already at Ohio State. He had been a teammate of mine in Hawaii. I figured, if I was going all the way from Hawaii to the Midwest, it would be better if there was someone I already knew."

Smith enlisted in the military in 1943 and was sent to the Great Lakes Naval Training Center, where he was permitted to train and compete in the AAU national championships.

He would win 15 separate titles in an assortment of races on that level while spending time as a swim instructor for the Navy in both California and Honolulu until the war ended.

That's when Smith made his way back to Ohio State to resume his college career and continue his unbeaten streak, which would include three titles apiece in the NCAA 200- and 500-meter freestyle from 1947-49.

Despite those achievements, and despite setting seven world

records during that time, Smith was approaching a decade of dedicated training without the reward he set out to attain as a child.

"My goal was always to make the Olympic team," Smith said. "That's what I trained for from the time I was a young man. My goal was, 'Olympics first, Olympics always.' If I thought I would never compete in the Olympics, I would have stopped swimming.

"So to compete from 1940-49 and never swim in an Olympic games was very disappointing to me, because I felt I missed a big part of the prime of my career."

Smith came by his Olympic fascination thanks to the exploits of Jesse Owens in the 1936 Games in Berlin, where the Cleveland native and Ohio State track phenom exposed the idiocy of Aryan supremacy by winning four gold medals.

"I remember reading the headlines in the newspaper about Jesse Owens," Smith said. "I thought, 'My goodness, that guy must be something else.' It made me think that I could achieve whatever I wanted if I worked hard enough."

Smith was on track to make the U.S. Olympic team in 1940, but Japan withdrew as the host in the summer of 1938 because it was at war with China and the Games were quickly transferred to Helsinki.

The Fins feverishly prepared to stage the competition until being invaded by the Soviet Union in 1939, and Germany's invasion of Poland soon afterward put the world at war and scuttled the Games until 1948.

By then, Smith was no longer the favorite for gold, finishing behind Jimmy McLane at the U.S. Olympic trials in the 400-meter freestyle.

But when he arrived in London, Smith got a double-barreled boost from the coaches who had meant the most to him.

Ohio State's Mike Peppe was Team USA's diving coach and would guide OSU's Bruce Harlan and Miller Anderson to a gold- and silver-medal performance, respectively, in the springboard event.

Smith's youth coach in Hawaii, Soichi Sakamoto, was also at the Games and huddled with his protégé before the 400-meter final.

"I was his first swimmer ever to compete in the Olympic games, so he came to London to see it," Smith said. "We had a long discussion before the event. We talked about goal setting, and how long I had trained for that moment. He told me, 'You can win this event. Just take it out fast and swim like you used to.' "

Inspired by that and by a similar motivational speech from Peppe, Smith stunned McLane by bursting to a six-meter lead early and never faltered.

Smith never lost a race while at OSU.

He triumphed in an Olympic-record time of 4:41.0 that gave him a two-second victory over his USA teammate.

Later, Smith and McLane teamed with Wally Ris and Wally Wolf for a world-record of 8:46.0 to win gold in the 800-meter freestyle relay.

"I had waited so long to make the team that just to get to the Olympics was extremely exciting," Smith said. "I was so proud of that, and then to win two gold medals, that was an amazing experience.

"Standing on the podium, waiting for the presentation, all I could think about was my parents, my teammates, Mike Peppe, Soichi Sakamoto. It really hit me that I had achieved what I set out to do."

David
ALBRITTON

He Scaled the Heights as a Friend

Athletes are competitive by nature, for without that drive to succeed, to rise above all others in achievement and recognition, success would go unclaimed.

The truest measure of an athlete, however, is not only the results that define their performance, but whether honor and unselfishness are trademarks of their persona.

None can question those aspects of the legacy left by David Albritton, whose career as an Ohio State high-jumper would have claimed much greater renown had it not coincided with the achievements of the incomparable Jesse Owens.

Albritton was not only Owens's teammate at OSU, he was his teammate and friend at Cleveland's East Technical High School, in junior high before that, in grade school before that, and in childhood before that.

Such a long association might have given birth to some resentment among lesser men, but not between Albritton and Owens.

The world, of course, would come to know Owens as a breaker of both world-records and Hitler's ridiculous assertion of Aryan supremacy.

All the while, Albritton was there, excelling himself athletically, but more importantly, proving his worth as a sportsman of the highest caliber by never once resenting his friend's fame.

"We were a pair," Albritton once said of his friendship with Owens. "I was his biggest booster and he was mine."

Their association began as five-year-olds in Alabama, where the two resided in nearby towns.

"He was from Oakville and I was from Danville," Albritton said. "They were within walking distance of each other, about four or five miles. We met on a Sunday afternoon when our brothers got together to play baseball.

"Jesse and I were too young to play, so we used to sit and watch our brothers."

Owens and Albritton would soon make a name for themselves athletically.

Owens's marks in the long jump and the sprints are well documented. What Ohio State fans may not know is that Albritton was a three-time All-American and three-time national champion high jumper for the Buckeyes under legendary track coach Larry Snyder.

Albritton set a school record as a freshman and broke the world record as a sophomore, giving him a spot on the 1936 Olympic team with Owens in Berlin.

Albritton and Cornelius Johnson both cleared 6-9 3/4 to set a world record at the Olympic Trials.

Only a greater number of misses at the winning height forced Albritton to settle for the silver medal in those Games, with Johnson winning the gold.

Albritton was one of first high jumpers to use the straddle technique, which served him well during a career of nearly three decades, during which he won numerous titles.

Albritton won or tied for seven national AAU outdoor titles

David Albritton (right) seated with Jesse Owens.

from 1936 to 1950 and tied for three national collegiate titles.

Citizens in Montgomery County, near Dayton, elected Albritton as their Ohio House representative for 18 years.

He was inducted into the Ohio State Athletic Hall of Fame in 1979.

Albritton died on May 14, 1994 at the age of 81.

Glenn DAVIS

Sage Advice, Wisely Heeded

It's no secret that Ohio State's football program flourished throughout Woody Hayes's 28 seasons as head coach in part because of his skills as an accomplished recruiter.

What most people don't know is that Hayes's skills as a "de-cruiter" figured prominently in one of OSU's greatest track and field success stories.

On the heels of winning his first national championship in 1954, Hayes had a replacement for Heisman Trophy-winner Howard "Hopalong" Cassady just waiting to become eligible as a sophomore.

His name was Glenn Davis, and now his legacy is well-known as a three-time gold medallist, five-time NCAA champion, and six-time world record holder.

Back in 1955, however, as an Ohio State freshman, Davis was as serious about playing football for Hayes as he was about starring for Larry Snyder's track team.

"I was ready to play football," Davis said. "Woody Hayes had talked to me after I captained the North all-stars at the North-South game in Springfield in the spring of 1955. It was all set, except Larry Snyder didn't want me to play football at all. He wasn't going to let me do it, because he was afraid I'd get hurt and that would ruin me for track.

"He saw me run the 400 hurdles the first time and said, 'No one's going to stop you. You're going all the way.' Well, I thought I could, too, but I still wanted to play football. So after my fresh-man year, I quit school and came home. I was going to transfer some place where they'd let me play football and run track, both."

Snyder didn't get to be a Hall of Fame coach by letting talents like Davis slip away, so he mar-shaled Hayes's assistance, and the two of them hopped in a car and headed toward Akron for a heart-to-heart with Davis.

"I was looking at Michigan and a couple of other schools out west," Davis said. "Well, that never happened, because Larry Snyder and Woody Hayes showed up at my house and talked me into coming back down.

"They said if I really wanted to play I could do both sports, so we all agreed to that and then I got in the car with them to go back to Columbus.

"Well, on the way back, Larry kept talking to me about track and how dangerous football could be to me becoming an Olympic champion. He talked about how, if I broke a bone, I wouldn't be able to compete.

"Woody joined right in with him, and by the time we got back to campus, he was actually en-couraging me to stick with the Olympics. He said he hadn't really taken the chance to think about it before, but now that he had, he knew I had the chance to set some world records, and so I'd be better off just sticking with track."

There's no telling how success-ful Davis might have been as an OSU tailback, but he was good enough after retiring from the track to play two seasons as a wide receiver with the NFL's Detroit Lions.

On the track, though, he was uncatchable, setting world records in both the 400 and the 400 hurdles.

"I had natural talent, but I worked hard to get better," Davis said. "If you have the gift, you have to work to get where you want to go and I did that. Even when I was a kid, I always knew I wanted to run in the Olympics.

"I can remember in high school, someone asking me to autograph a picture. I signed it and wrote on there that some day I would be making the Olympic team."

True to his word, Davis followed his 1956 NCAA championships in the indoor and outdoor 440-yard hurdles by setting a world record in the metric equivalent of that event at the U.S. Olympic Trials that summer.

He won the gold at the Summer Games later that year in Melbourne, then returned to OSU to win three more NCAA individual titles in the 440-yard dash and gain the 1958 Sullivan Award as the nation's top amateur athlete.

Davis dominated his era in the hurdles.

Davis went to Rome in 1960 and defended his Olympic gold in the hurdles and also joined the 4x400 relay to win another gold medal.

After those Games, he went on a brief competitive tour of five foreign countries with Team USA and then began his pro football career in Detroit.

"I played two seasons and about half of another one, but I banged up my shoulder quite a bit," Davis said. "It kept getting hurt because I kept dislocating it."

Given those unfortunate circumstances, Davis looks back now and realizes the wisdom of Snyder's and Hayes's advice that he stick to track and field.

"It was probably one of the smartest things I did," he said. "I still owe them a thank you for talking me into not playing football at Ohio State."

Jesse OWENS

More Than an Olympic Hero

Ohio State University athletes have made their mark in every sport across the spectrum, exhibiting their talents not just in Columbus, throughout the Big Ten Conference and across the country, but on the international stage via the Olympic Games.

None however, have had the impact on the world, not just the athletic world, but also the consciousness of the entire planet, like the immortal Jesse Owens.

The son of a sharecropper from Alabama, Owens matriculated to OSU by way of Cleveland and later struck an unforgettable blow against racism with his riveting performance at the 1936 Berlin Olympics.

A gold medal-winner in four events—the 100- and 200-meter dashes, long jump, and 400-meter relay—Owens exposed German dictator Adolf Hitler's contention of Aryan supremacy for the fraud it was.

Owens's winning performances in the four events would have

been good for Olympic medals as late as 1960, but more important than what he did on the track was the way he humbly used the platform afforded him by his Olympic success to press for better treatment of blacks in the United States once he returned to a hero's welcome.

"In America," Owens once said in his understated eloquence, "anybody can become a somebody."

J.C. Owens—Jesse was a name given to him by elementary school teachers—was one of eight children his father and mother brought north to Cleveland during World War I when Owens was nine.

A chronically-ill child, he suffered from both bronchial congestion and several bouts of pneumonia.

Owens, though, had the good fortune to hook up with coach Charles Riley at Cleveland's Fairmont Junior High School, and together they would begin a relationship that would set track and field on its ear and change the

course of race relations in the world.

Owens's first look at the Ohio State campus came as a sophomore at East Technical High School, when he came to Columbus for the state scholastic meet.

Foreshadowing the success he would experience as a Buckeye, Owens set a new state long jump record of 22-3 7/9, finished second in the 200-yard dash and fourth in the 100.

One year later, Owens returned to Columbus for the state meet and tied the Ohio prep record with a winning time of 9.9 in the 100-yard dash, while also winning the 200 in 22.6 seconds and the long jump with a new mark of 22-11 1/4.

"Believe me, ladies and gentlemen," Owens told the cheering throng over the public address system that day, "when I run in college, it will be for you, because you have made me want to run."

True to his word, Owens arrived at Ohio State in the fall of 1933 and set about an All-

American career that would culminate in the greatest single-day performance in track and field history.

That came not in Berlin, but in Ann Arbor, Mich., on May 25, 1935.

Mill Marsh, writing in the *Ann Arbor News* the day after those Big Ten Conference championships, wrote, "There will never be another meet like it."

So far, there hasn't been.

In just over one hour, Owens tied one world record and broke five others to rocket to international prominence some 15 months before he would spoil Hitler's party in Berlin.

Owens had won four events at the Big Ten meet the year before, but wasn't even certain he would compete that day, having injured his back in a fall down the stairs just one week before.

But Owens not only competed, he did so in such a way to lend credence to a statement he would later make.

"When people come out to see you perform, you have to give them the best you have within you," he said.

Hence, in his first event that afternoon, Owens tied the world record in the 100-yard dash with a winning time of 9.4 seconds.

Not bad, but it would be Owens's least-spectacular performance of the day.

He came back 30 minutes later to shatter by three-tenths of a second his own world record in the 220-yard dash, and in so doing passed the mark for the 200 meters in what also stood as world-record time.

In between those two sprints, Owens headed to the long jump pit and made his approach toward the take-off board on his first attempt.

He soared into the air and astonished the 7,000 onlookers by landing nearly six inches beyond the world record with a new standard of 26 feet 8 1/4 inches. That mark would stand for a quarter-century, longer than any other record in modern track and field history.

Ohio State coach Larry Snyder, not wanting Owens to risk a reinjury to his back, made his star bypass his later attempts to rest for the 220-yard low hurdles.

That was Owens's weakest event, and having done all that he had so far, another record performance seemed out of the question.

To everyone else, maybe, but not to Owens.

He again ran away from the pack and extended his lead until he was 10 yards clear of the field at the finish, again setting a world record for his race (22.6) and also beating the existing standard when he passed the mark at 200 meters.

Thus ended the most remarkable day in track and field history, a performance that to those who witnessed it made what would transpire in Berlin only an extension of the legend Owens formulated first as an Ohio State Buckeye.

Owens foreshadowed his Olympic success in Ohio Stadium.

Butch
REYNOLDS

A Blur in the Quarter-Mile

Harry "Butch" Reynolds may have shocked the world with his stunning world-record 400-meter run on Aug. 18, 1988, but those who saw him compete at OSU the two seasons prior to that saw nothing surprising in the shattering of what was then the second-oldest world record on the books.

Reynolds flashed his speed from his first workout with the Buckeyes after transferring to OSU from Butler County Community College, running a time on the tight turns of French Field House that caught the attention of head coach Frank Zubovich.

"The first indoor (400) time he ran here was a 46.6," Zubovich said. "Anybody who can run that fast in practice has to be something special."

Reynolds more than delivered on the promise he had already flashed in winning the indoor junior college national championship, while also setting an outdoor

JC record and winning the national championship in the spring of 1984.

Reynolds reached the semifinals of the Olympic Trials that summer, but his Olympic potential and world-class speed was still in its infancy at that stage.

He came to OSU in 1985 with personal-best 400-meter times from junior college that were better than the Buckeyes' existing school records both indoors and outdoors, so it was only a matter of time before Reynolds began engraving his name in school history.

The Akron Hoban High School graduate began what would become an illustrious career by setting a new school outdoor 400 record (45.36) at the Big Ten meet in 1986, scoring points not only in that event, but in the 400- and 1,600-meter relays, as well.

Reynolds matched that time at the Jesse Owens Track Classic that year and won the 400, defeating 1985 world champion Mitchell

Franks to foreshadow a huge year on the horizon in 1987.

That year started with Reynolds's world-record time in the 600-meter run indoors (1:06.87), shattering by nearly one second a mark that had stood since 1970.

Once the weather warmed and the season shifted outdoors, Reynolds turned the conference meet into his own personal highlight film, breaking Jesse Owens's Big Ten-record of 20.7 in the 200 with a 20.46 clocking in the prelims.

Reynolds was only slightly slower (20.51) in winning the 200 finals, and he put that together with a winning time of 45-flat in the 400 to crush the conference record by .32 of a second.

Those victories, together with Reynolds's anchoring of the winning 4x400-meter relay prompted coaches to unanimously award him the meet's outstanding athlete award.

Now Reynolds was ready to go

global with his talents, and he did so by burning to a 44.09 clocking in the Owens Classic 400 on a windy, cold and rainy day that June.

The time was the fastest 400 ever in a race not run at altitude, and served notice that Lee Evans's world-record time of 43.86 run in the rarified air of Mexico City in 1968 was on borrowed time.

Sure enough, just over a year later, Reynolds stepped onto the track in Zurich, Switzerland and made headlines around the world.

Having continued to train at OSU under Zubovich, rather than move to a warmer climate, Reynolds was still contending with the after effects of a hamstring pull suffered on French Fieldhouse's tight turns that winter.

"Truthfully," Reynolds said of that night in Switzerland, "I didn't feel like racing."

Rating himself only at about 80 percent of his maximum abilities, Reynolds nevertheless blazed through a 43.29 400 with his trademark powerful finish, then fell into the waiting arms of his brother, Jeff.

"As soon as I crossed the finish line, my brother grabbed me and said, 'You've got the world record. You crushed it,'" Reynolds said. "I thought it would be in the 43.8s. When I turned around and saw the scoreboard and it said, '43.29, official.' I couldn't think of anything. I was just speechless."

Reynolds took the silver medal at the 400 at the Seoul Olympics in 1988 and also won the gold on the United States' 4x400-meter relay team, which set a world record.

His dominance of the 400 was interrupted by the politics of his sport, however, when the International Amateur Athletic Federation declared Reynolds ineligible in 1990 for testing positive for steroid use.

Reynolds fought the charge in the courts and was vindicated in his assertion that the test was poorly administered and flawed. U.S. courts awarded him a $27-million judgment that the IAAF never paid.

The legal wrangling cost Reynolds a berth on the 1992 Olympic squad.

He returned to Ohio State in the early 1990s and served several years as an assistant with the school's track program.

Reynolds was an immediate star at OSU.

Mal
WHITFIELD

Winning the Race of Life

Nicknames get hung on a person for a myriad of reasons, often as an attempt at humor, sometimes for sarcasm and occasionally because the sound is simply melodious to the ear.

It's rare when a nickname is applied in youth and remains appropriate into adulthood, and rarer, still, when the recipient achieves so extensively that he renders what was intended as a tribute wholly inadequate to typify his life's work.

Mal Whitfield, "Marvelous Mal," as he became known during his Ohio State track career, is among those exceptional individuals.

Marvelous, while laudable and complimentary in its meaning as an adjective, cannot begin to quantify the array of contributions Whitfield made to his sport, his nation, and the world.

He was an athlete of elite status, winning three gold medals, a silver and a bronze in two Olympics, but he was much more than that.

Whitfield was also an inspiration in the way he overcame his humble beginnings in the roughest section of Los Angeles, where he lost his father at age four and his mother at age 12.

He was a patriot, a war hero and a diligent servant of the U.S. government who, for 34 years, served in some 132 countries to build valuable diplomatic relationships that have proven crucial to American interests.

Whitfield's foundation has arranged more than 5,000 athletic scholarships at U.S. colleges and universities for African athletes, where his work with that continent's Olympic program caused 1968 gold medalist Kip Keino to refer to him as, "the father of organized athletics" in Africa.

Keino, Ethiopia's Mamo Wolde, and Uganda's John Akibua are among the gold medallists whose careers were assisted by the work Whitfield completed in Africa to nurture its nation's Olympic programs.

Doing so was a way for

Whitfield to repay the break he was given as a U.S. Airman stationed at Lockburn Air Base in Columbus in 1946.

It was then that he and some other soldiers were invited to Ohio State one day to compete against the Buckeyes' track and field squad.

OSU coach Larry Snyder took one look at Whitfield's effortless stride and amazing speed and set about procuring his talents for the scarlet and gray.

"Strangely enough, I had always wanted to go to Ohio State because of Jesse Owens and the great success he had in the 1936 Olympics," Whitfield said. "Coach Snyder went in to talk to the commanding officer of the 477th Bomb Group, Col. Benjamin O. Davis, to see if I could attend college while serving in the military. That was the first time they had ever had that sort of request.

"A couple of days later, I got a call that I was to report to the commanding officer. Right away I thought, 'What does he want with me? What did I do?' That's the first thing that enters an enlisted man's mind. Then they told me to dress up in my khakis and I knew then that I wasn't in any sort of trouble."

Whitfield still didn't know what was about to occur until he walked into the office and saw Snyder seated in an adjacent chair, smiling at him.

"The Colonel said something to the effect that I must have really shaken them up on campus, because he had a telex in his hand from the Pentagon approving me to attend Ohio State full time in something called the Bootstrap Training Program. Man, was that a thrill."

Whitfield would soon return the favor to Snyder and anyone else who saw him run for the Buckeyes, winning two NCAA championships with an amazing range that allowed him to run as fast as 10.7 for the 100 meters and sustain that speed for a mile as fast as 4:12.

"It didn't take long for me to really succeed," Whitfield said. "I had always liked track and field, and I was fast enough and had endurance enough as a result of hard training. I took everything serious, even my studies. The program I was in was tough on me, because I still had to put in four hours every day on the military base, plus time at the stadium for practice and in classes.

"It wasn't easy. It was serious business. But I felt I had a great opportunity and I was determined to take advantage of it. When your ambition is to be a winner, an achiever, you overcome obstacles along the way by keeping your mind on your objective. The power of concentration is the most essential thing in everything you undertake in life."

Whitfield's discipline and determination made him nearly unbeatable at the middle distances from 1946-55, a span during which he won 66 of 69 major races from 800-1,000 meters.

He made his first Olympic team in 1948, winning the gold medal in the 800-meter run in an Olympic-record 1:49.2.

Whitfield also ran a leg on the United States' gold-medal 4x400-meter relay team and won a bronze medal in the 400-meter run.

After that, he returned to OSU and won 1949 NCAA half-mile, then rejoined his unit on active duty and flew 37 combat missions as an aerial gunner in the Korean War.

Whitfield defended his 800-meter gold medal at the 1952 Summer Games in London, pulling away with 250 meters to go in a time that equaled his Olympic record from four years earlier.

He also gained a silver medal in the 4x400 relay.

"Standing on the top step of the awards stand while the American flag was raised, with the national anthem playing in the background, was one of the great moments of my life," Whitfield said. "I felt great on the stand in 1948, but even better in 1952, because we had prevailed against the Soviet Union."

Whitfield eventually dropped his 880-world record to 1:48.6 and also established a world-record in the 1,000 meters (2:20.8) on the same day he set an American record of 46.2 in the 440-yard run.

Those achievements helped him become the 1954 Sullivan Award winner, the first black athlete honored as the nation's top amateur athlete.

Whitfield's distinguished government service career followed his retirement from the track and culminated in his forging key diplomatic relationships that convinced the African nations to support Atlanta's bid to host the 1996 Summer Games.

For that work, and for his five Olympic medals, Whitfield was selected as one of the top 100 living Olympians.

Mal Whitfield: Simply marvelous.

INDEX OF ATHLETES

PHOTO CREDITS

p. 65, courtesy of Buckeye Sports Bulletin. Used with permission.

p. 113, courtesy of Buckeye Sports Bulletin. Used with permission.

p. 119, courtesy of Buckeye Sports Bulletin. Used with permission.

p. 147, courtesy of Alice Hohlmayer. Used with permission.

p. 175, copyright Bettmann/CORBIS. Used with permission.

p. 177, copyright Bettmann/CORBIS. Used with permission.

p. 179, courtesy of the Hawaii Sports Hall of Fame. Used with permission.

p. 185, courtesy of the Hawaii Sports Hall of Fame. Used with permission.

p. 189, courtesy of the Hawaii Sports Hall of Fame. Used with permission.

p. 191, copyright Bettmann/CORBIS. Used with permission.

All other photos courtesy of Ohio State University.

Celebrate the Heroes of Ohio Sports

in These Other Acclaimed Titles from Sports Publishing!